THOR

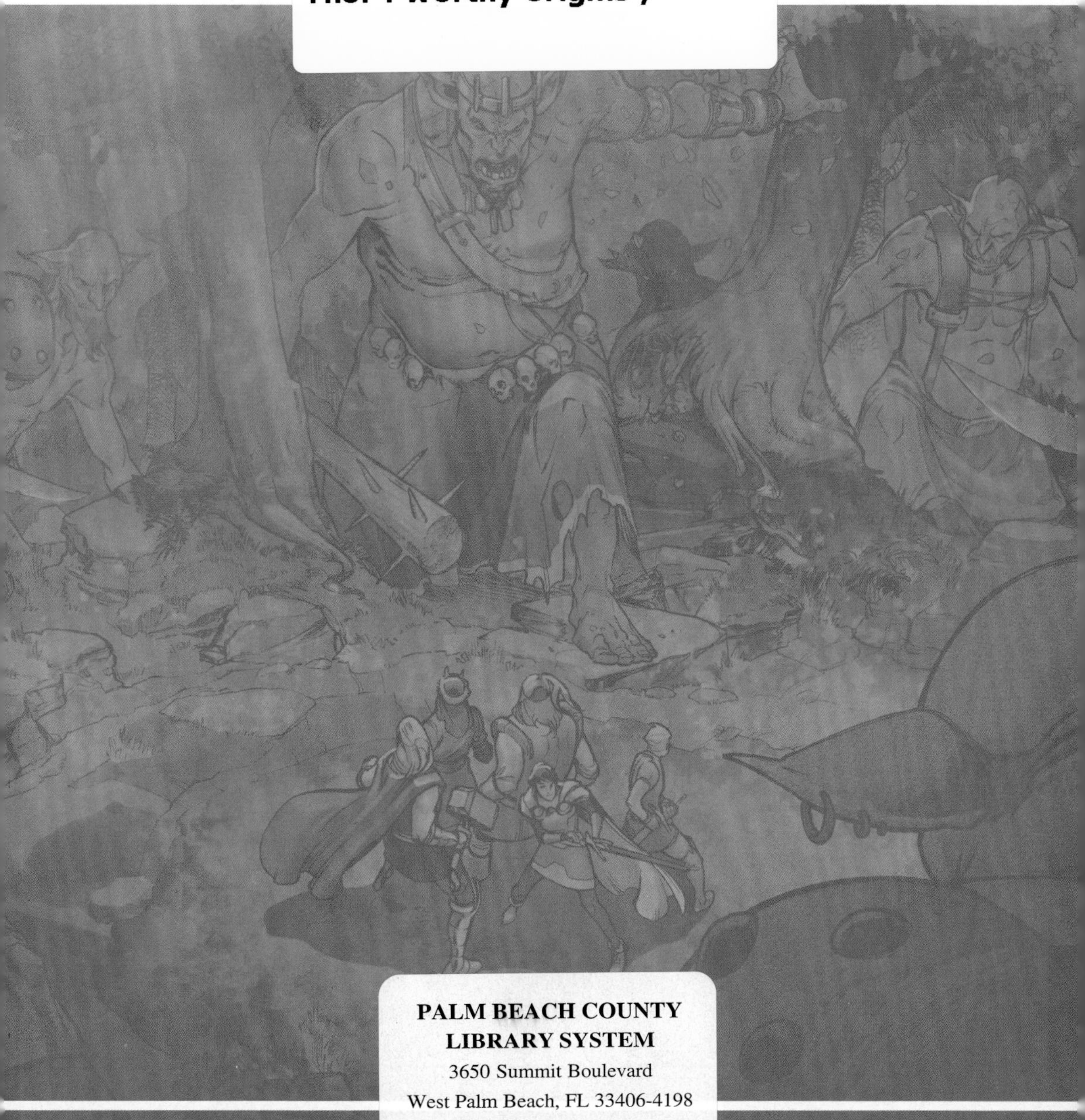

COLLECTION EDITOR: **JENNIFER GRÜNWALD**
ASSISTANT EDITOR: **CAITLIN O'CONNELL**
ASSOCIATE MANAGING EDITOR: **KATERI WOODY**
EDITOR, SPECIAL PROJECTS: **MARK D. BEAZLEY**
VP PRODUCTION & SPECIAL PROJECTS: **JEFF YOUNGQUIST**
SVP PRINT, SALES & MARKETING: **DAVID GABRIEL**
BOOK DESIGN: **JEFF POWELL**

EDITOR IN CHIEF: **AXEL ALONSO**
CHIEF CREATIVE OFFICER: **JOE QUESADA**
PRESIDENT: **DAN BUCKLEY**
EXECUTIVE PRODUCER: **ALAN FINE**

THOR: WORTHY ORIGINS. Contains material originally published in magazine form as THOR: SEASON ONE and THOR: GOD OF THUNDER #1. First printing 2017. ISBN# 978-0-7851-8476-8. Published by MARVEL WORLDWIDE, INC., a subsidiary of MARVEL ENTERTAINMENT, LLC. OFFICE OF PUBLICATION: 135 West 50th Street, New York, NY 10020. Copyright © 2017 MARVEL No similarity between any of the names, characters, persons, and/or institutions in this magazine with those of any living or dead person or institution is intended, and any such similarity which may exist is purely coincidental. **Printed in Canada.** DAN BUCKLEY, President, Marvel Entertainment; JOE QUESADA, Chief Creative Officer; TOM BREVOORT, SVP of Publishing; DAVID BOGART, SVP of Business Affairs & Operations, Publishing & Partnership; C.B. CEBULSKI, VP of Brand Management & Development, Asia; DAVID GABRIEL, SVP of Sales & Marketing, Publishing; JEFF YOUNGQUIST, VP of Production & Special Projects; DAN CARR, Executive Director of Publishing Technology; ALEX MORALES, Director of Publishing Operations; SUSAN CRESPI, Production Manager; STAN LEE, Chairman Emeritus. For information regarding advertising in Marvel Comics or on Marvel.com, please contact Vit DeBellis, Integrated Sales Manager, at vdebellis@marvel.com. For Marvel subscription inquiries, please call 888-511-5480. **Manufactured between 7/28/2017 and 8/29/2017 by SOLISCO PRINTERS, SCOTT, QC, CANADA.**

10 9 8 7 6 5 4 3 2 1

THOR

WRITER
LILAH STURGES

ARTIST
PEPE LARRAZ

COLOR ARTIST
WIL QUINTANA

LETTERER
VC'S CORY PETIT

COVER ARTIST
JULIAN TOTINO TEDESCO

ASSISTANT EDITORS
JAKE THOMAS
WITH **JON MOISAN**

EDITOR
LAUREN SANKOVITCH

THOR CREATED BY STAN LEE,
LARRY LIEBER & JACK KIRBY

WORTHY ORIGINS

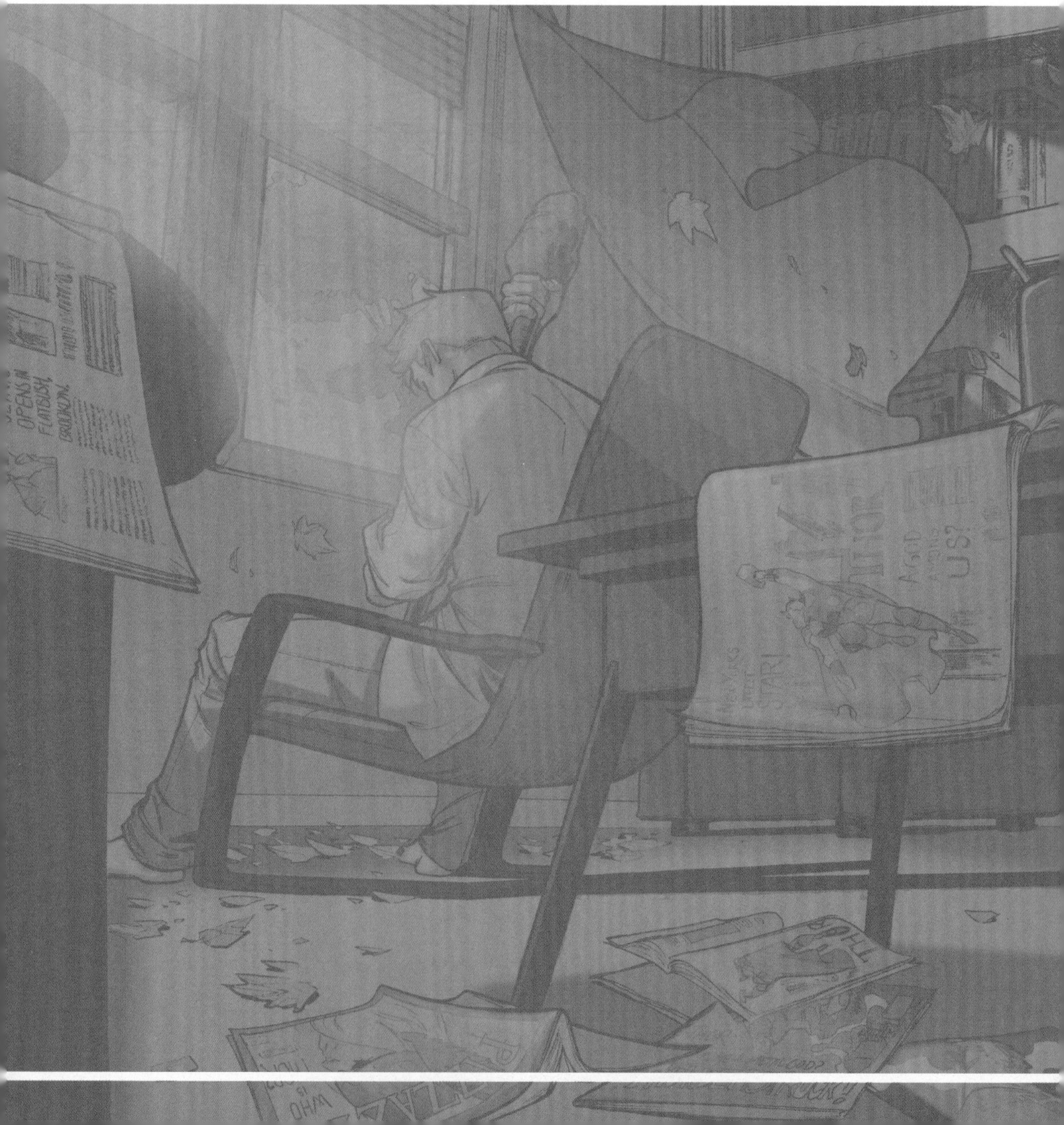

OPENS IN FLATBUSH, BROOKLYN

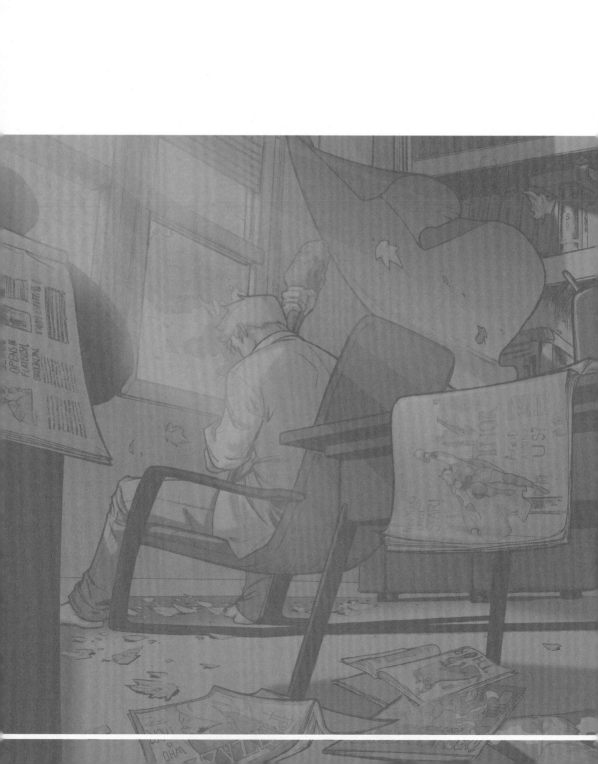

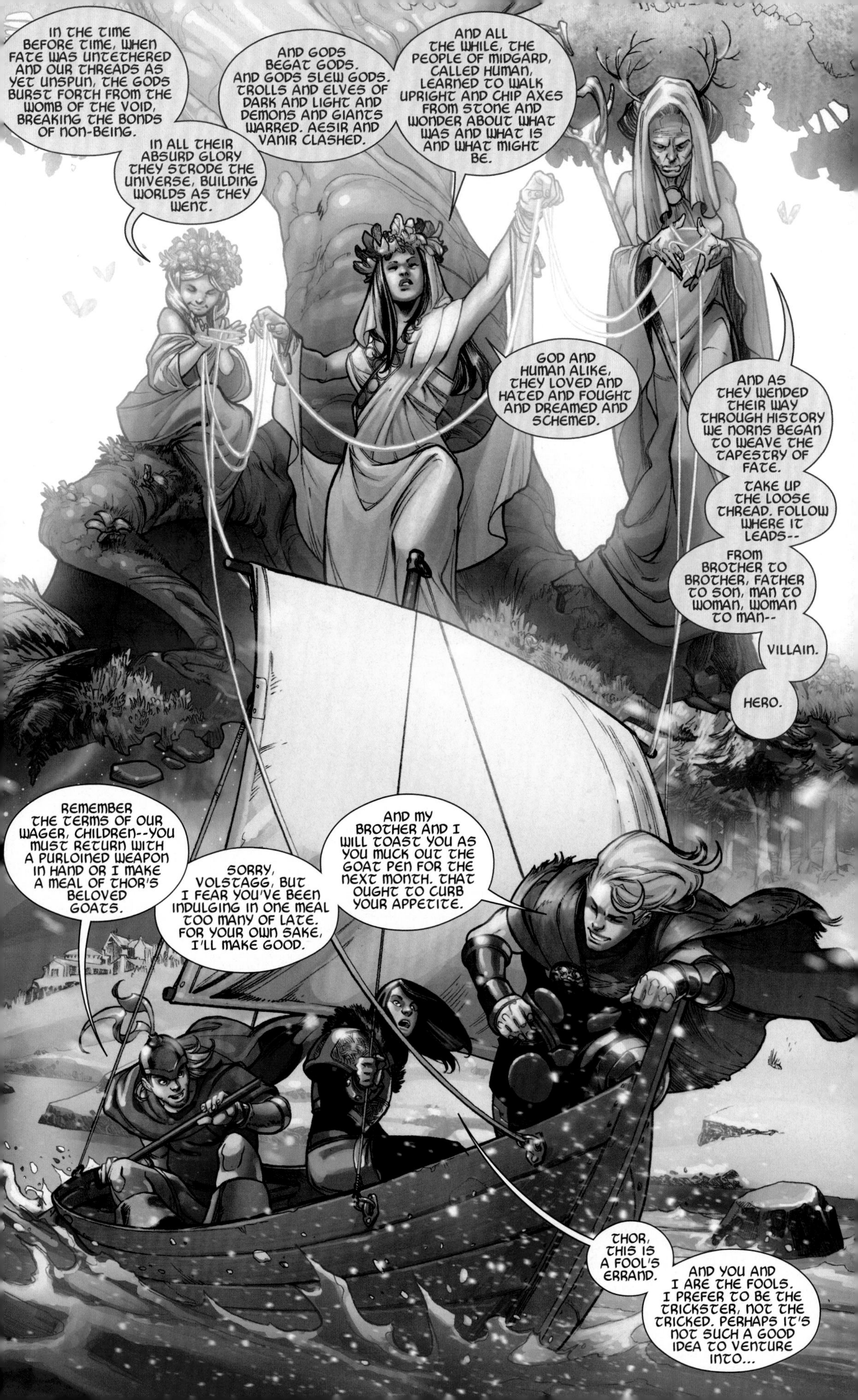
IN THE TIME BEFORE TIME, WHEN FATE WAS UNTETHERED AND OUR THREADS AS YET UNSPUN, THE GODS BURST FORTH FROM THE WOMB OF THE VOID, BREAKING THE BONDS OF NON-BEING.
IN ALL THEIR ABSURD GLORY THEY STRODE THE UNIVERSE, BUILDING WORLDS AS THEY WENT.
AND GODS BEGAT GODS. AND GODS SLEW GODS. TROLLS AND ELVES OF DARK AND LIGHT AND DEMONS AND GIANTS WARRED. AESIR AND VANIR CLASHED.
AND ALL THE WHILE, THE PEOPLE OF MIDGARD, CALLED HUMAN, LEARNED TO WALK UPRIGHT AND CHIP AXES FROM STONE AND WONDER ABOUT WHAT WAS AND WHAT IS AND WHAT MIGHT BE.
GOD AND HUMAN ALIKE, THEY LOVED AND HATED AND FOUGHT AND DREAMED AND SCHEMED.
AND AS THEY WENDED THEIR WAY THROUGH HISTORY WE NORNS BEGAN TO WEAVE THE TAPESTRY OF FATE.
TAKE UP THE LOOSE THREAD. FOLLOW WHERE IT LEADS--
FROM BROTHER TO BROTHER, FATHER TO SON, MAN TO WOMAN, WOMAN TO MAN--
VILLAIN.
HERO.
REMEMBER THE TERMS OF OUR WAGER, CHILDREN--YOU MUST RETURN WITH A PURLOINED WEAPON IN HAND OR I MAKE A MEAL OF THOR'S BELOVED GOATS.
SORRY, VOLSTAGG, BUT I FEAR YOU'VE BEEN INDULGING IN ONE MEAL TOO MANY OF LATE. FOR YOUR OWN SAKE, I'LL MAKE GOOD.
AND MY BROTHER AND I WILL TOAST YOU AS YOU MUCK OUT THE GOAT PEN FOR THE NEXT MONTH. THAT OUGHT TO CURB YOUR APPETITE.
THOR, THIS IS A FOOL'S ERRAND.
AND YOU AND I ARE THE FOOLS. I PREFER TO BE THE TRICKSTER, NOT THE TRICKED. PERHAPS IT'S NOT SUCH A GOOD IDEA TO VENTURE INTO...

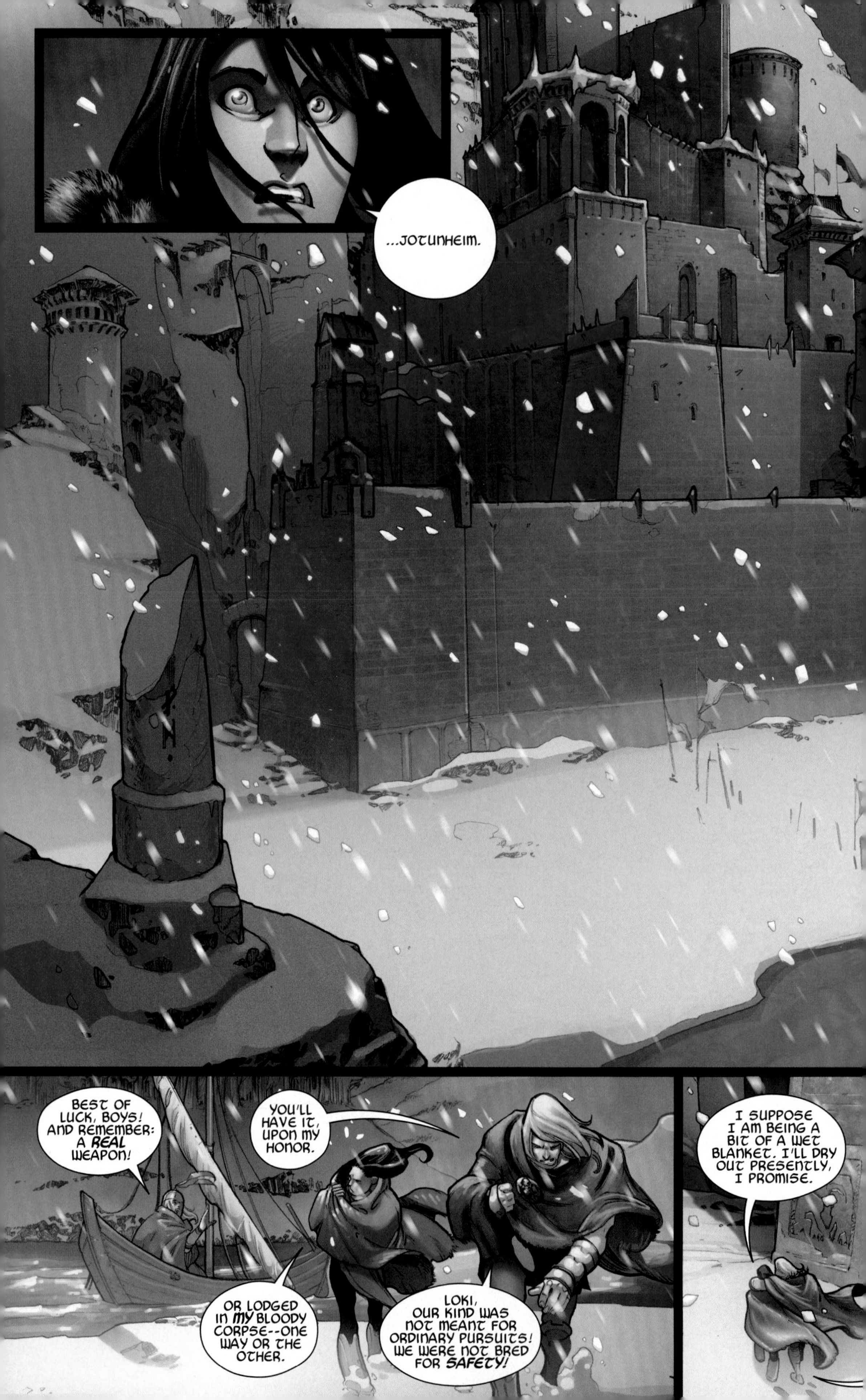
...JOTUNHEIM.
BEST OF LUCK, BOYS! AND REMEMBER: A REAL WEAPON!
YOU'LL HAVE IT, UPON MY HONOR.
OR LODGED IN MY BLOODY CORPSE--ONE WAY OR THE OTHER.
LOKI, OUR KIND WAS NOT MEANT FOR ORDINARY PURSUITS! WE WERE NOT BRED FOR SAFETY!
I SUPPOSE I AM BEING A BIT OF A WET BLANKET. I'LL DRY OUT PRESENTLY, I PROMISE.

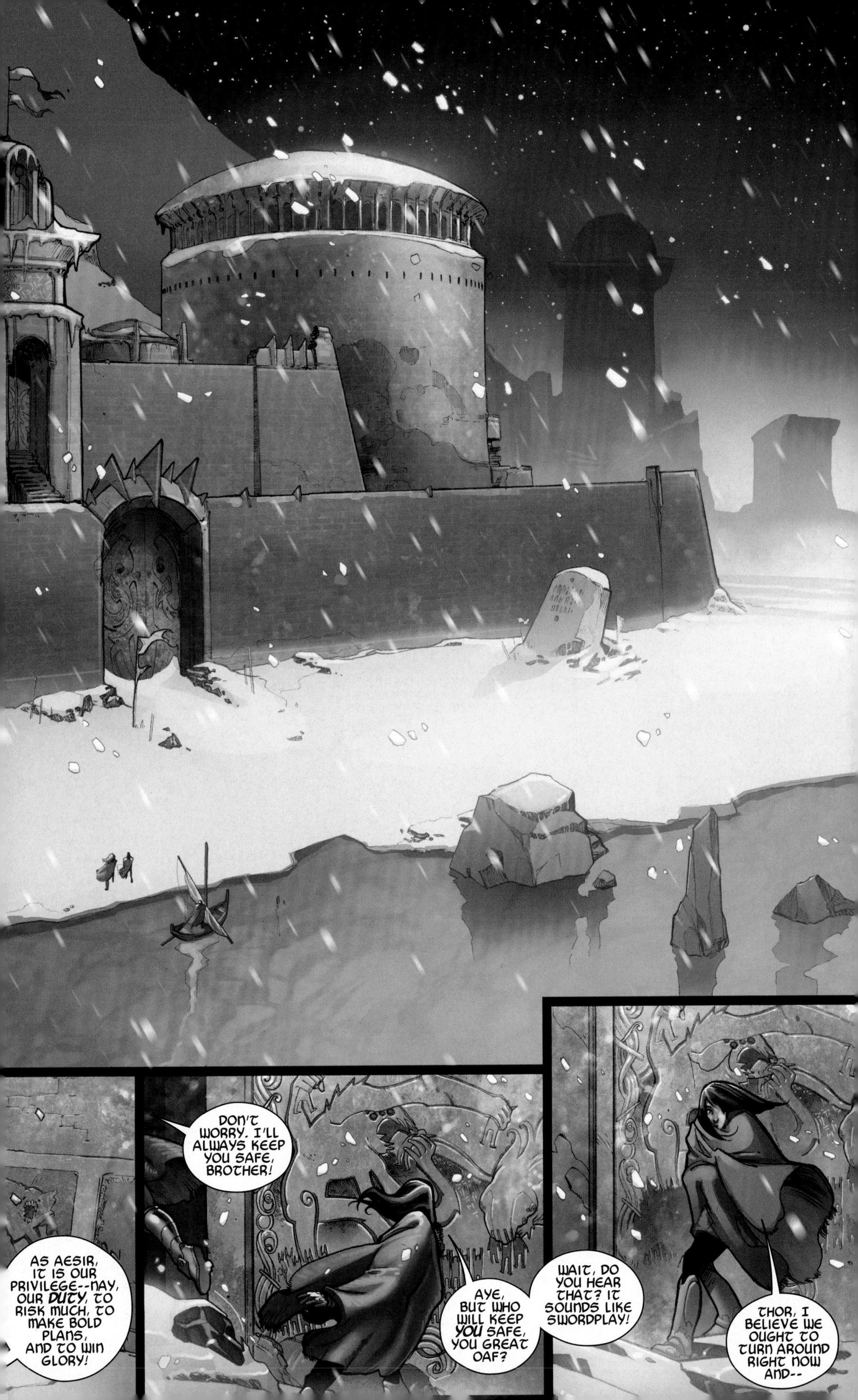
AS AESIR, IT IS OUR PRIVILEGE--NAY, OUR DUTY, TO RISK MUCH, TO MAKE BOLD PLANS, AND TO WIN GLORY!
DON'T WORRY. I'LL ALWAYS KEEP YOU SAFE, BROTHER!
AYE, BUT WHO WILL KEEP YOU SAFE, YOU GREAT OAF?
WAIT, DO YOU HEAR THAT? IT SOUNDS LIKE SWORDPLAY!
THOR, I BELIEVE WE OUGHT TO TURN AROUND RIGHT NOW AND--

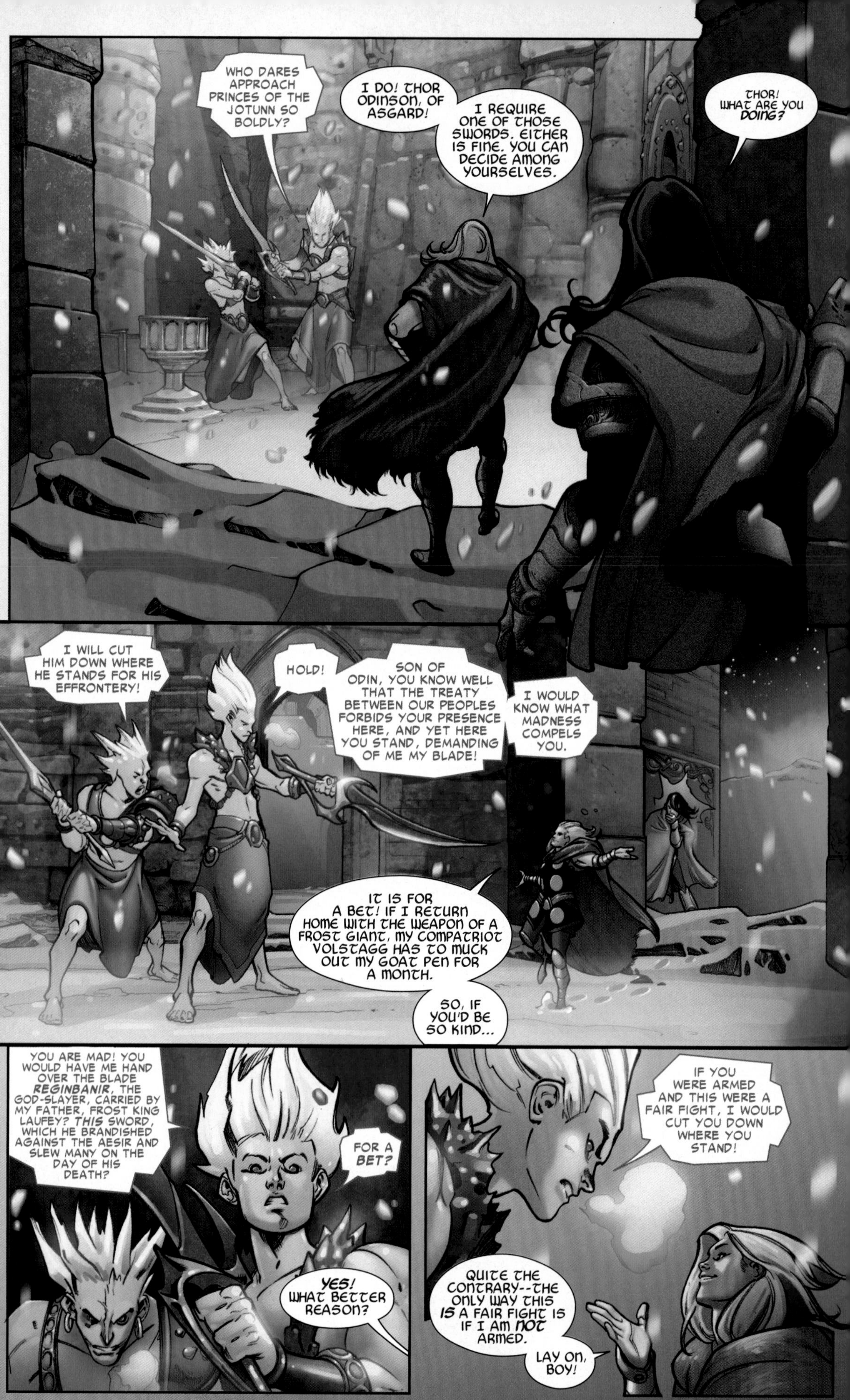
WHO DARES APPROACH PRINCES OF THE JOTUNN SO BOLDLY?
I DO! THOR ODINSON, OF ASGARD!
I REQUIRE ONE OF THOSE SWORDS. EITHER IS FINE. YOU CAN DECIDE AMONG YOURSELVES.
THOR! WHAT ARE YOU DOING?
I WILL CUT HIM DOWN WHERE HE STANDS FOR HIS EFFRONTERY!
HOLD!
SON OF ODIN, YOU KNOW WELL THAT THE TREATY BETWEEN OUR PEOPLES FORBIDS YOUR PRESENCE HERE, AND YET HERE YOU STAND, DEMANDING OF ME MY BLADE!
I WOULD KNOW WHAT MADNESS COMPELS YOU.
IT IS FOR A BET! IF I RETURN HOME WITH THE WEAPON OF A FROST GIANT, MY COMPATRIOT VOLSTAGG HAS TO MUCK OUT MY GOAT PEN FOR A MONTH.
SO, IF YOU'D BE SO KIND...
YOU ARE MAD! YOU WOULD HAVE ME HAND OVER THE BLADE REGINBANIR, THE GOD-SLAYER, CARRIED BY MY FATHER, FROST KING LAUFEY? THIS SWORD, WHICH HE BRANDISHED AGAINST THE AESIR AND SLEW MANY ON THE DAY OF HIS DEATH?
FOR A BET?
YES! WHAT BETTER REASON?
IF YOU WERE ARMED AND THIS WERE A FAIR FIGHT, I WOULD CUT YOU DOWN WHERE YOU STAND!
QUITE THE CONTRARY--THE ONLY WAY THIS IS A FAIR FIGHT IS IF I AM NOT ARMED.
LAY ON, BOY!

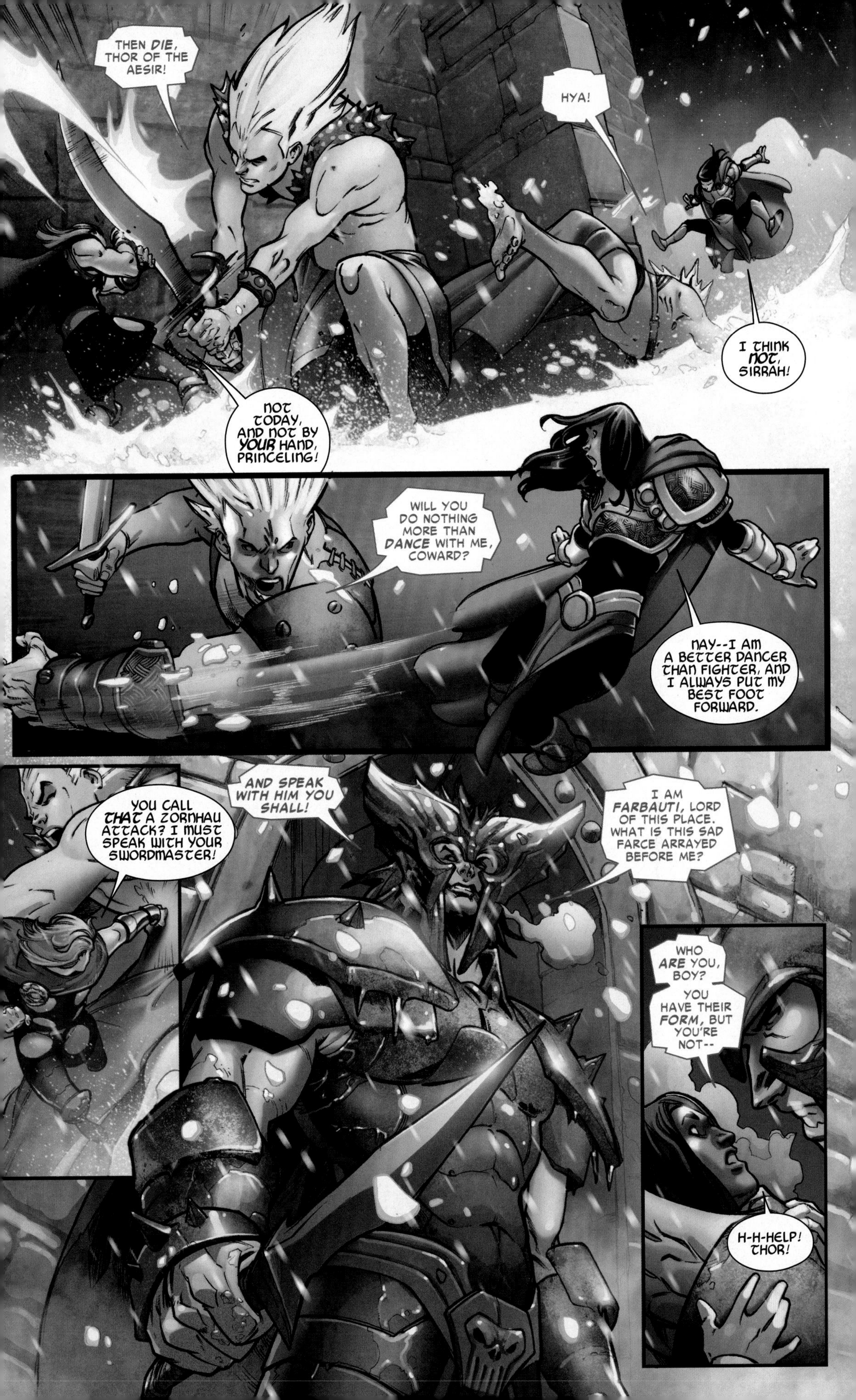
THEN DIE, THOR OF THE AESIR!
HYA!
I THINK NOT, SIRRAH!
NOT TODAY, AND NOT BY YOUR HAND, PRINCELING!
WILL YOU DO NOTHING MORE THAN DANCE WITH ME, COWARD?
NAY--I AM A BETTER DANCER THAN FIGHTER, AND I ALWAYS PUT MY BEST FOOT FORWARD.
YOU CALL THAT A ZORNHAU ATTACK? I MUST SPEAK WITH YOUR SWORDMASTER!
AND SPEAK WITH HIM YOU SHALL!
I AM FARBAUTI, LORD OF THIS PLACE. WHAT IS THIS SAD FARCE ARRAYED BEFORE ME?
WHO ARE YOU, BOY?
YOU HAVE THEIR FORM, BUT YOU'RE NOT--
H-H-HELP! THOR!

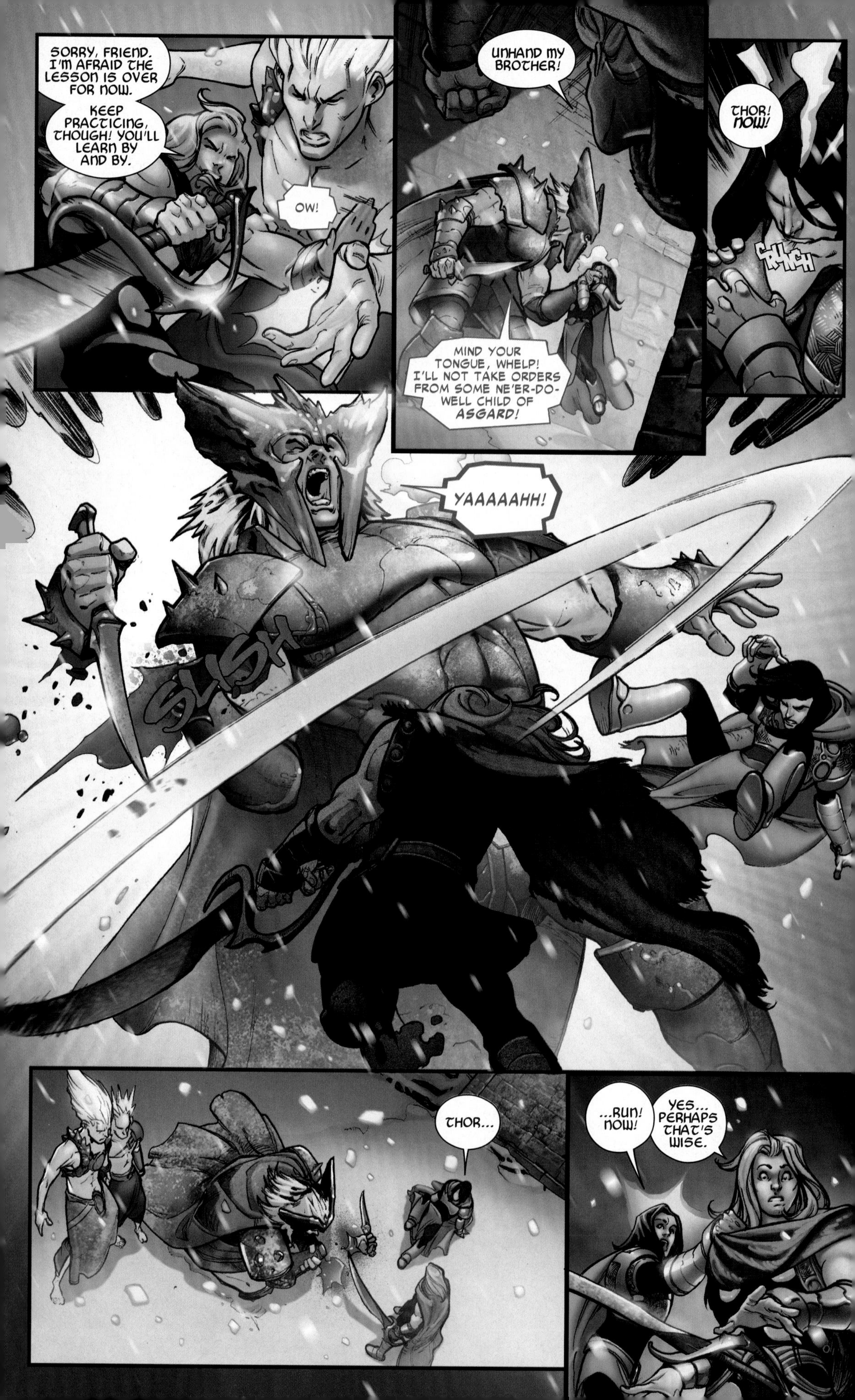
SORRY, FRIEND. I'M AFRAID THE LESSON IS OVER FOR NOW.
KEEP PRACTICING, THOUGH! YOU'LL LEARN BY AND BY.
OW!
UNHAND MY BROTHER!
MIND YOUR TONGUE, WHELP! I'LL NOT TAKE ORDERS FROM SOME NE'ER-DO-WELL CHILD OF ASGARD!
THOR! NOW!
CRUNCH
YAAAAAHH!
SLISH
THOR...
...RUN! NOW!
YES... PERHAPS THAT'S WISE.

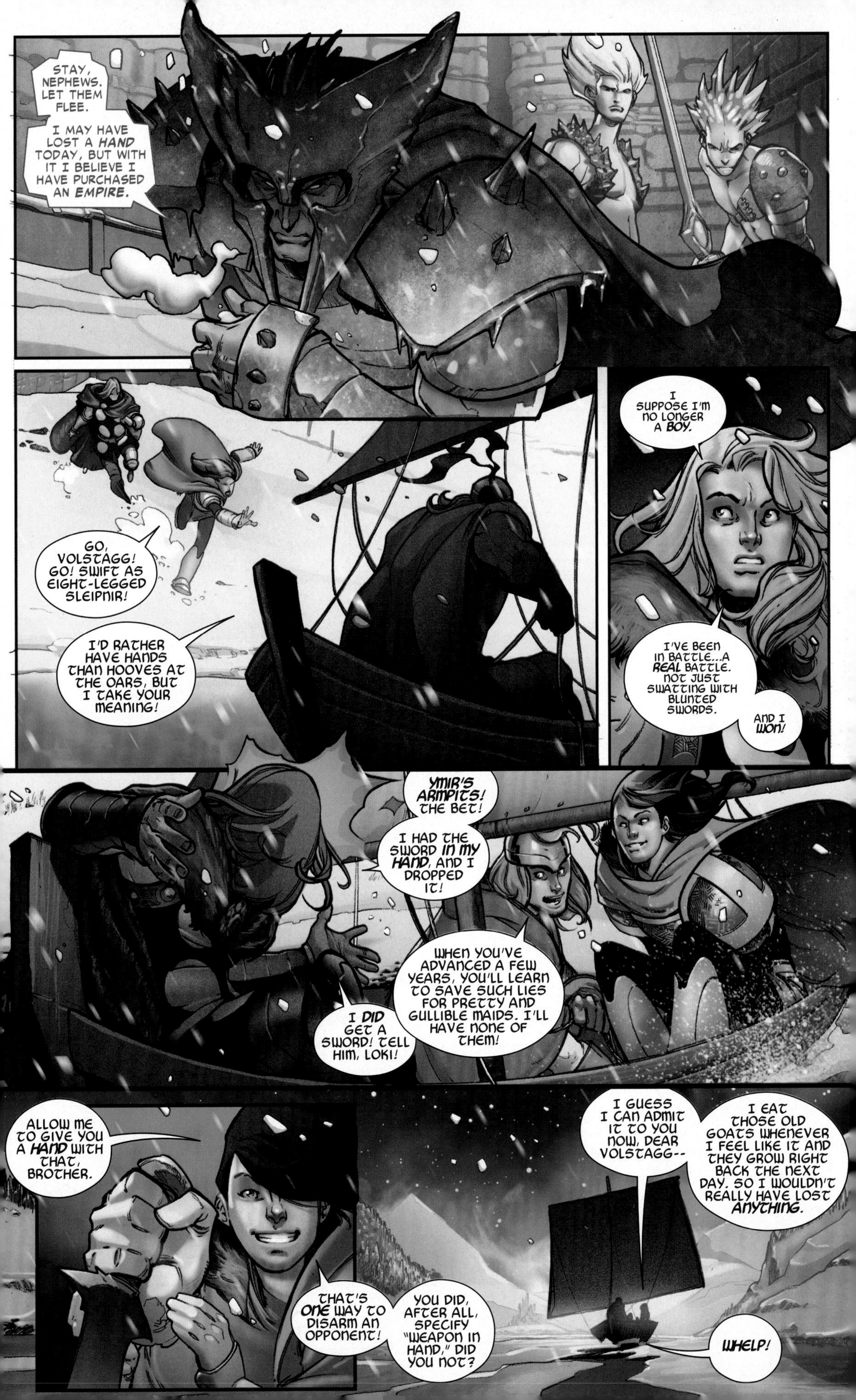
STAY, NEPHEWS. LET THEM FLEE.
I MAY HAVE LOST A HAND TODAY, BUT WITH IT I BELIEVE I HAVE PURCHASED AN EMPIRE.
GO, VOLSTAGG! GO! SWIFT AS EIGHT-LEGGED SLEIPNIR!
I'D RATHER HAVE HANDS THAN HOOVES AT THE OARS, BUT I TAKE YOUR MEANING!
I SUPPOSE I'M NO LONGER A BOY.
I'VE BEEN IN BATTLE...A REAL BATTLE. NOT JUST SWATTING WITH BLUNTED SWORDS.
AND I WON!
YMIR'S ARMPITS! THE BET!
I HAD THE SWORD IN MY HAND, AND I DROPPED IT!
WHEN YOU'VE ADVANCED A FEW YEARS, YOU'LL LEARN TO SAVE SUCH LIES FOR PRETTY AND GULLIBLE MAIDS. I'LL HAVE NONE OF THEM!
I DID GET A SWORD! TELL HIM, LOKI!
ALLOW ME TO GIVE YOU A HAND WITH THAT, BROTHER.
THAT'S ONE WAY TO DISARM AN OPPONENT!
YOU DID, AFTER ALL, SPECIFY "WEAPON IN HAND," DID YOU NOT?
I GUESS I CAN ADMIT IT TO YOU NOW, DEAR VOLSTAGG--
I EAT THOSE OLD GOATS WHENEVER I FEEL LIKE IT AND THEY GROW RIGHT BACK THE NEXT DAY. SO I WOULDN'T REALLY HAVE LOST ANYTHING.
WHELP!

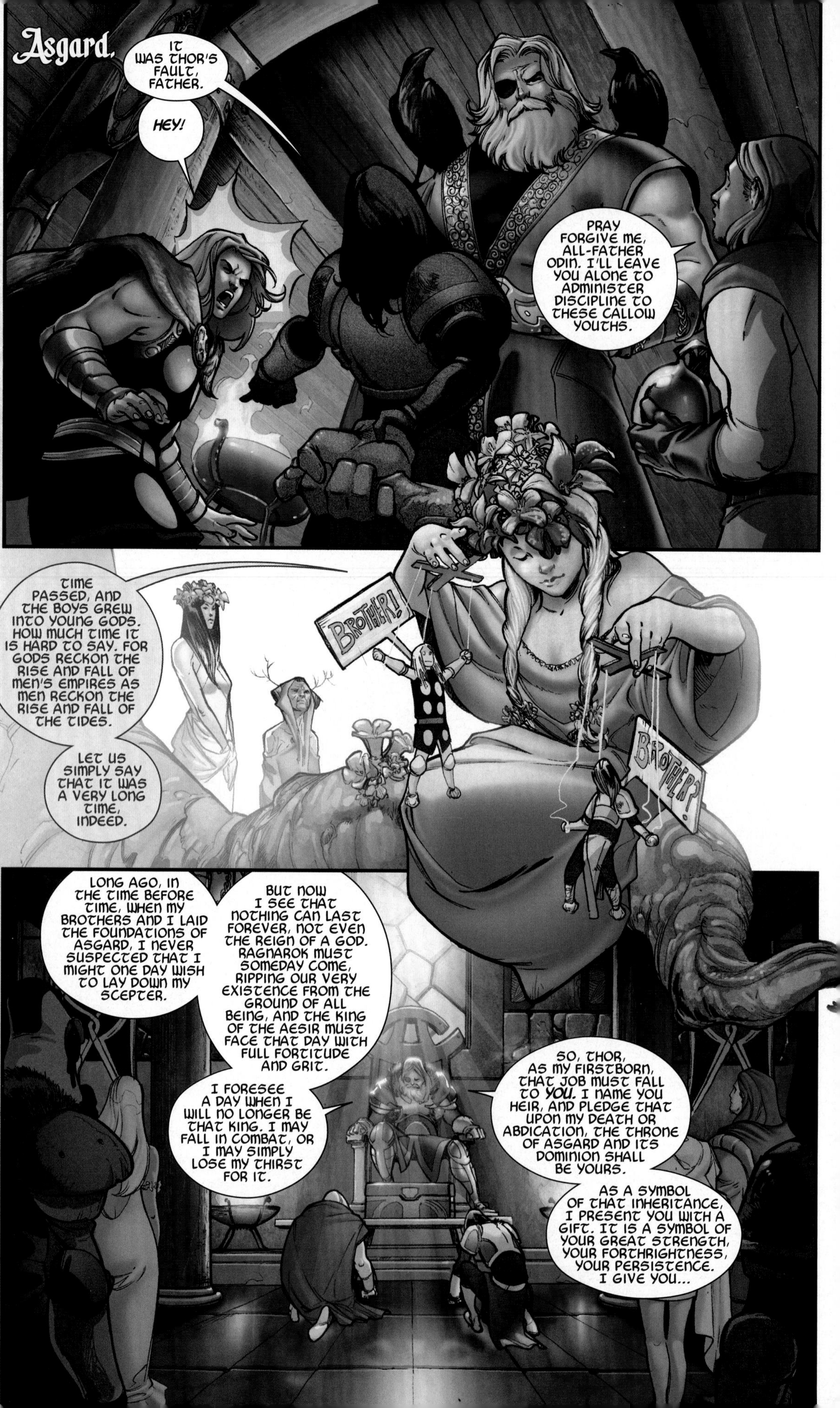
Asgard,
IT WAS THOR'S FAULT, FATHER.
HEY!
PRAY FORGIVE ME, ALL-FATHER ODIN. I'LL LEAVE YOU ALONE TO ADMINISTER DISCIPLINE TO THESE CALLOW YOUTHS.
TIME PASSED, AND THE BOYS GREW INTO YOUNG GODS. HOW MUCH TIME IT IS HARD TO SAY. FOR GODS RECKON THE RISE AND FALL OF MEN'S EMPIRES AS MEN RECKON THE RISE AND FALL OF THE TIDES.
LET US SIMPLY SAY THAT IT WAS A VERY LONG TIME, INDEED.
BROTHER!
BROTHER?
LONG AGO, IN THE TIME BEFORE TIME, WHEN MY BROTHERS AND I LAID THE FOUNDATIONS OF ASGARD, I NEVER SUSPECTED THAT I MIGHT ONE DAY WISH TO LAY DOWN MY SCEPTER.
BUT NOW I SEE THAT NOTHING CAN LAST FOREVER, NOT EVEN THE REIGN OF A GOD. RAGNAROK MUST SOMEDAY COME, RIPPING OUR VERY EXISTENCE FROM THE GROUND OF ALL BEING, AND THE KING OF THE AESIR MUST FACE THAT DAY WITH FULL FORTITUDE AND GRIT.
I FORESEE A DAY WHEN I WILL NO LONGER BE THAT KING. I MAY FALL IN COMBAT, OR I MAY SIMPLY LOSE MY THIRST FOR IT.
SO, THOR, AS MY FIRSTBORN, THAT JOB MUST FALL TO YOU. I NAME YOU HEIR, AND PLEDGE THAT UPON MY DEATH OR ABDICATION, THE THRONE OF ASGARD AND ITS DOMINION SHALL BE YOURS.
AS A SYMBOL OF THAT INHERITANCE, I PRESENT YOU WITH A GIFT. IT IS A SYMBOL OF YOUR GREAT STRENGTH, YOUR FORTHRIGHTNESS, YOUR PERSISTENCE. I GIVE YOU...

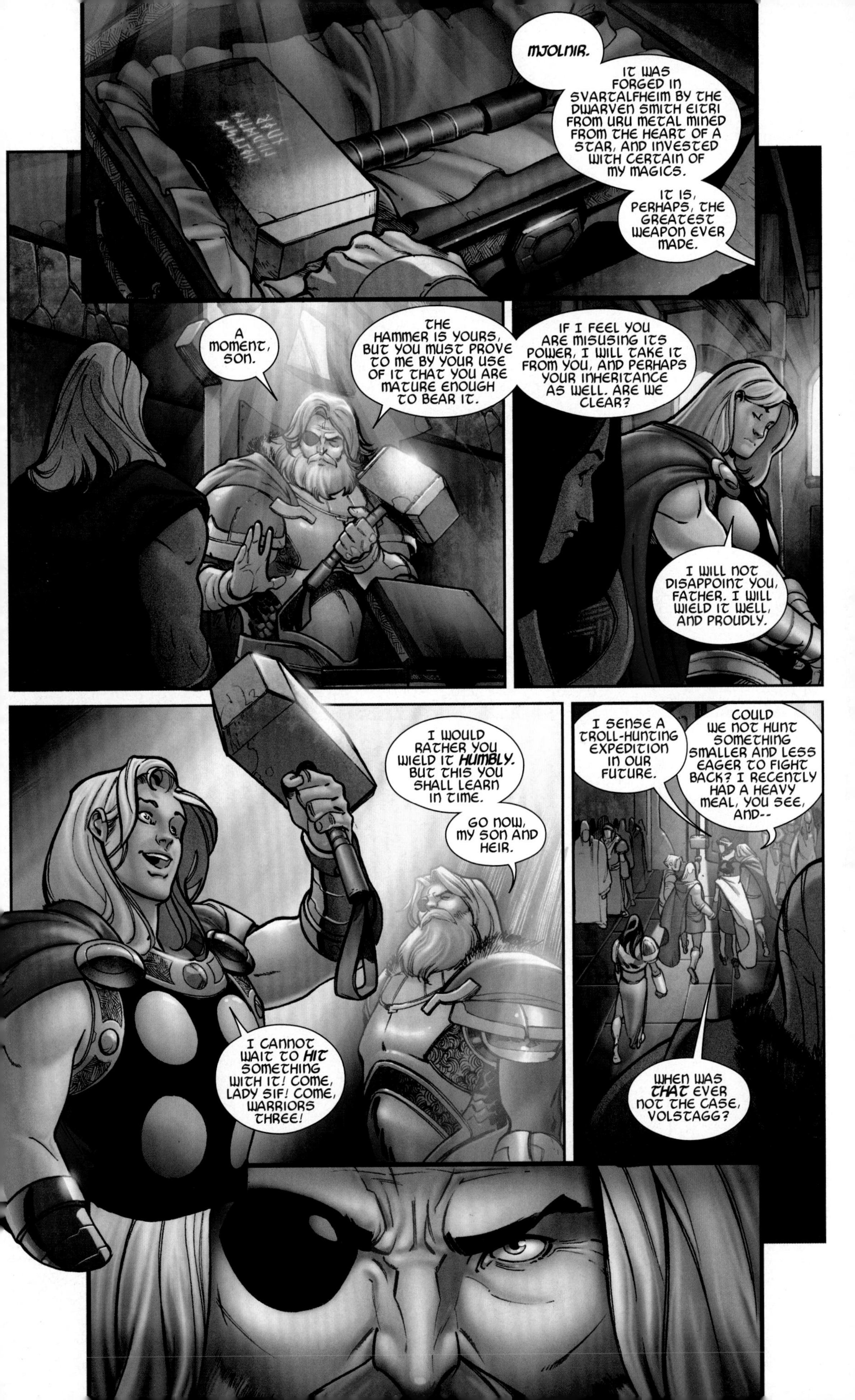
MJOLNIR.
IT WAS FORGED IN SVARTALFHEIM BY THE DWARVEN SMITH EITRI FROM URU METAL MINED FROM THE HEART OF A STAR, AND INVESTED WITH CERTAIN OF MY MAGICS.
IT IS, PERHAPS, THE GREATEST WEAPON EVER MADE.
A MOMENT, SON.
THE HAMMER IS YOURS, BUT YOU MUST PROVE TO ME BY YOUR USE OF IT THAT YOU ARE MATURE ENOUGH TO BEAR IT.
IF I FEEL YOU ARE MISUSING ITS POWER, I WILL TAKE IT FROM YOU, AND PERHAPS YOUR INHERITANCE AS WELL. ARE WE CLEAR?
I WILL NOT DISAPPOINT YOU, FATHER. I WILL WIELD IT WELL, AND PROUDLY.
I WOULD RATHER YOU WIELD IT HUMBLY. BUT THIS YOU SHALL LEARN IN TIME.
GO NOW, MY SON AND HEIR.
I CANNOT WAIT TO HIT SOMETHING WITH IT! COME, LADY SIF! COME, WARRIORS THREE!
I SENSE A TROLL-HUNTING EXPEDITION IN OUR FUTURE.
COULD WE NOT HUNT SOMETHING SMALLER AND LESS EAGER TO FIGHT BACK? I RECENTLY HAD A HEAVY MEAL, YOU SEE, AND--
WHEN WAS THAT EVER NOT THE CASE, VOLSTAGG?

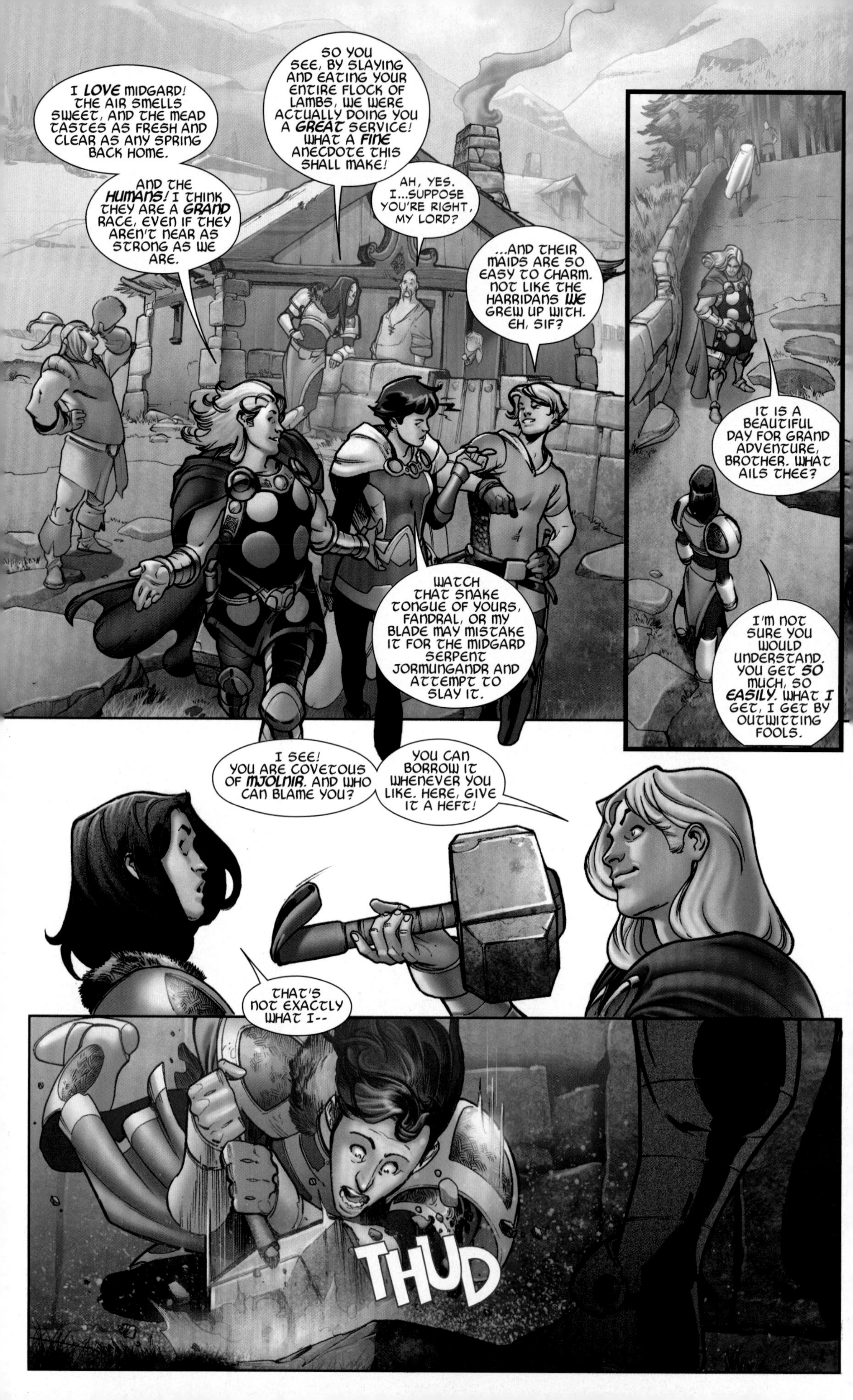

I LOVE MIDGARD! THE AIR SMELLS SWEET, AND THE MEAD TASTES AS FRESH AND CLEAR AS ANY SPRING BACK HOME.
AND THE HUMANS! I THINK THEY ARE A GRAND RACE, EVEN IF THEY AREN'T NEAR AS STRONG AS WE ARE.
SO YOU SEE, BY SLAYING AND EATING YOUR ENTIRE FLOCK OF LAMBS, WE WERE ACTUALLY DOING YOU A GREAT SERVICE! WHAT A FINE ANECDOTE THIS SHALL MAKE!
AH, YES. I...SUPPOSE YOU'RE RIGHT, MY LORD?
...AND THEIR MAIDS ARE SO EASY TO CHARM. NOT LIKE THE HARRIDANS WE GREW UP WITH. EH, SIF?
WATCH THAT SNAKE TONGUE OF YOURS, FANDRAL, OR MY BLADE MAY MISTAKE IT FOR THE MIDGARD SERPENT JORMUNGANDR AND ATTEMPT TO SLAY IT.
IT IS A BEAUTIFUL DAY FOR GRAND ADVENTURE, BROTHER. WHAT AILS THEE?
I'M NOT SURE YOU WOULD UNDERSTAND. YOU GET SO MUCH, SO EASILY. WHAT I GET, I GET BY OUTWITTING FOOLS.
I SEE! YOU ARE COVETOUS OF MJOLNIR. AND WHO CAN BLAME YOU?
YOU CAN BORROW IT WHENEVER YOU LIKE. HERE, GIVE IT A HEFT!
THAT'S NOT EXACTLY WHAT I--
THUD

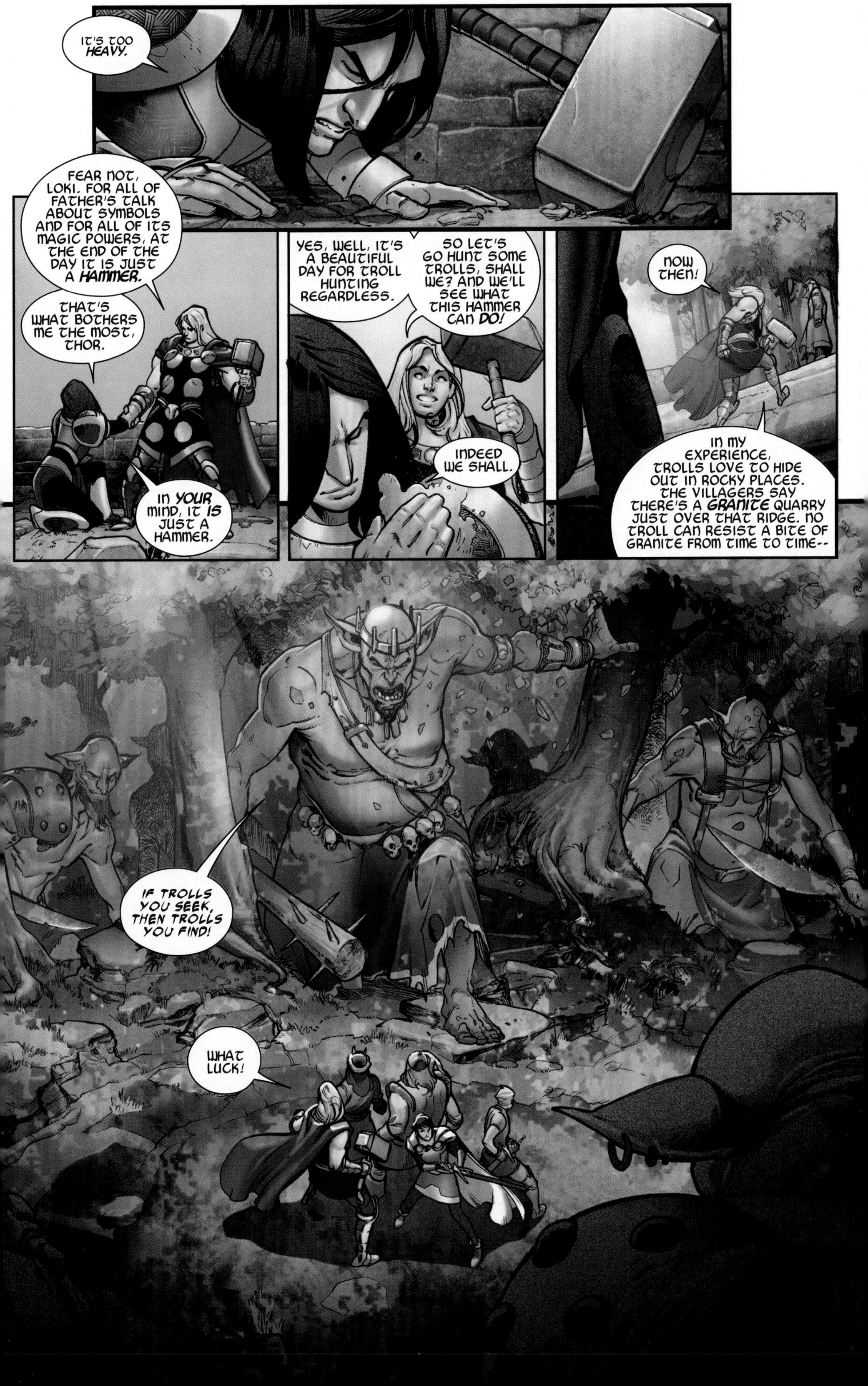
IT'S TOO HEAVY.
FEAR NOT, LOKI. FOR ALL OF FATHER'S TALK ABOUT SYMBOLS AND FOR ALL OF ITS MAGIC POWERS, AT THE END OF THE DAY IT IS JUST A HAMMER.
THAT'S WHAT BOTHERS ME THE MOST, THOR.
IN YOUR MIND, IT IS JUST A HAMMER.
YES, WELL, IT'S A BEAUTIFUL DAY FOR TROLL HUNTING REGARDLESS.
SO LET'S GO HUNT SOME TROLLS, SHALL WE? AND WE'LL SEE WHAT THIS HAMMER CAN DO!
INDEED WE SHALL.
NOW THEN!
IN MY EXPERIENCE, TROLLS LOVE TO HIDE OUT IN ROCKY PLACES. THE VILLAGERS SAY THERE'S A GRANITE QUARRY JUST OVER THAT RIDGE. NO TROLL CAN RESIST A BITE OF GRANITE FROM TIME TO TIME--
IF TROLLS YOU SEEK, THEN TROLLS YOU FIND!
WHAT LUCK!

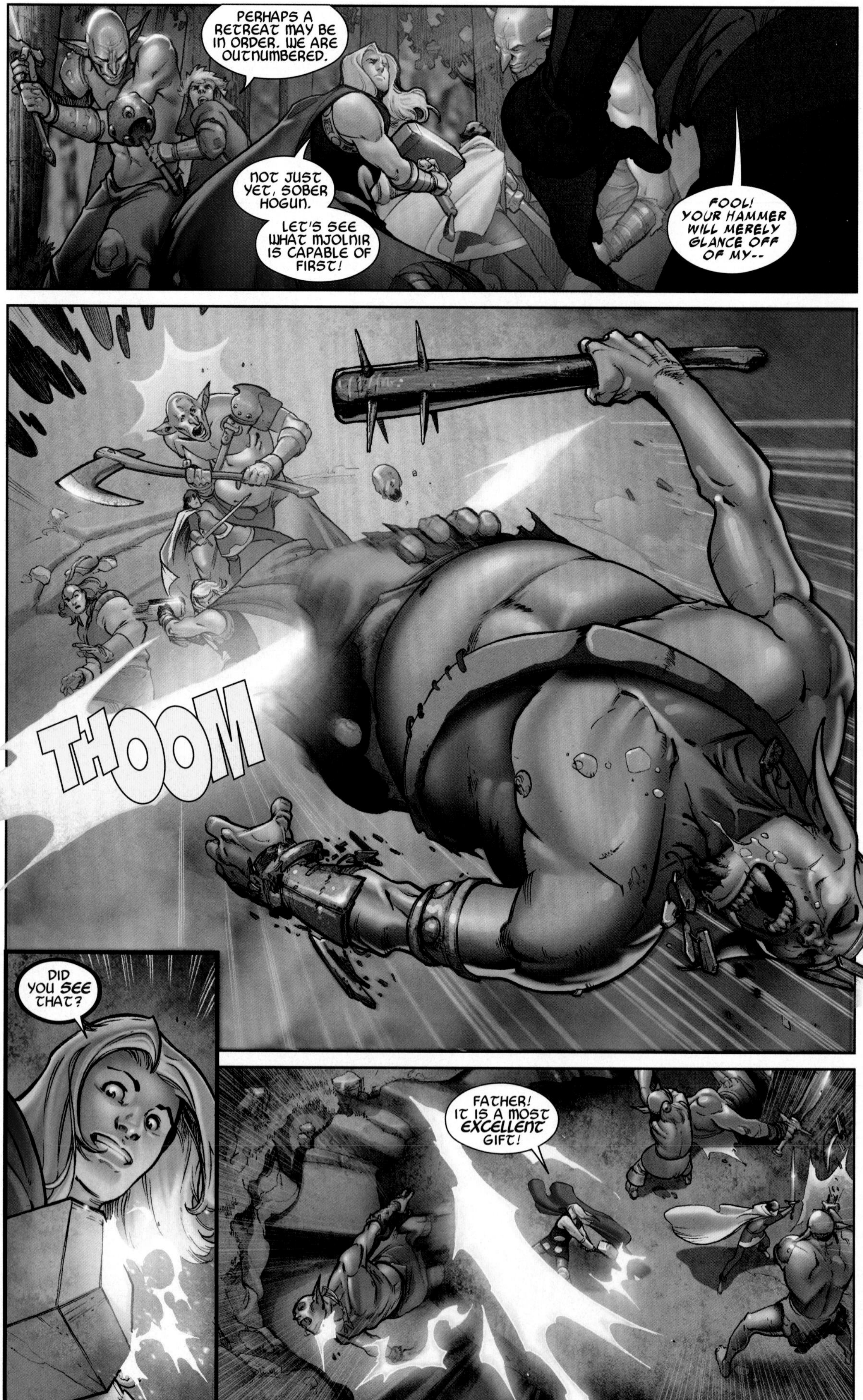
PERHAPS A RETREAT MAY BE IN ORDER. WE ARE OUTNUMBERED.
NOT JUST YET, SOBER HOGUN.
LET'S SEE WHAT MJOLNIR IS CAPABLE OF FIRST!
FOOL! YOUR HAMMER WILL MERELY GLANCE OFF OF MY--
THOOM
DID YOU SEE THAT?
FATHER! IT IS A MOST EXCELLENT GIFT!

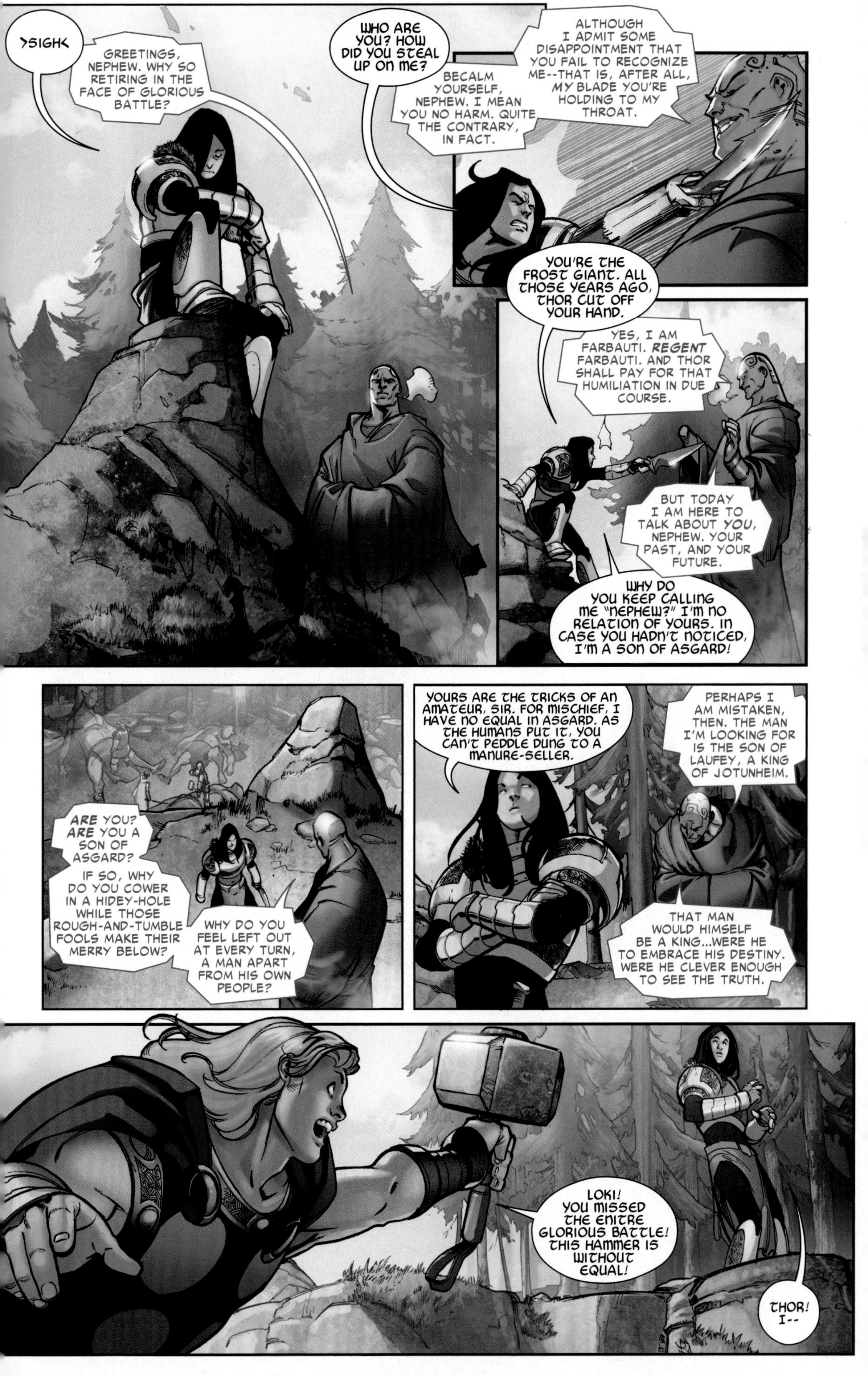
>SIGH<
GREETINGS, NEPHEW. WHY SO RETIRING IN THE FACE OF GLORIOUS BATTLE?
WHO ARE YOU? HOW DID YOU STEAL UP ON ME?
BECALM YOURSELF, NEPHEW. I MEAN YOU NO HARM. QUITE THE CONTRARY, IN FACT.
ALTHOUGH I ADMIT SOME DISAPPOINTMENT THAT YOU FAIL TO RECOGNIZE ME--THAT IS, AFTER ALL, MY BLADE YOU'RE HOLDING TO MY THROAT.
YOU'RE THE FROST GIANT. ALL THOSE YEARS AGO, THOR CUT OFF YOUR HAND.
YES, I AM FARBAUTI. REGENT FARBAUTI. AND THOR SHALL PAY FOR THAT HUMILIATION IN DUE COURSE.
BUT TODAY I AM HERE TO TALK ABOUT YOU, NEPHEW. YOUR PAST, AND YOUR FUTURE.
WHY DO YOU KEEP CALLING ME "NEPHEW?" I'M NO RELATION OF YOURS. IN CASE YOU HADN'T NOTICED, I'M A SON OF ASGARD!
ARE YOU? ARE YOU A SON OF ASGARD?
IF SO, WHY DO YOU COWER IN A HIDEY-HOLE WHILE THOSE ROUGH-AND-TUMBLE FOOLS MAKE THEIR MERRY BELOW?
WHY DO YOU FEEL LEFT OUT AT EVERY TURN, A MAN APART FROM HIS OWN PEOPLE?
YOURS ARE THE TRICKS OF AN AMATEUR, SIR. FOR MISCHIEF, I HAVE NO EQUAL IN ASGARD. AS THE HUMANS PUT IT, YOU CAN'T PEDDLE DUNG TO A MANURE-SELLER.
PERHAPS I AM MISTAKEN, THEN. THE MAN I'M LOOKING FOR IS THE SON OF LAUFEY, A KING OF JOTUNHEIM.
THAT MAN WOULD HIMSELF BE A KING...WERE HE TO EMBRACE HIS DESTINY. WERE HE CLEVER ENOUGH TO SEE THE TRUTH.
LOKI! YOU MISSED THE ENITRE GLORIOUS BATTLE! THIS HAMMER IS WITHOUT EQUAL!
THOR! I--

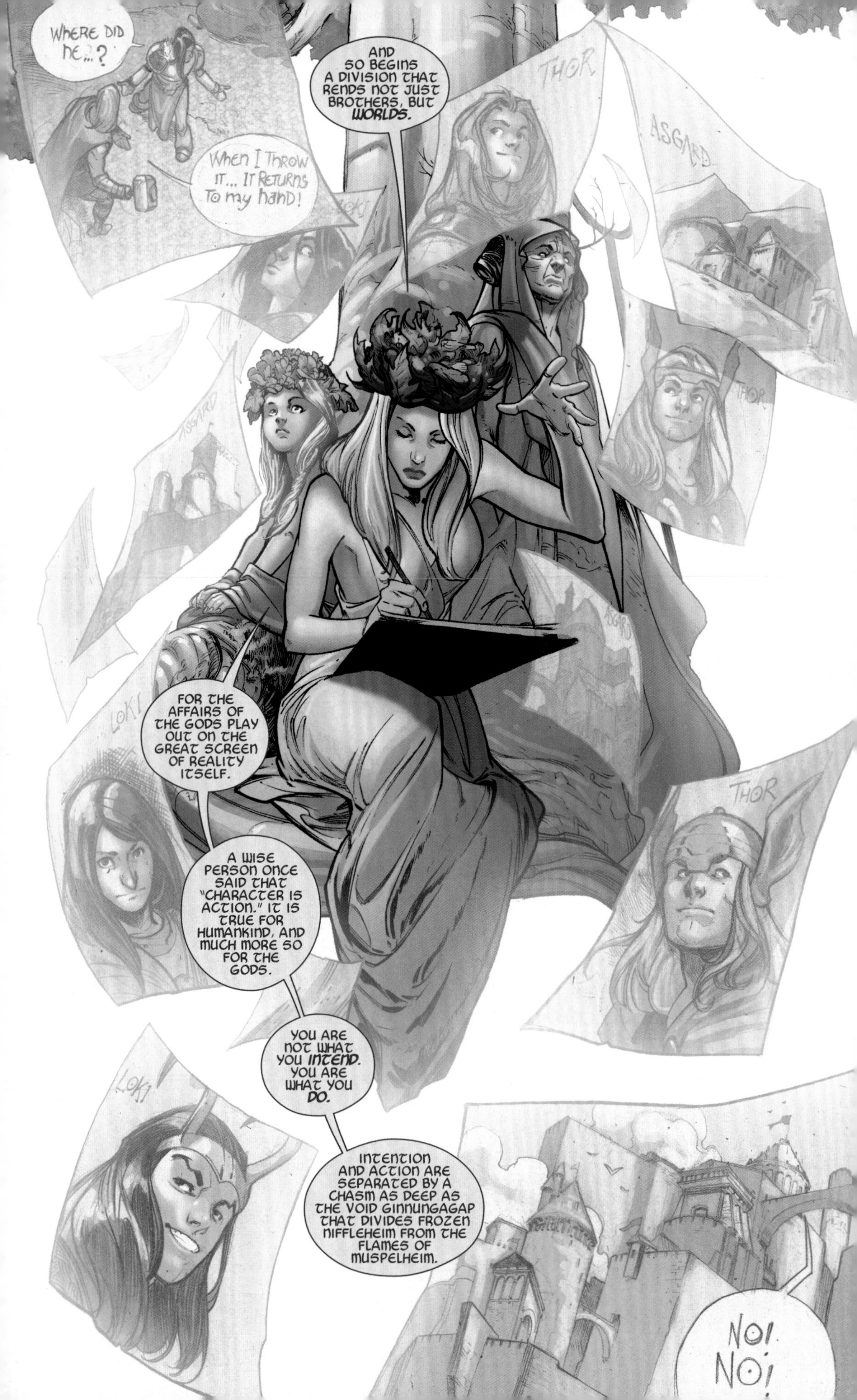
WHERE DID HE...?
WHEN I THROW IT... IT RETURNS TO MY HAND!
AND SO BEGINS A DIVISION THAT RENDS NOT JUST BROTHERS, BUT WORLDS.
THOR
ASGARD
LOKI
ASGARD
THOR
ASGARD
FOR THE AFFAIRS OF THE GODS PLAY OUT ON THE GREAT SCREEN OF REALITY ITSELF.
LOKI
THOR
A WISE PERSON ONCE SAID THAT "CHARACTER IS ACTION." IT IS TRUE FOR HUMANKIND, AND MUCH MORE SO FOR THE GODS.
YOU ARE NOT WHAT YOU INTEND. YOU ARE WHAT YOU DO.
LOKI
INTENTION AND ACTION ARE SEPARATED BY A CHASM AS DEEP AS THE VOID GINNUNGAGAP THAT DIVIDES FROZEN NIFFLEHEIM FROM THE FLAMES OF MUSPELHEIM.
NO! NO!

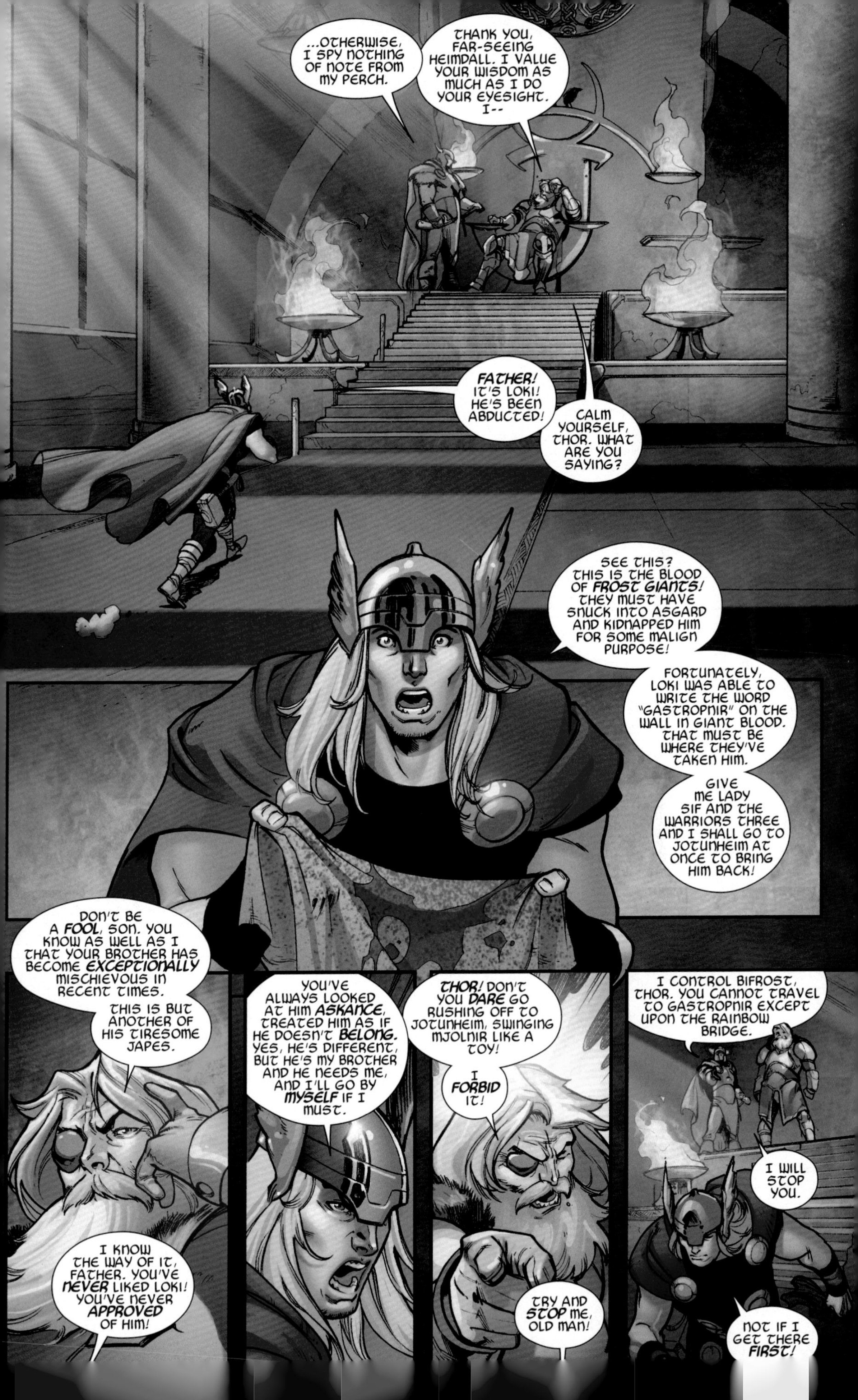

...OTHERWISE, I SPY NOTHING OF NOTE FROM MY PERCH.
THANK YOU, FAR-SEEING HEIMDALL. I VALUE YOUR WISDOM AS MUCH AS I DO YOUR EYESIGHT. I--
FATHER! IT'S LOKI! HE'S BEEN ABDUCTED!
CALM YOURSELF, THOR. WHAT ARE YOU SAYING?
SEE THIS? THIS IS THE BLOOD OF FROST GIANTS! THEY MUST HAVE SNUCK INTO ASGARD AND KIDNAPPED HIM FOR SOME MALIGN PURPOSE!
FORTUNATELY, LOKI WAS ABLE TO WRITE THE WORD "GASTROPNIR" ON THE WALL IN GIANT BLOOD. THAT MUST BE WHERE THEY'VE TAKEN HIM.
GIVE ME LADY SIF AND THE WARRIORS THREE AND I SHALL GO TO JOTUNHEIM AT ONCE TO BRING HIM BACK!
DON'T BE A FOOL, SON. YOU KNOW AS WELL AS I THAT YOUR BROTHER HAS BECOME EXCEPTIONALLY MISCHIEVOUS IN RECENT TIMES.
THIS IS BUT ANOTHER OF HIS TIRESOME JAPES.
I KNOW THE WAY OF IT, FATHER. YOU'VE NEVER LIKED LOKI! YOU'VE NEVER APPROVED OF HIM!
YOU'VE ALWAYS LOOKED AT HIM ASKANCE, TREATED HIM AS IF HE DOESN'T BELONG. YES, HE'S DIFFERENT, BUT HE'S MY BROTHER AND HE NEEDS ME, AND I'LL GO BY MYSELF IF I MUST.
THOR! DON'T YOU DARE GO RUSHING OFF TO JOTUNHEIM, SWINGING MJOLNIR LIKE A TOY!
I FORBID IT!
TRY AND STOP ME, OLD MAN!
I CONTROL BIFROST, THOR. YOU CANNOT TRAVEL TO GASTROPNIR EXCEPT UPON THE RAINBOW BRIDGE.
I WILL STOP YOU.
NOT IF I GET THERE FIRST!

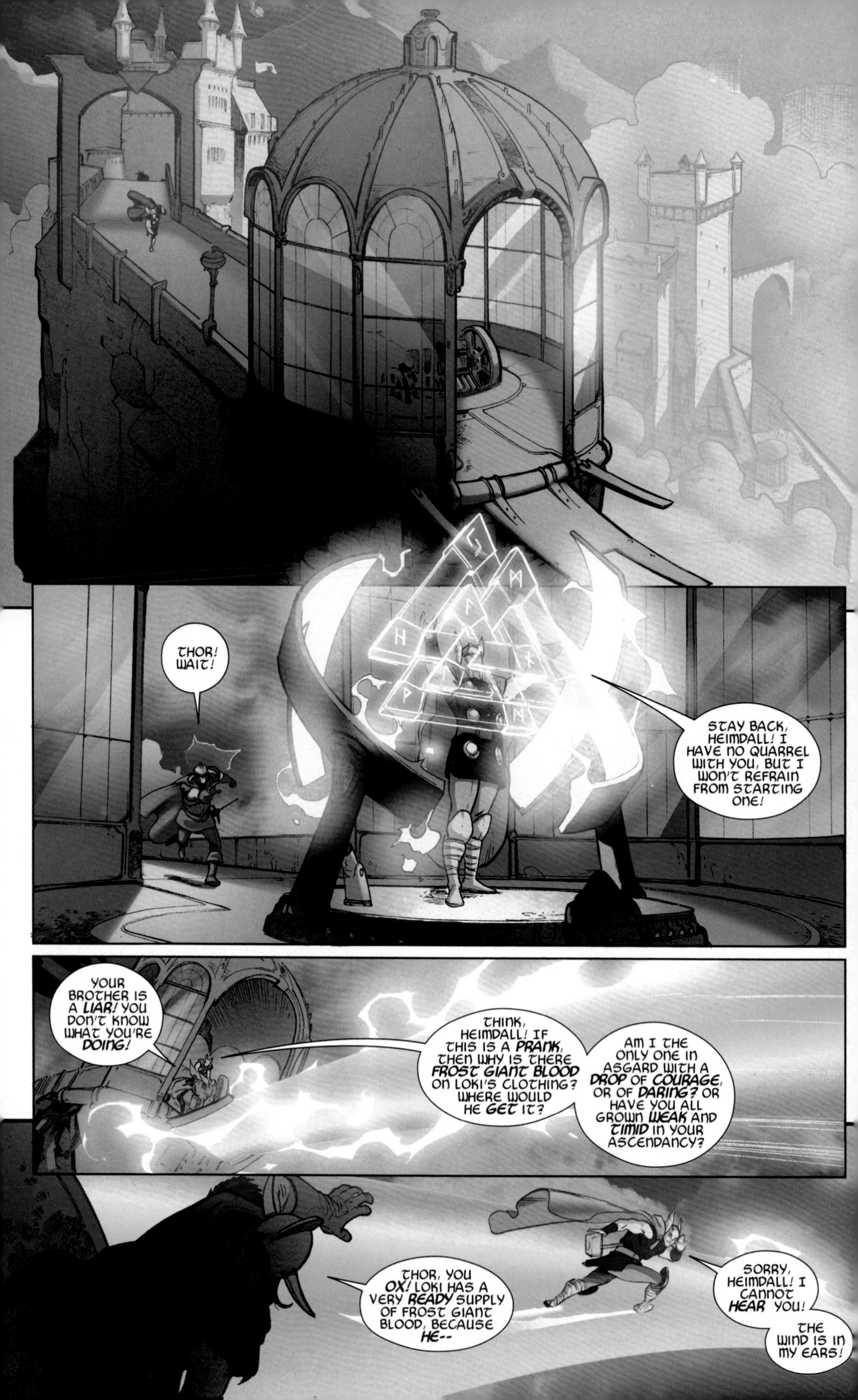
THOR! WAIT!
STAY BACK, HEIMDALL! I HAVE NO QUARREL WITH YOU, BUT I WON'T REFRAIN FROM STARTING ONE!
YOUR BROTHER IS A LIAR! YOU DON'T KNOW WHAT YOU'RE DOING!
THINK, HEIMDALL! IF THIS IS A PRANK, THEN WHY IS THERE FROST GIANT BLOOD ON LOKI'S CLOTHING? WHERE WOULD HE GET IT?
AM I THE ONLY ONE IN ASGARD WITH A DROP OF COURAGE, OR OF DARING? OR HAVE YOU ALL GROWN WEAK AND TIMID IN YOUR ASCENDANCY?
THOR, YOU OX! LOKI HAS A VERY READY SUPPLY OF FROST GIANT BLOOD, BECAUSE HE--
SORRY, HEIMDALL! I CANNOT HEAR YOU!
THE WIND IS IN MY EARS!

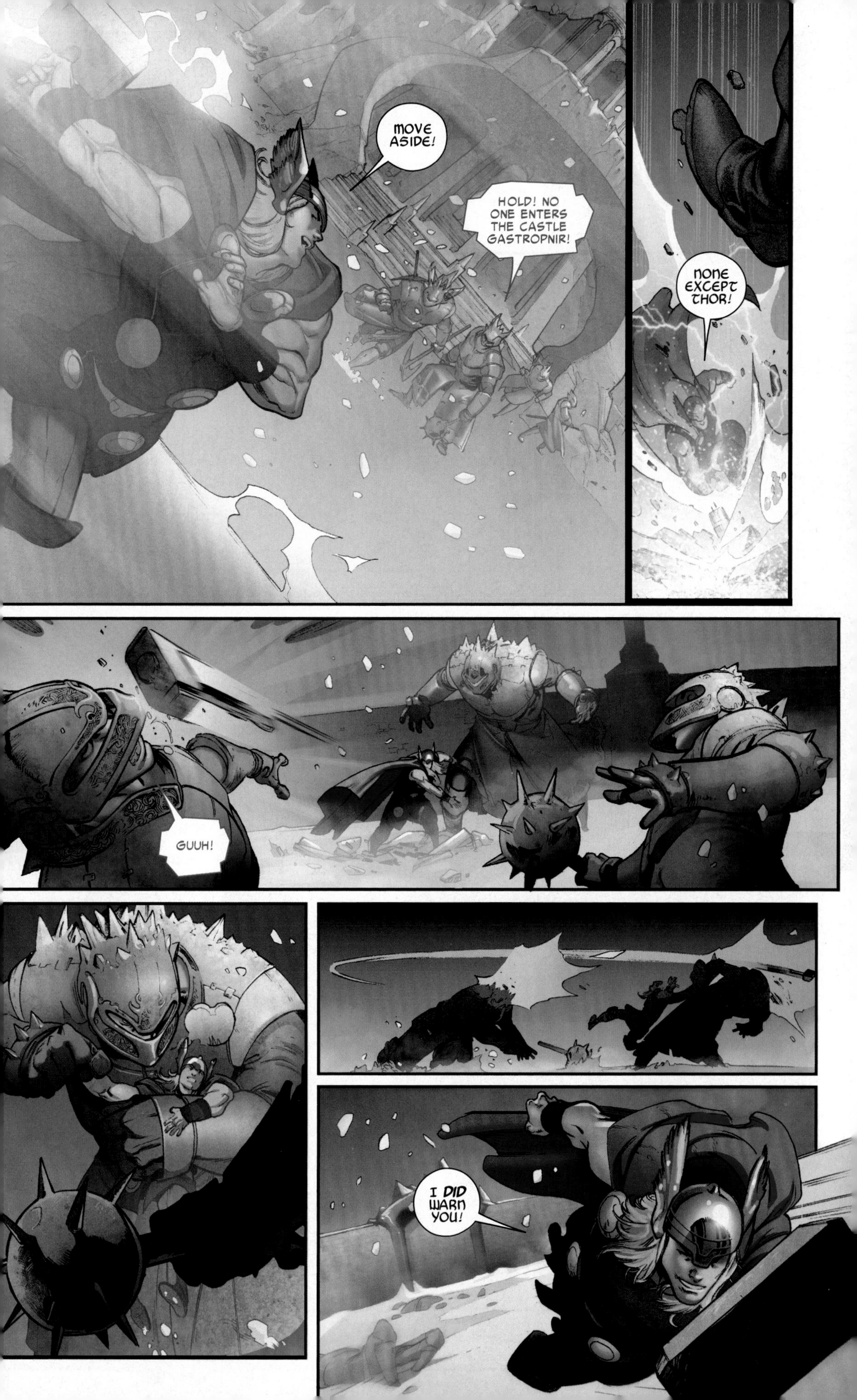
MOVE ASIDE!
HOLD! NO ONE ENTERS THE CASTLE GASTROPNIR!
NONE EXCEPT THOR!
GUUH!
I DID WARN YOU!

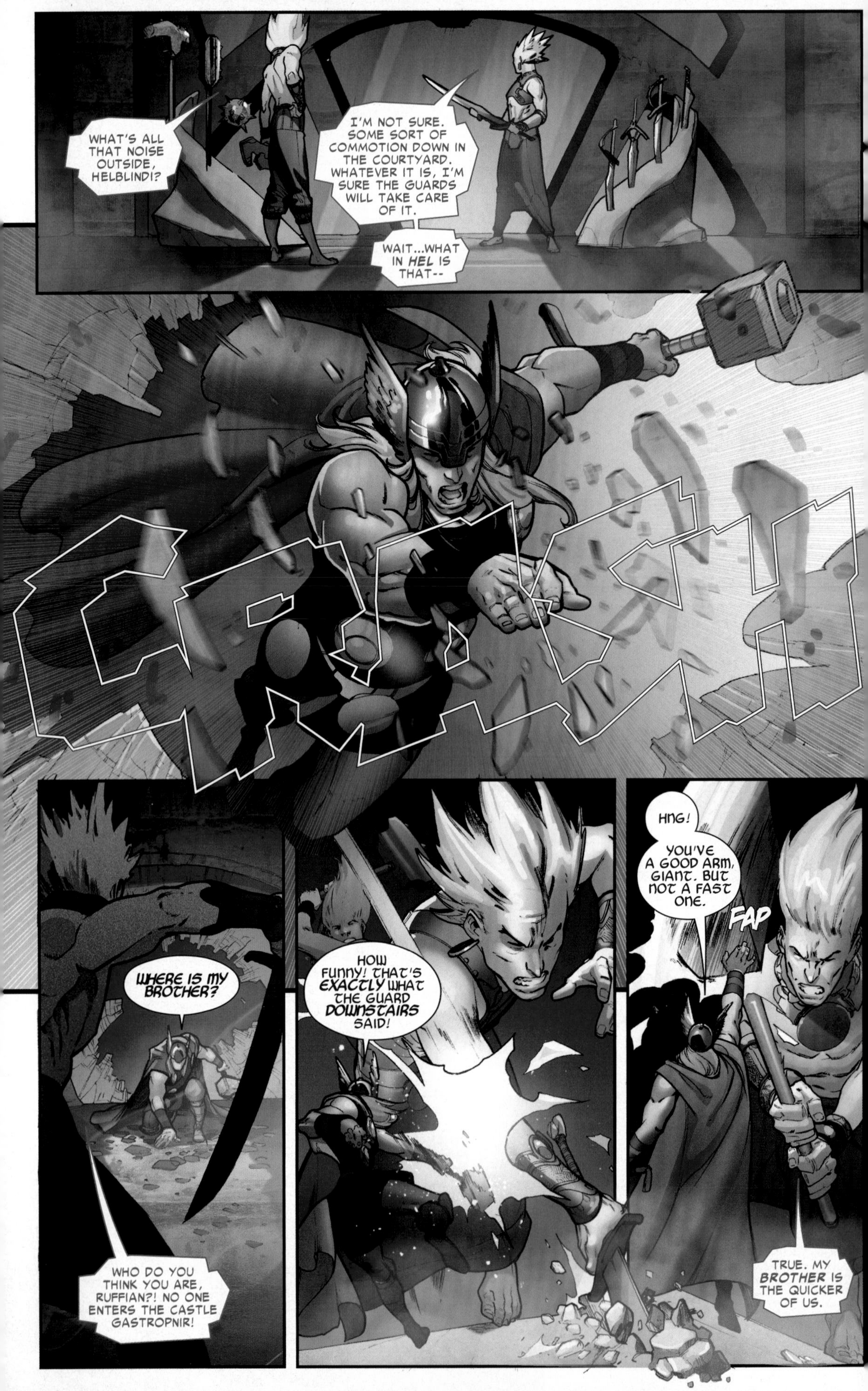
WHAT'S ALL THAT NOISE OUTSIDE, HELBLINDI?
I'M NOT SURE. SOME SORT OF COMMOTION DOWN IN THE COURTYARD. WHATEVER IT IS, I'M SURE THE GUARDS WILL TAKE CARE OF IT.
WAIT...WHAT IN HEL IS THAT--
CRASH
WHERE IS MY BROTHER?
WHO DO YOU THINK YOU ARE, RUFFIAN?! NO ONE ENTERS THE CASTLE GASTROPNIR!
HOW FUNNY! THAT'S EXACTLY WHAT THE GUARD DOWNSTAIRS SAID!
HNG!
YOU'VE A GOOD ARM, GIANT. BUT NOT A FAST ONE.
FAP
TRUE. MY BROTHER IS THE QUICKER OF US.

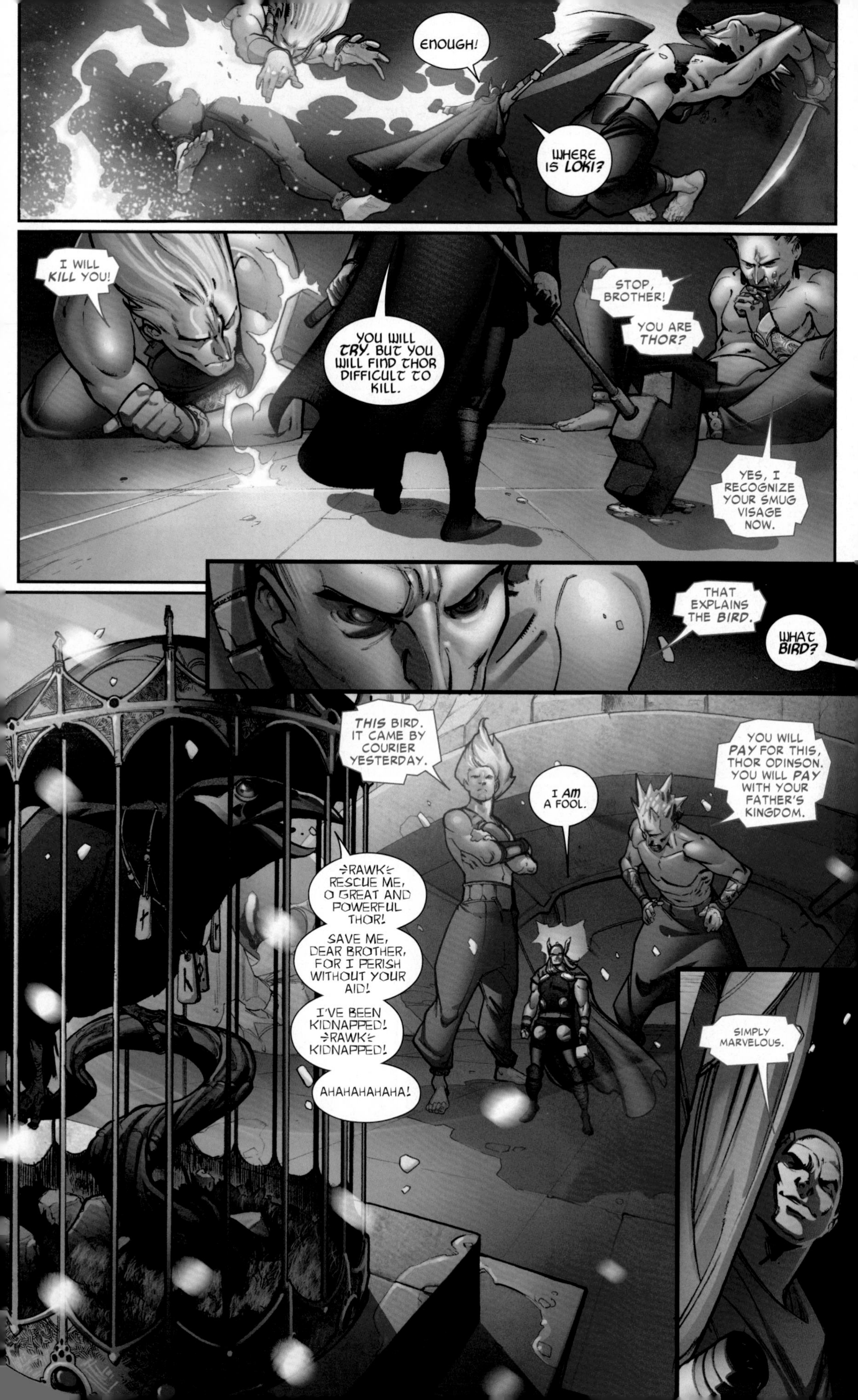
ENOUGH!
WHERE IS LOKI?
I WILL KILL YOU!
YOU WILL TRY. BUT YOU WILL FIND THOR DIFFICULT TO KILL.
STOP, BROTHER!
YOU ARE THOR?
YES, I RECOGNIZE YOUR SMUG VISAGE NOW.
THAT EXPLAINS THE BIRD.
WHAT BIRD?
THIS BIRD. IT CAME BY COURIER YESTERDAY.
I AM A FOOL.
YOU WILL PAY FOR THIS, THOR ODINSON. YOU WILL PAY WITH YOUR FATHER'S KINGDOM.
RAWK RESCUE ME, O GREAT AND POWERFUL THOR!
SAVE ME, DEAR BROTHER, FOR I PERISH WITHOUT YOUR AID!
I'VE BEEN KIDNAPPED! RAWK KIDNAPPED!
AHAHAHAHAHA!
SIMPLY MARVELOUS.

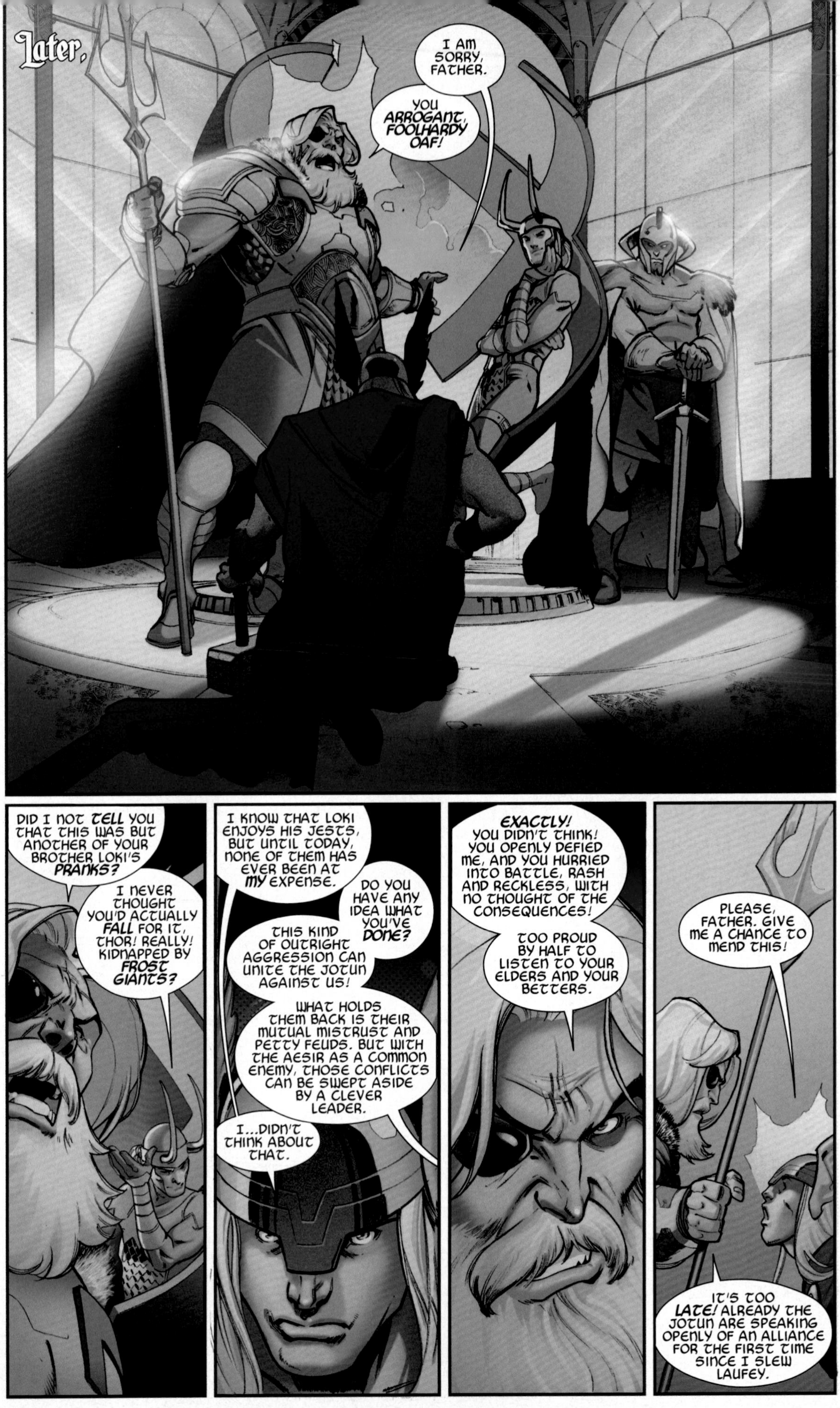
Later,
I AM SORRY, FATHER.
YOU ARROGANT, FOOLHARDY OAF!
DID I NOT TELL YOU THAT THIS WAS BUT ANOTHER OF YOUR BROTHER LOKI'S PRANKS?
I NEVER THOUGHT YOU'D ACTUALLY FALL FOR IT, THOR! REALLY! KIDNAPPED BY FROST GIANTS?
I KNOW THAT LOKI ENJOYS HIS JESTS, BUT UNTIL TODAY, NONE OF THEM HAS EVER BEEN AT MY EXPENSE.
DO YOU HAVE ANY IDEA WHAT YOU'VE DONE?
THIS KIND OF OUTRIGHT AGGRESSION CAN UNITE THE JOTUN AGAINST US!
WHAT HOLDS THEM BACK IS THEIR MUTUAL MISTRUST AND PETTY FEUDS. BUT WITH THE AESIR AS A COMMON ENEMY, THOSE CONFLICTS CAN BE SWEPT ASIDE BY A CLEVER LEADER.
I...DIDN'T THINK ABOUT THAT.
EXACTLY! YOU DIDN'T THINK! YOU OPENLY DEFIED ME, AND YOU HURRIED INTO BATTLE, RASH AND RECKLESS, WITH NO THOUGHT OF THE CONSEQUENCES!
TOO PROUD BY HALF TO LISTEN TO YOUR ELDERS AND YOUR BETTERS.
PLEASE, FATHER. GIVE ME A CHANCE TO MEND THIS!
IT'S TOO LATE! ALREADY THE JOTUN ARE SPEAKING OPENLY OF AN ALLIANCE FOR THE FIRST TIME SINCE I SLEW LAUFEY.

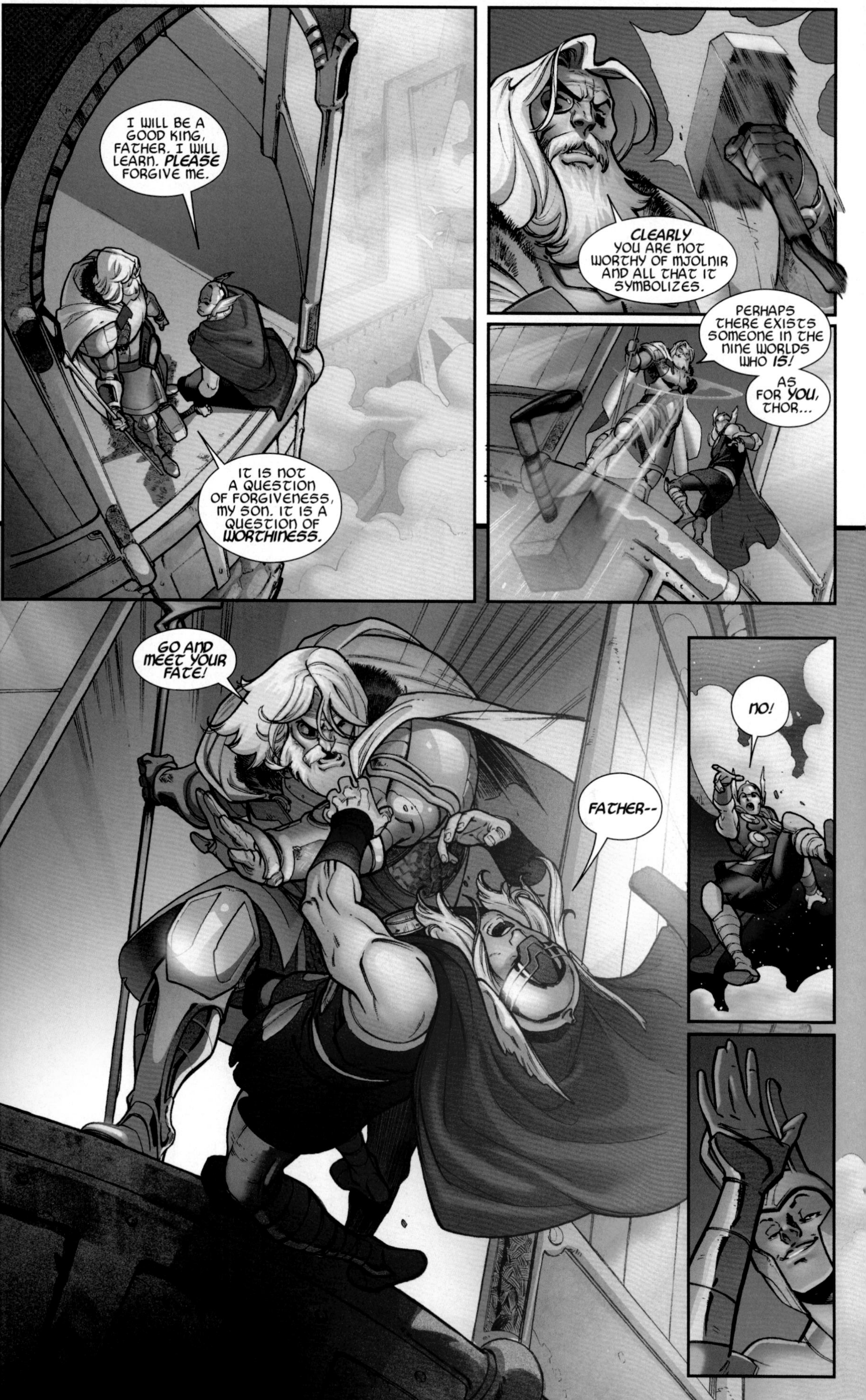
I WILL BE A GOOD KING, FATHER. I WILL LEARN. PLEASE FORGIVE ME.
IT IS NOT A QUESTION OF FORGIVENESS, MY SON. IT IS A QUESTION OF WORTHINESS.
CLEARLY YOU ARE NOT WORTHY OF MJOLNIR AND ALL THAT IT SYMBOLIZES.
PERHAPS THERE EXISTS SOMEONE IN THE NINE WORLDS WHO IS!
AS FOR YOU, THOR...
GO AND MEET YOUR FATE!
FATHER--
NO!

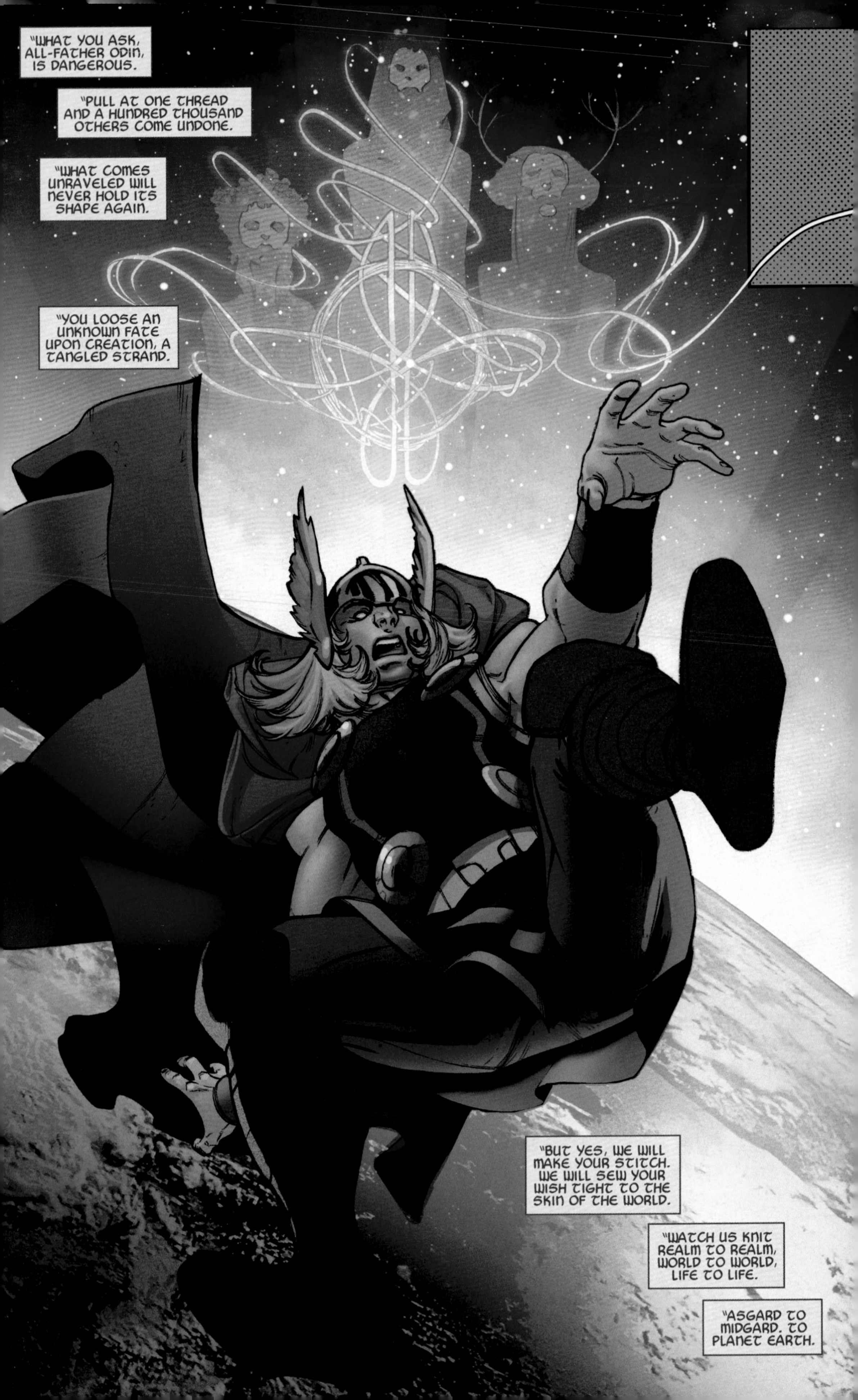
"WHAT YOU ASK, ALL-FATHER ODIN, IS DANGEROUS.
"PULL AT ONE THREAD AND A HUNDRED THOUSAND OTHERS COME UNDONE.
"WHAT COMES UNRAVELED WILL NEVER HOLD ITS SHAPE AGAIN.
"YOU LOOSE AN UNKNOWN FATE UPON CREATION, A TANGLED STRAND.
"BUT YES, WE WILL MAKE YOUR STITCH. WE WILL SEW YOUR WISH TIGHT TO THE SKIN OF THE WORLD.
"WATCH US KNIT REALM TO REALM, WORLD TO WORLD, LIFE TO LIFE.
"ASGARD TO MIDGARD. TO PLANET EARTH.

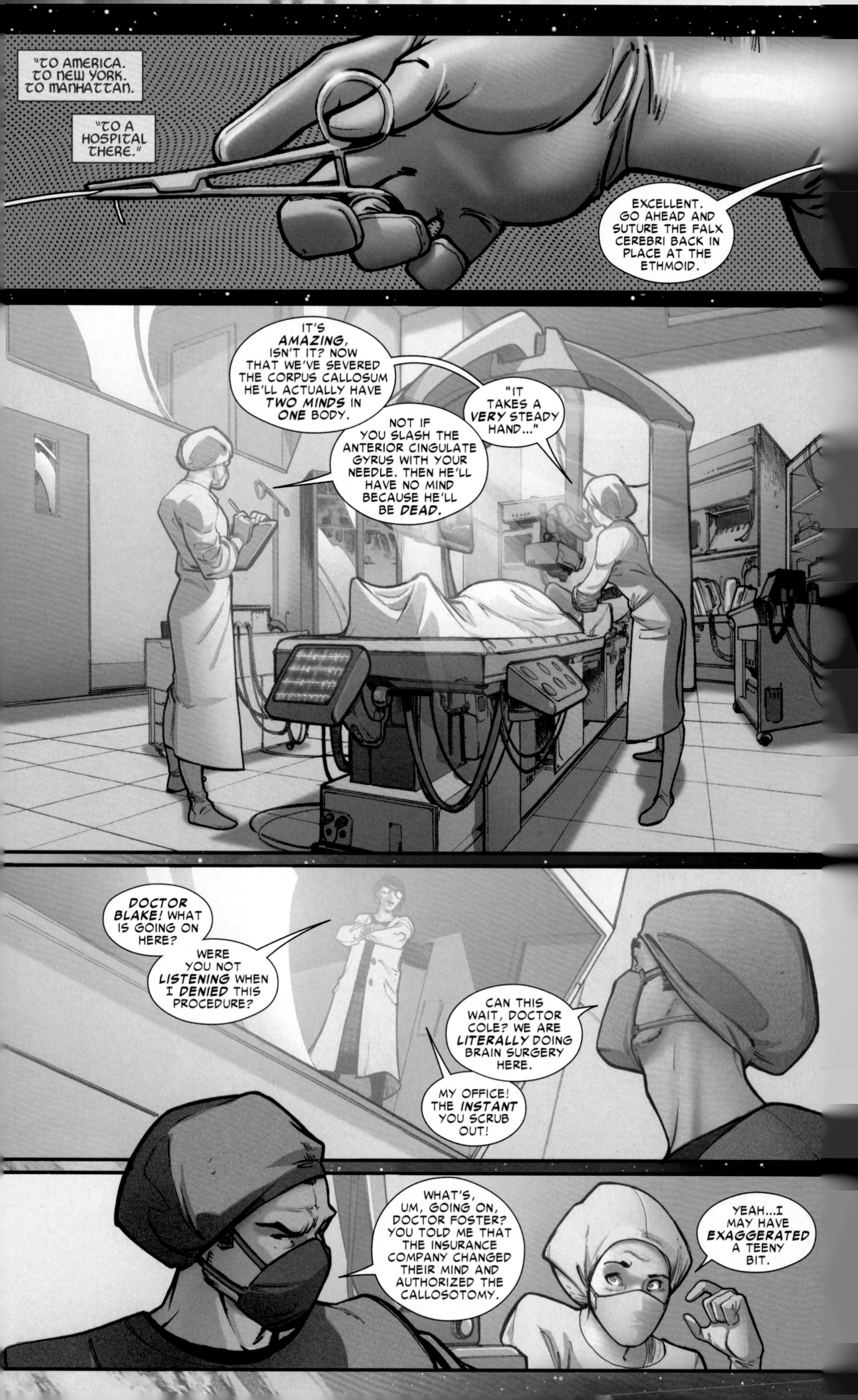
"TO AMERICA. TO NEW YORK. TO MANHATTAN.
"TO A HOSPITAL THERE."
EXCELLENT. GO AHEAD AND SUTURE THE FALX CEREBRI BACK IN PLACE AT THE ETHMOID.
IT'S AMAZING, ISN'T IT? NOW THAT WE'VE SEVERED THE CORPUS CALLOSUM HE'LL ACTUALLY HAVE TWO MINDS IN ONE BODY.
"IT TAKES A VERY STEADY HAND..."
NOT IF YOU SLASH THE ANTERIOR CINGULATE GYRUS WITH YOUR NEEDLE. THEN HE'LL HAVE NO MIND BECAUSE HE'LL BE DEAD.
DOCTOR BLAKE! WHAT IS GOING ON HERE?
WERE YOU NOT LISTENING WHEN I DENIED THIS PROCEDURE?
CAN THIS WAIT, DOCTOR COLE? WE ARE LITERALLY DOING BRAIN SURGERY HERE.
MY OFFICE! THE INSTANT YOU SCRUB OUT!
WHAT'S, UM, GOING ON, DOCTOR FOSTER? YOU TOLD ME THAT THE INSURANCE COMPANY CHANGED THEIR MIND AND AUTHORIZED THE CALLOSOTOMY.
YEAH...I MAY HAVE EXAGGERATED A TEENY BIT.

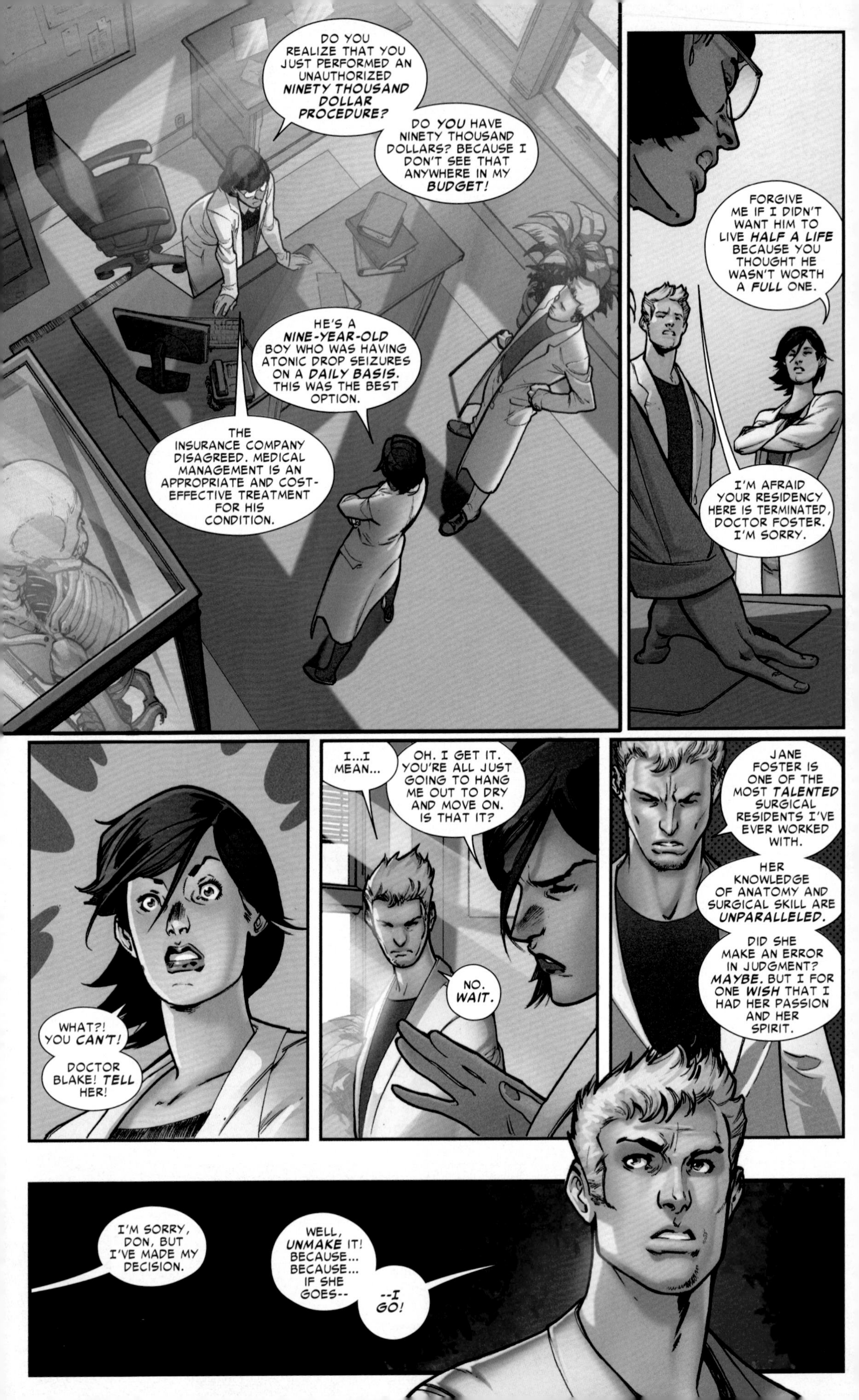

DO YOU REALIZE THAT YOU JUST PERFORMED AN UNAUTHORIZED NINETY THOUSAND DOLLAR PROCEDURE?
DO YOU HAVE NINETY THOUSAND DOLLARS? BECAUSE I DON'T SEE THAT ANYWHERE IN MY BUDGET!
HE'S A NINE-YEAR-OLD BOY WHO WAS HAVING ATONIC DROP SEIZURES ON A DAILY BASIS. THIS WAS THE BEST OPTION.
THE INSURANCE COMPANY DISAGREED. MEDICAL MANAGEMENT IS AN APPROPRIATE AND COST-EFFECTIVE TREATMENT FOR HIS CONDITION.
FORGIVE ME IF I DIDN'T WANT HIM TO LIVE HALF A LIFE BECAUSE YOU THOUGHT HE WASN'T WORTH A FULL ONE.
I'M AFRAID YOUR RESIDENCY HERE IS TERMINATED, DOCTOR FOSTER. I'M SORRY.
WHAT?! YOU CAN'T!
DOCTOR BLAKE! TELL HER!
I...I MEAN...
OH. I GET IT. YOU'RE ALL JUST GOING TO HANG ME OUT TO DRY AND MOVE ON. IS THAT IT?
NO. WAIT.
JANE FOSTER IS ONE OF THE MOST TALENTED SURGICAL RESIDENTS I'VE EVER WORKED WITH.
HER KNOWLEDGE OF ANATOMY AND SURGICAL SKILL ARE UNPARALLELED.
DID SHE MAKE AN ERROR IN JUDGMENT? MAYBE. BUT I FOR ONE WISH THAT I HAD HER PASSION AND HER SPIRIT.
I'M SORRY, DON, BUT I'VE MADE MY DECISION.
WELL, UNMAKE IT! BECAUSE... BECAUSE... IF SHE GOES--
--I GO!

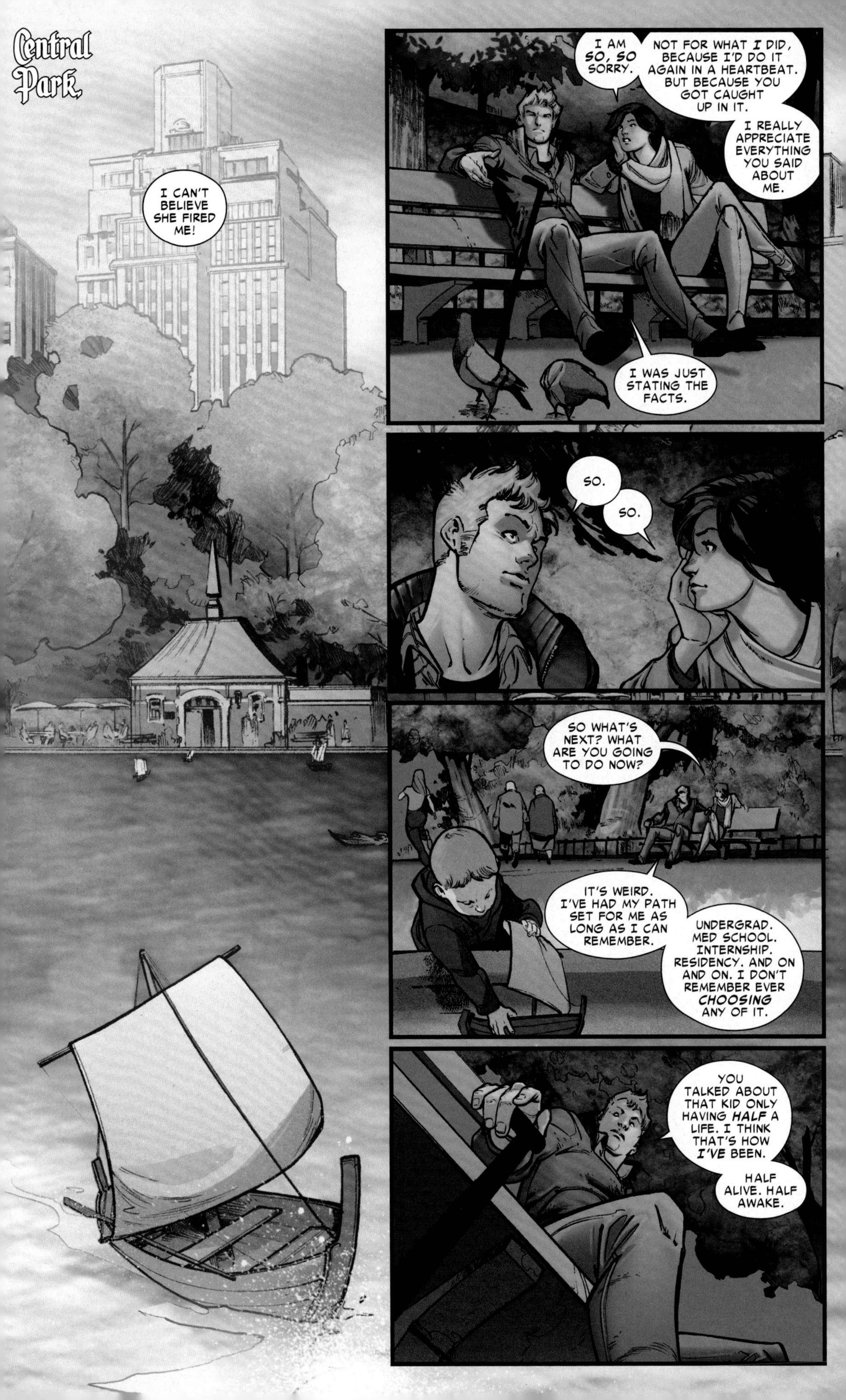
Central Park
I CAN'T BELIEVE SHE FIRED ME!
I AM SO, SO SORRY.
NOT FOR WHAT I DID, BECAUSE I'D DO IT AGAIN IN A HEARTBEAT. BUT BECAUSE YOU GOT CAUGHT UP IN IT.
I REALLY APPRECIATE EVERYTHING YOU SAID ABOUT ME.
I WAS JUST STATING THE FACTS.
SO.
SO.
SO WHAT'S NEXT? WHAT ARE YOU GOING TO DO NOW?
IT'S WEIRD. I'VE HAD MY PATH SET FOR ME AS LONG AS I CAN REMEMBER.
UNDERGRAD. MED SCHOOL. INTERNSHIP. RESIDENCY. AND ON AND ON. I DON'T REMEMBER EVER CHOOSING ANY OF IT.
YOU TALKED ABOUT THAT KID ONLY HAVING HALF A LIFE. I THINK THAT'S HOW I'VE BEEN.
HALF ALIVE. HALF AWAKE.

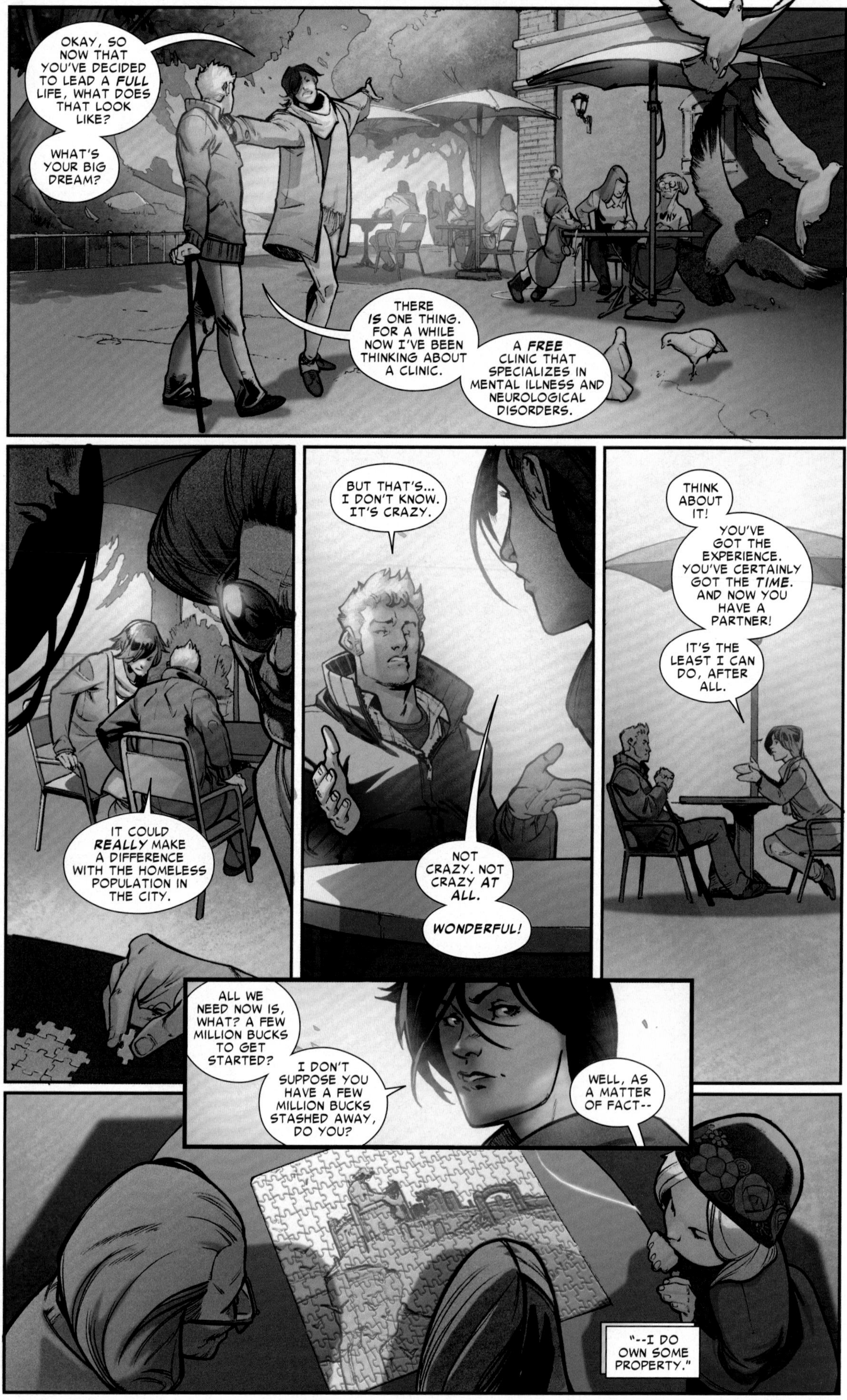
OKAY, SO NOW THAT YOU'VE DECIDED TO LEAD A FULL LIFE, WHAT DOES THAT LOOK LIKE?
WHAT'S YOUR BIG DREAM?
THERE IS ONE THING. FOR A WHILE NOW I'VE BEEN THINKING ABOUT A CLINIC.
A FREE CLINIC THAT SPECIALIZES IN MENTAL ILLNESS AND NEUROLOGICAL DISORDERS.
IT COULD REALLY MAKE A DIFFERENCE WITH THE HOMELESS POPULATION IN THE CITY.
BUT THAT'S... I DON'T KNOW. IT'S CRAZY.
NOT CRAZY. NOT CRAZY AT ALL.
WONDERFUL!
THINK ABOUT IT!
YOU'VE GOT THE EXPERIENCE. YOU'VE CERTAINLY GOT THE TIME. AND NOW YOU HAVE A PARTNER!
IT'S THE LEAST I CAN DO, AFTER ALL.
ALL WE NEED NOW IS, WHAT? A FEW MILLION BUCKS TO GET STARTED?
I DON'T SUPPOSE YOU HAVE A FEW MILLION BUCKS STASHED AWAY, DO YOU?
WELL, AS A MATTER OF FACT--
"--I DO OWN SOME PROPERTY."

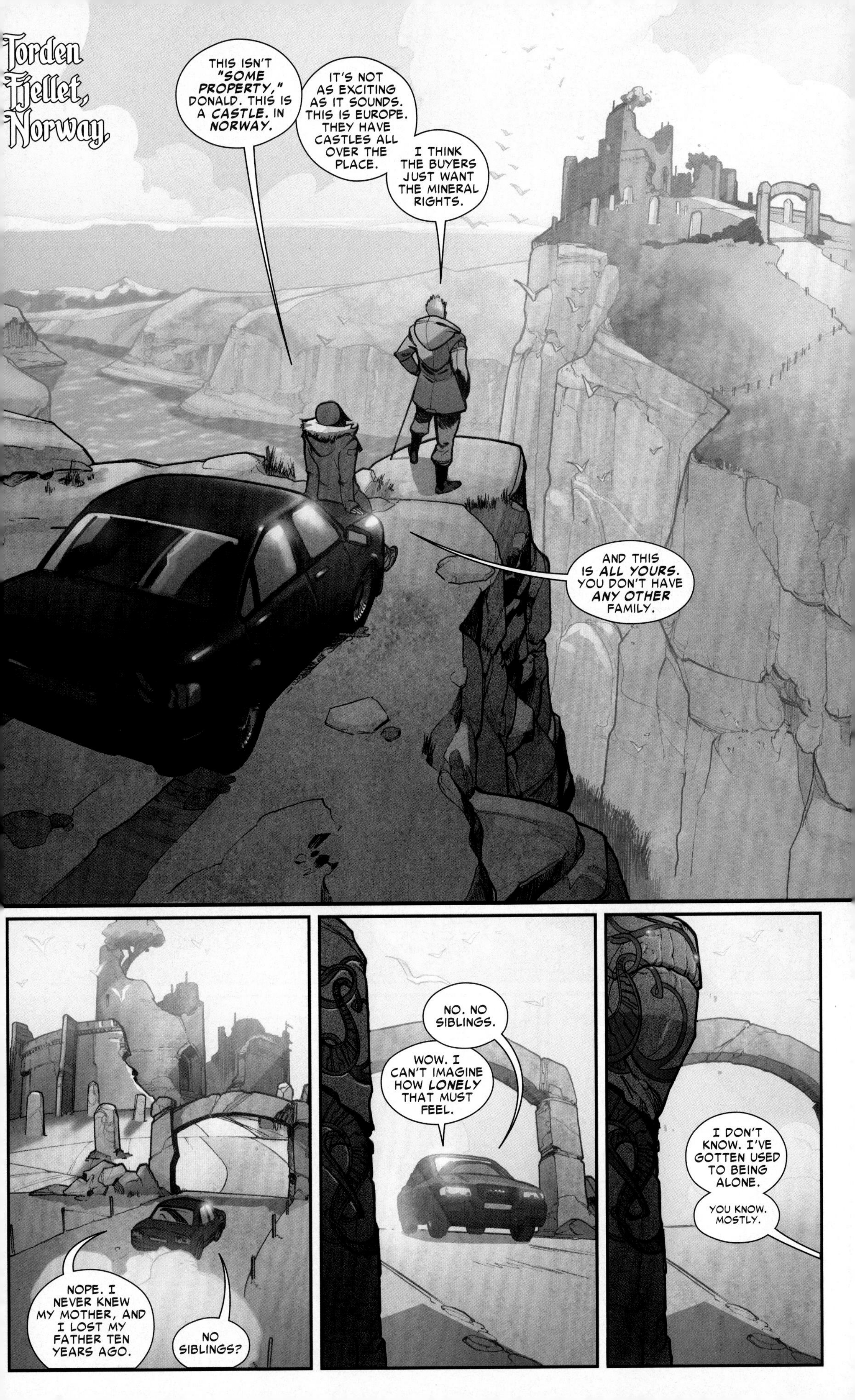

Torden Fjellet, Norway.
THIS ISN'T "SOME PROPERTY," DONALD. THIS IS A CASTLE. IN NORWAY.
IT'S NOT AS EXCITING AS IT SOUNDS. THIS IS EUROPE. THEY HAVE CASTLES ALL OVER THE PLACE.
I THINK THE BUYERS JUST WANT THE MINERAL RIGHTS.
AND THIS IS ALL YOURS. YOU DON'T HAVE ANY OTHER FAMILY.
NOPE. I NEVER KNEW MY MOTHER, AND I LOST MY FATHER TEN YEARS AGO.
NO SIBLINGS?
NO. NO SIBLINGS.
WOW. I CAN'T IMAGINE HOW LONELY THAT MUST FEEL.
I DON'T KNOW. I'VE GOTTEN USED TO BEING ALONE.
YOU KNOW. MOSTLY.

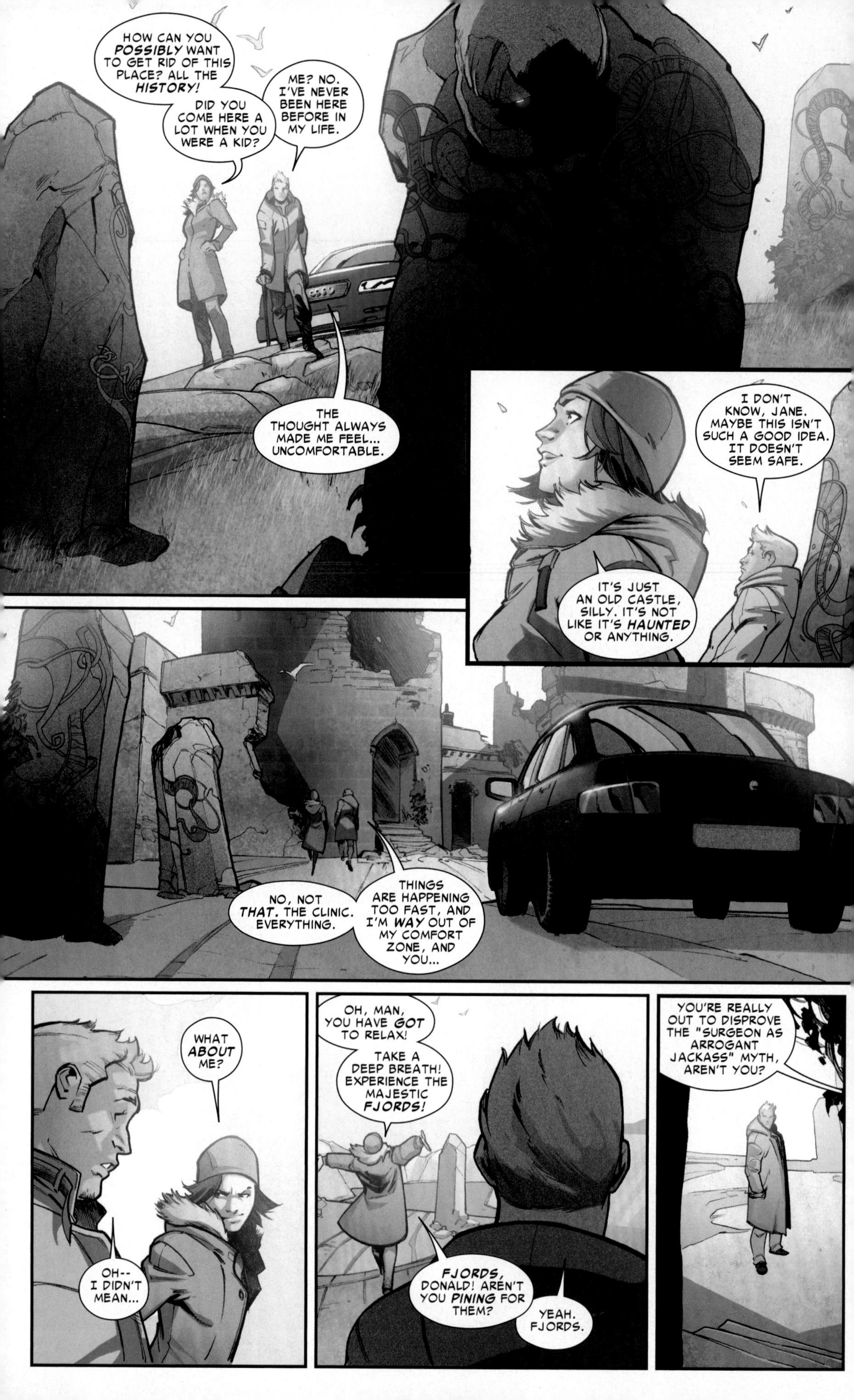
HOW CAN YOU POSSIBLY WANT TO GET RID OF THIS PLACE? ALL THE HISTORY!
DID YOU COME HERE A LOT WHEN YOU WERE A KID?
ME? NO. I'VE NEVER BEEN HERE BEFORE IN MY LIFE.
THE THOUGHT ALWAYS MADE ME FEEL... UNCOMFORTABLE.
I DON'T KNOW, JANE. MAYBE THIS ISN'T SUCH A GOOD IDEA. IT DOESN'T SEEM SAFE.
IT'S JUST AN OLD CASTLE, SILLY. IT'S NOT LIKE IT'S HAUNTED OR ANYTHING.
NO, NOT THAT. THE CLINIC. EVERYTHING.
THINGS ARE HAPPENING TOO FAST, AND I'M WAY OUT OF MY COMFORT ZONE, AND YOU...
WHAT ABOUT ME?
OH-- I DIDN'T MEAN...
OH, MAN, YOU HAVE GOT TO RELAX!
TAKE A DEEP BREATH! EXPERIENCE THE MAJESTIC FJORDS!
FJORDS, DONALD! AREN'T YOU PINING FOR THEM?
YEAH. FJORDS.
YOU'RE REALLY OUT TO DISPROVE THE "SURGEON AS ARROGANT JACKASS" MYTH, AREN'T YOU?

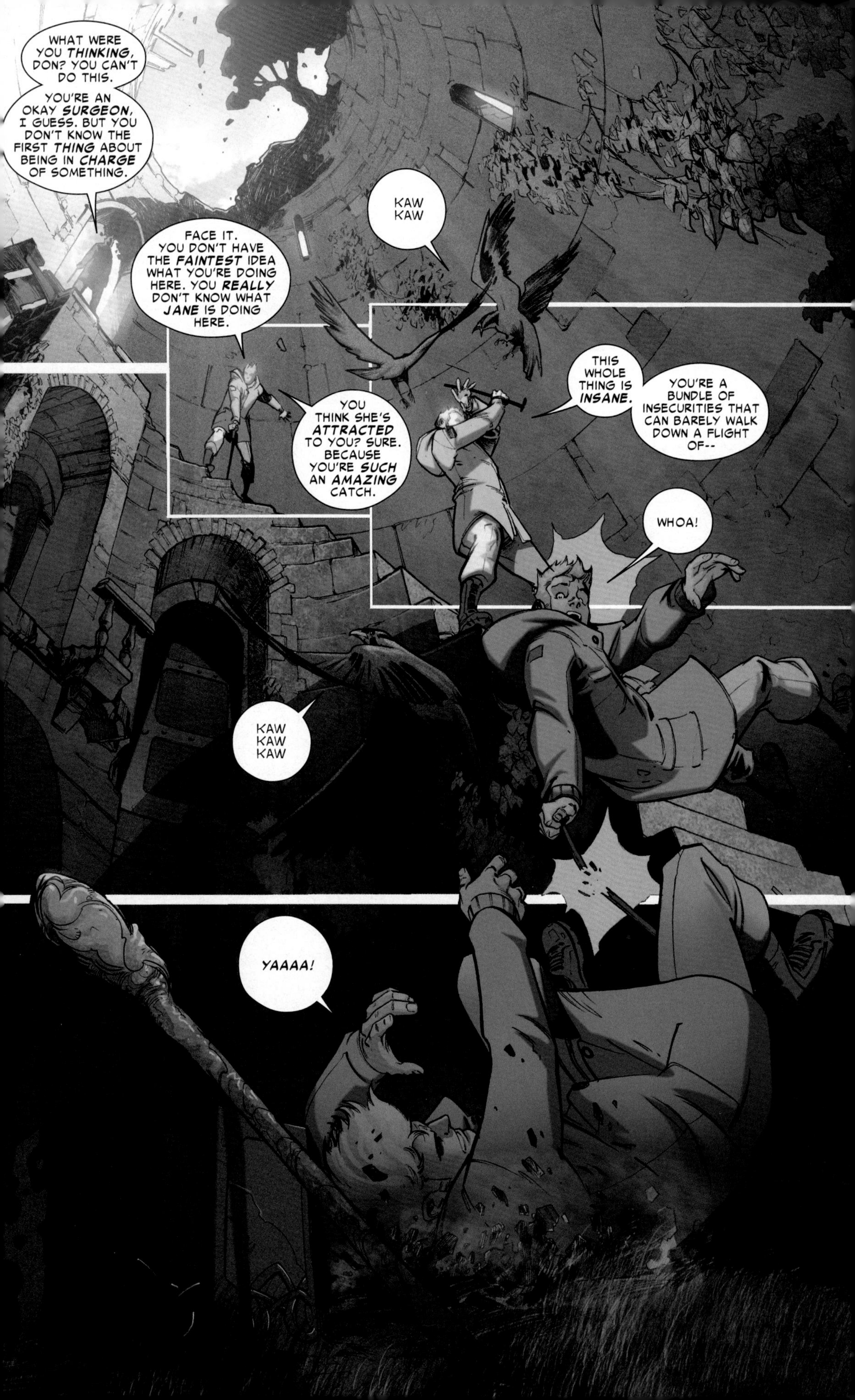
WHAT WERE YOU *THINKING*, DON? YOU CAN'T DO THIS.
YOU'RE AN OKAY *SURGEON*, I GUESS. BUT YOU DON'T KNOW THE FIRST *THING* ABOUT BEING IN *CHARGE* OF SOMETHING.
KAW KAW
FACE IT. YOU DON'T HAVE THE *FAINTEST* IDEA WHAT YOU'RE DOING HERE. YOU *REALLY* DON'T KNOW WHAT *JANE* IS DOING HERE.
YOU THINK SHE'S *ATTRACTED* TO YOU? SURE. BECAUSE YOU'RE *SUCH* AN *AMAZING* CATCH.
THIS WHOLE THING IS *INSANE*.
YOU'RE A BUNDLE OF INSECURITIES THAT CAN BARELY WALK DOWN A FLIGHT OF--
WHOA!
KAW KAW KAW
YAAAA!

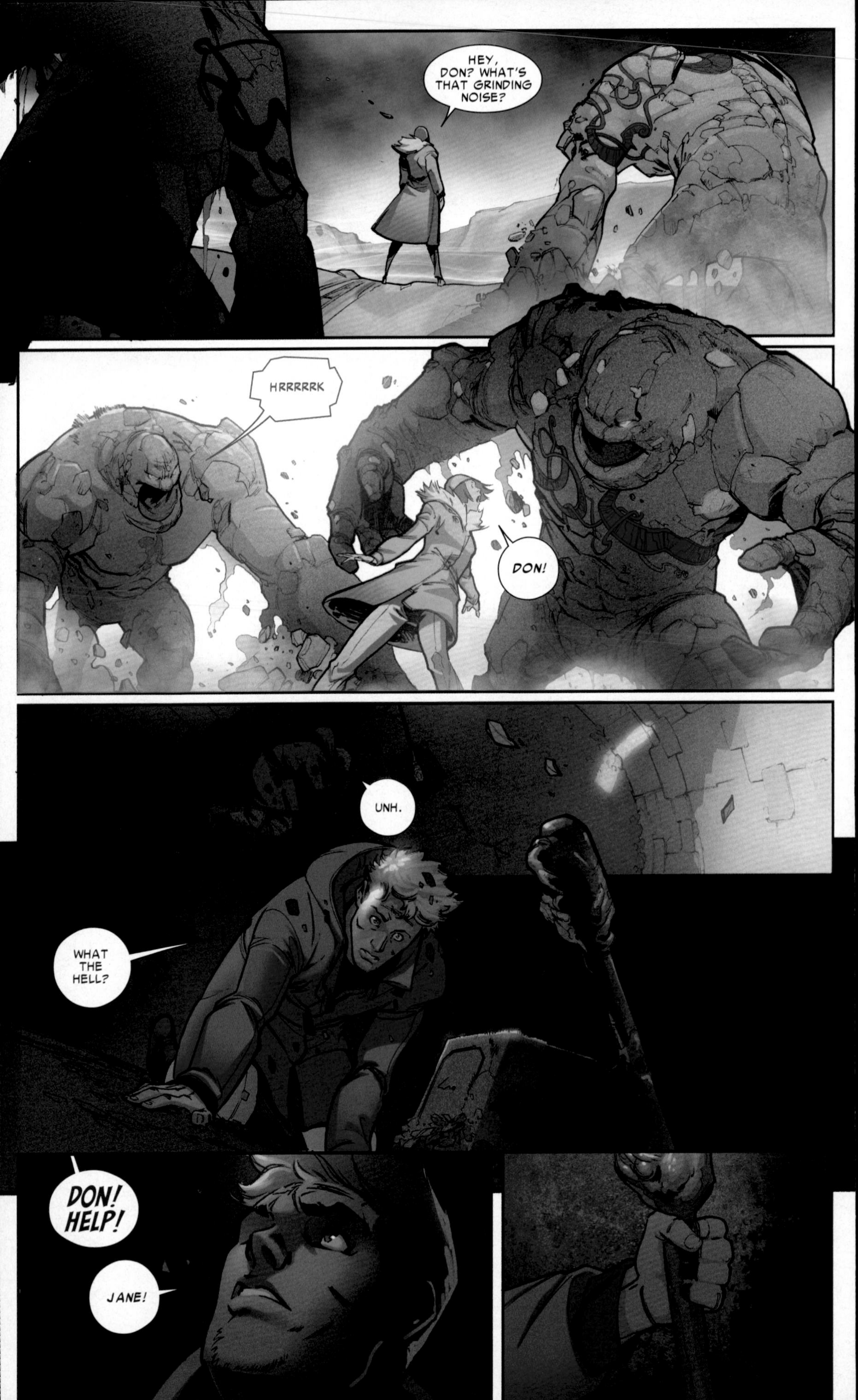
HEY, DON? WHAT'S THAT GRINDING NOISE?
HRRRRRK
DON!
UNH.
WHAT THE HELL?
DON! HELP!
JANE!

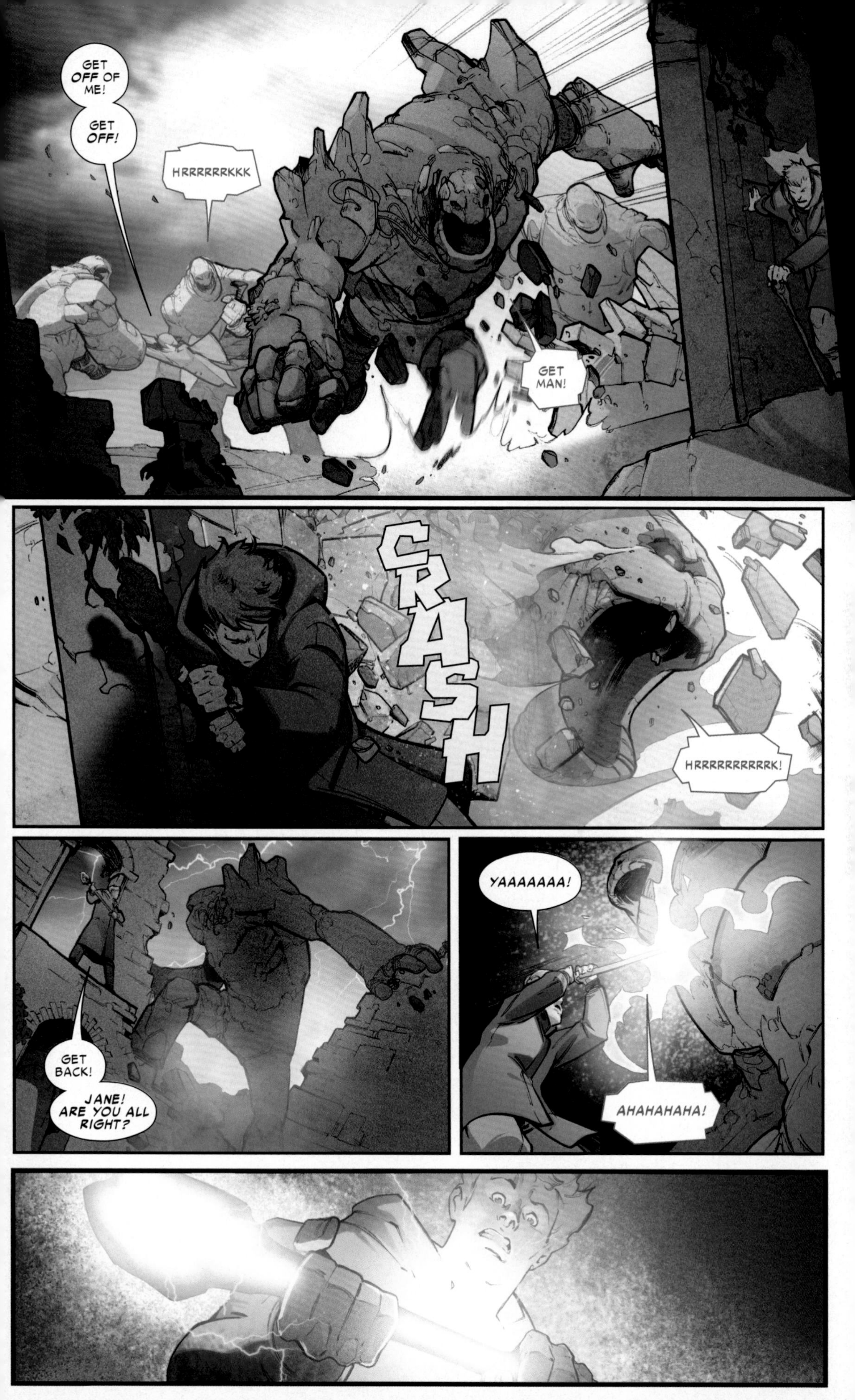
GET OFF OF ME!
GET OFF!
HRRRRRRKKK
GET MAN!
CRASH
HRRRRRRRRRK!
GET BACK!
JANE! ARE YOU ALL RIGHT?
YAAAAAAA!
AHAHAHAHA!

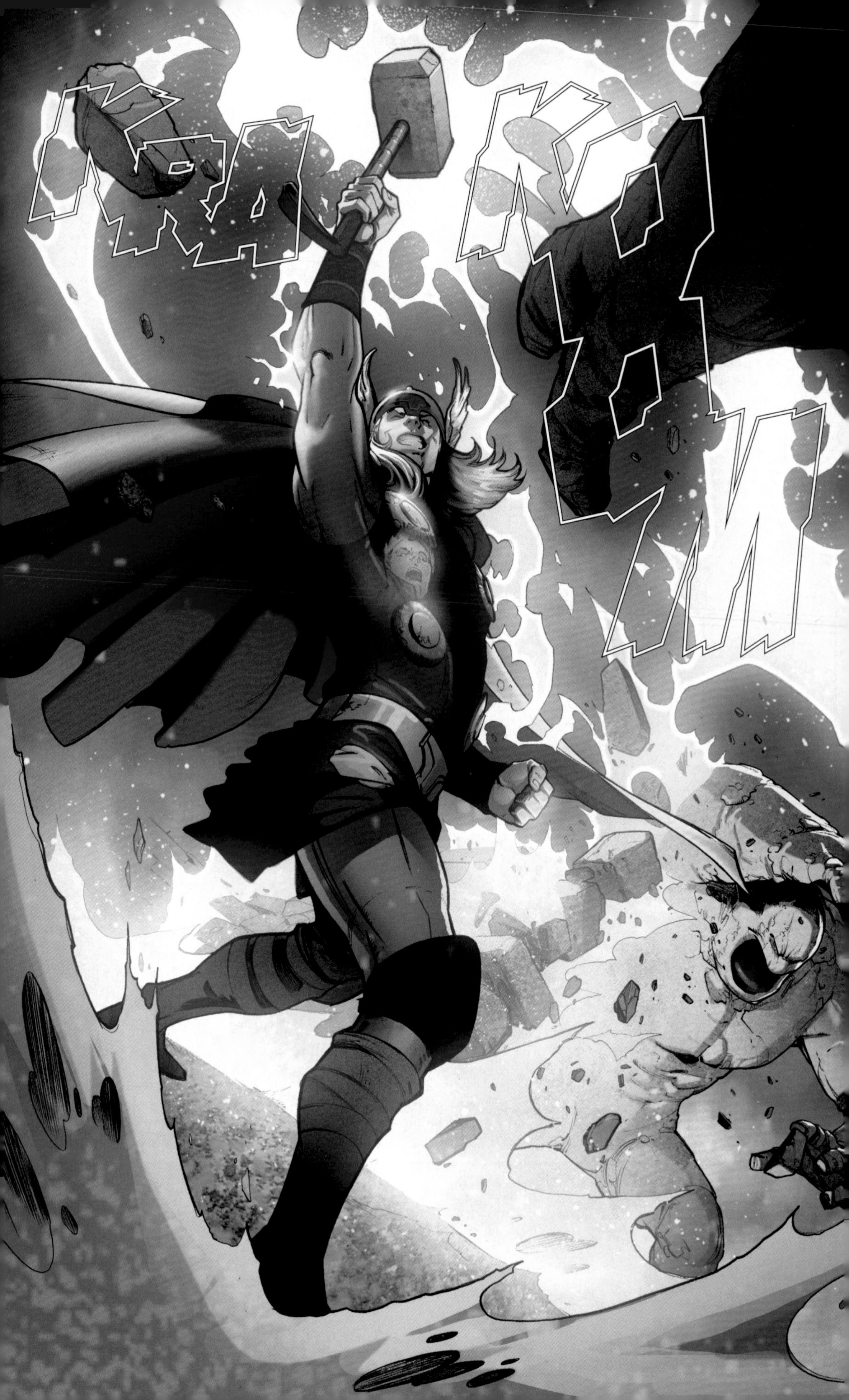
KRAKBAM

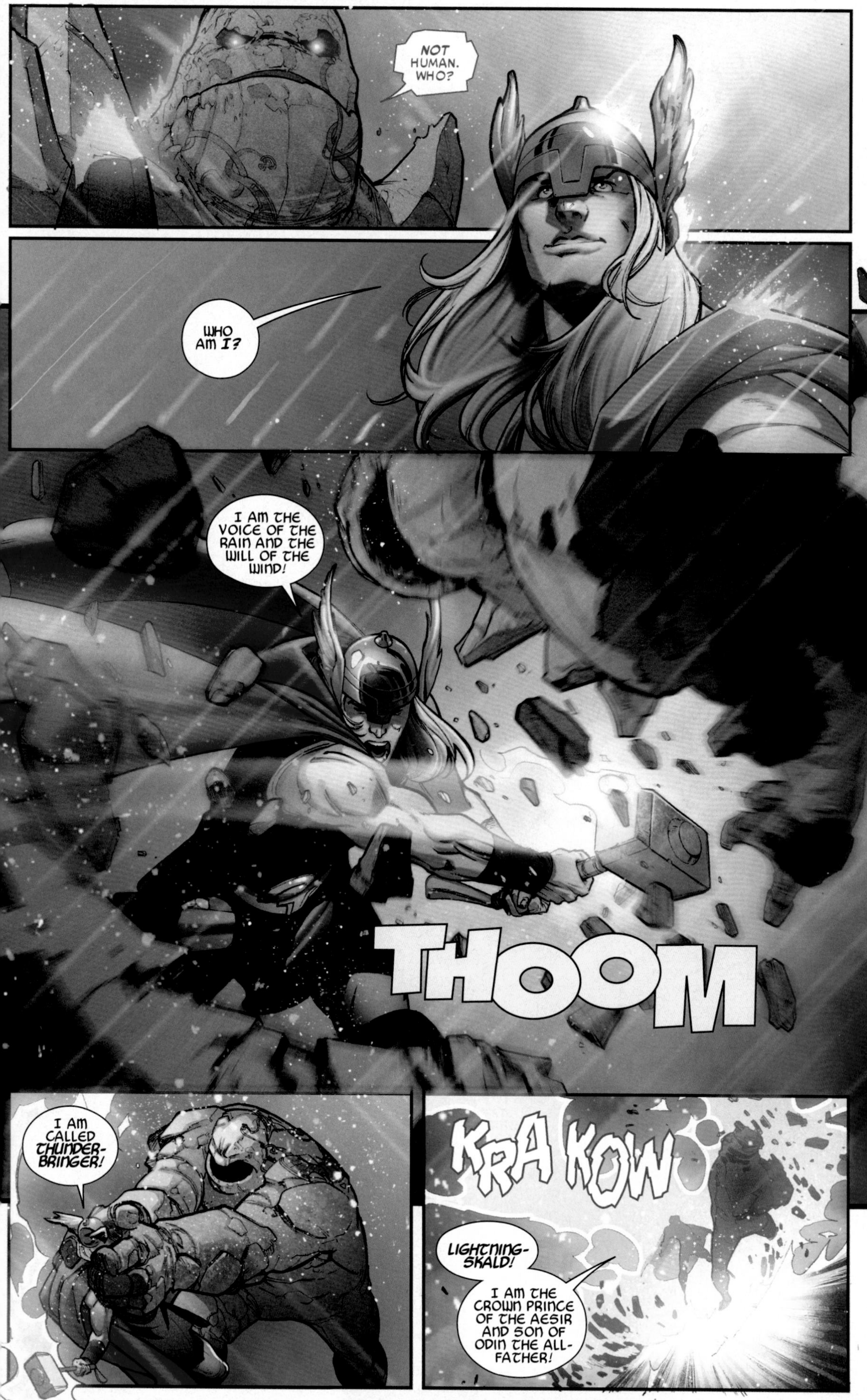

NOT HUMAN. WHO?
WHO AM I?
I AM THE VOICE OF THE RAIN AND THE WILL OF THE WIND!
THOOM
I AM CALLED THUNDER-BRINGER!
KRA KOW
LIGHTNING-SKALD!
I AM THE CROWN PRINCE OF THE AESIR AND SON OF ODIN THE ALL-FATHER!

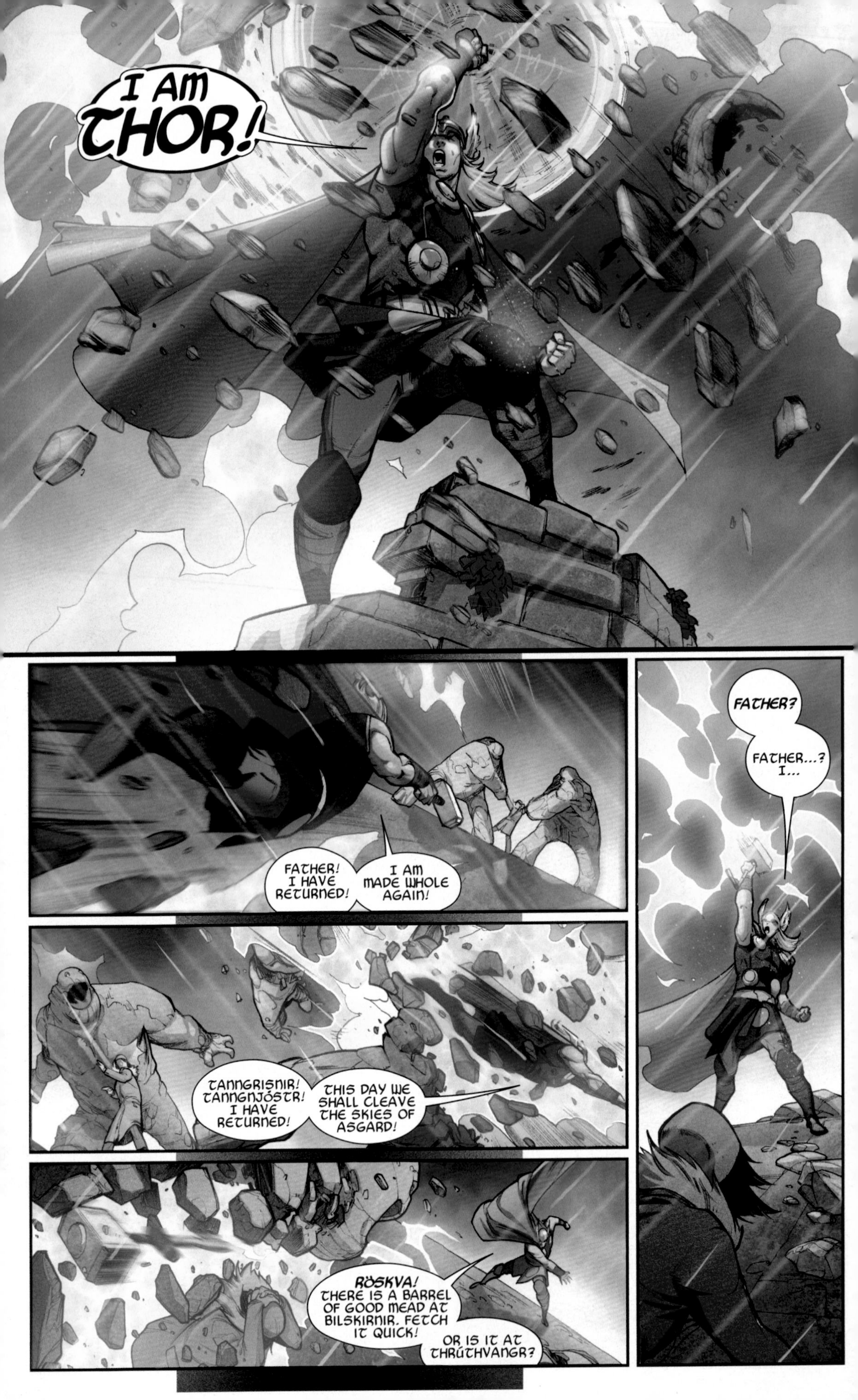
I AM THOR!
FATHER! I HAVE RETURNED!
I AM MADE WHOLE AGAIN!
TANNGRISNIR! TANNGNJÓSTR! I HAVE RETURNED!
THIS DAY WE SHALL CLEAVE THE SKIES OF ASGARD!
RÖSKVA! THERE IS A BARREL OF GOOD MEAD AT BILSKIRNIR. FETCH IT QUICK!
OR IS IT AT THRÚTHVANGR?
FATHER?
FATHER...? I...

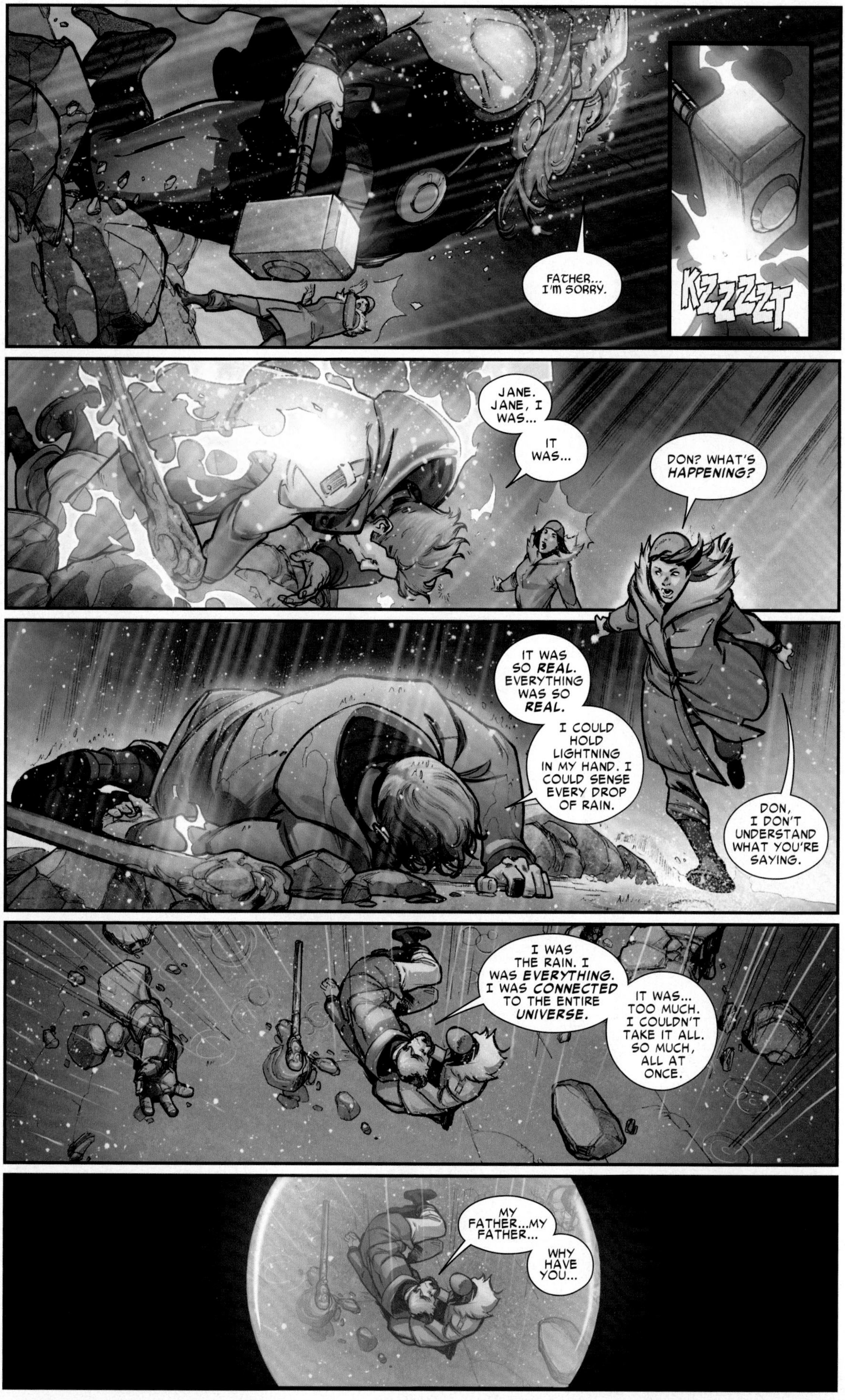
FATHER... I'M SORRY.
KZZZZZT
JANE. JANE, I WAS...
IT WAS...
DON? WHAT'S *HAPPENING?*
IT WAS SO *REAL*. EVERYTHING WAS SO *REAL*.
I COULD HOLD LIGHTNING IN MY HAND. I COULD SENSE EVERY DROP OF RAIN.
DON, I DON'T UNDERSTAND WHAT YOU'RE SAYING.
I WAS THE RAIN. I WAS *EVERYTHING*. I WAS *CONNECTED* TO THE ENTIRE *UNIVERSE*.
IT WAS... TOO MUCH. I COULDN'T TAKE IT ALL. SO MUCH, ALL AT ONCE.
MY FATHER...MY FATHER...
WHY HAVE YOU...

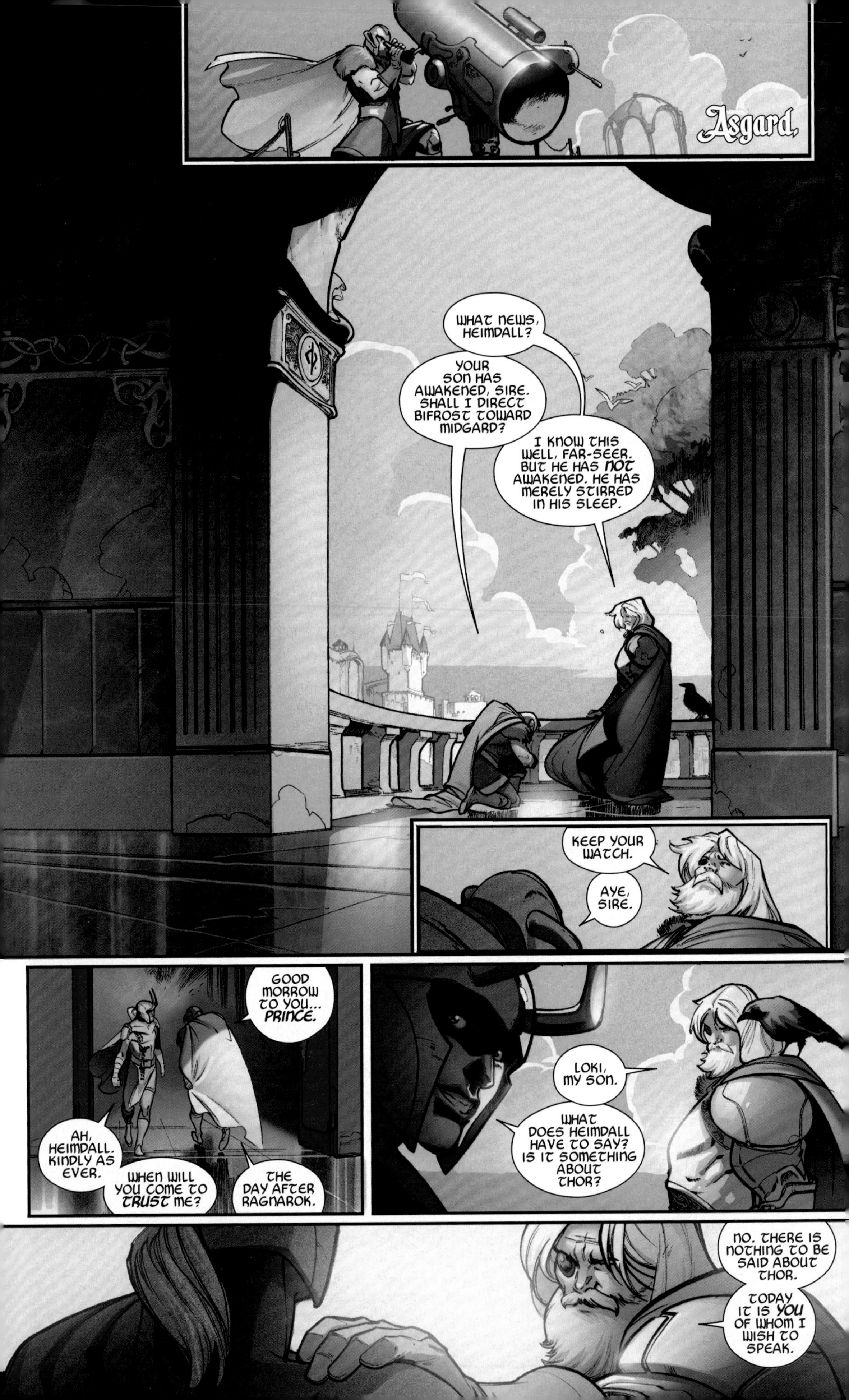
Asgard.
WHAT NEWS, HEIMDALL?
YOUR SON HAS AWAKENED, SIRE. SHALL I DIRECT BIFROST TOWARD MIDGARD?
I KNOW THIS WELL, FAR-SEER. BUT HE HAS NOT AWAKENED. HE HAS MERELY STIRRED IN HIS SLEEP.
KEEP YOUR WATCH.
AYE, SIRE.
GOOD MORROW TO YOU... PRINCE.
AH, HEIMDALL. KINDLY AS EVER.
WHEN WILL YOU COME TO TRUST ME?
THE DAY AFTER RAGNAROK.
LOKI, MY SON.
WHAT DOES HEIMDALL HAVE TO SAY? IS IT SOMETHING ABOUT THOR?
NO. THERE IS NOTHING TO BE SAID ABOUT THOR.
TODAY IT IS YOU OF WHOM I WISH TO SPEAK.

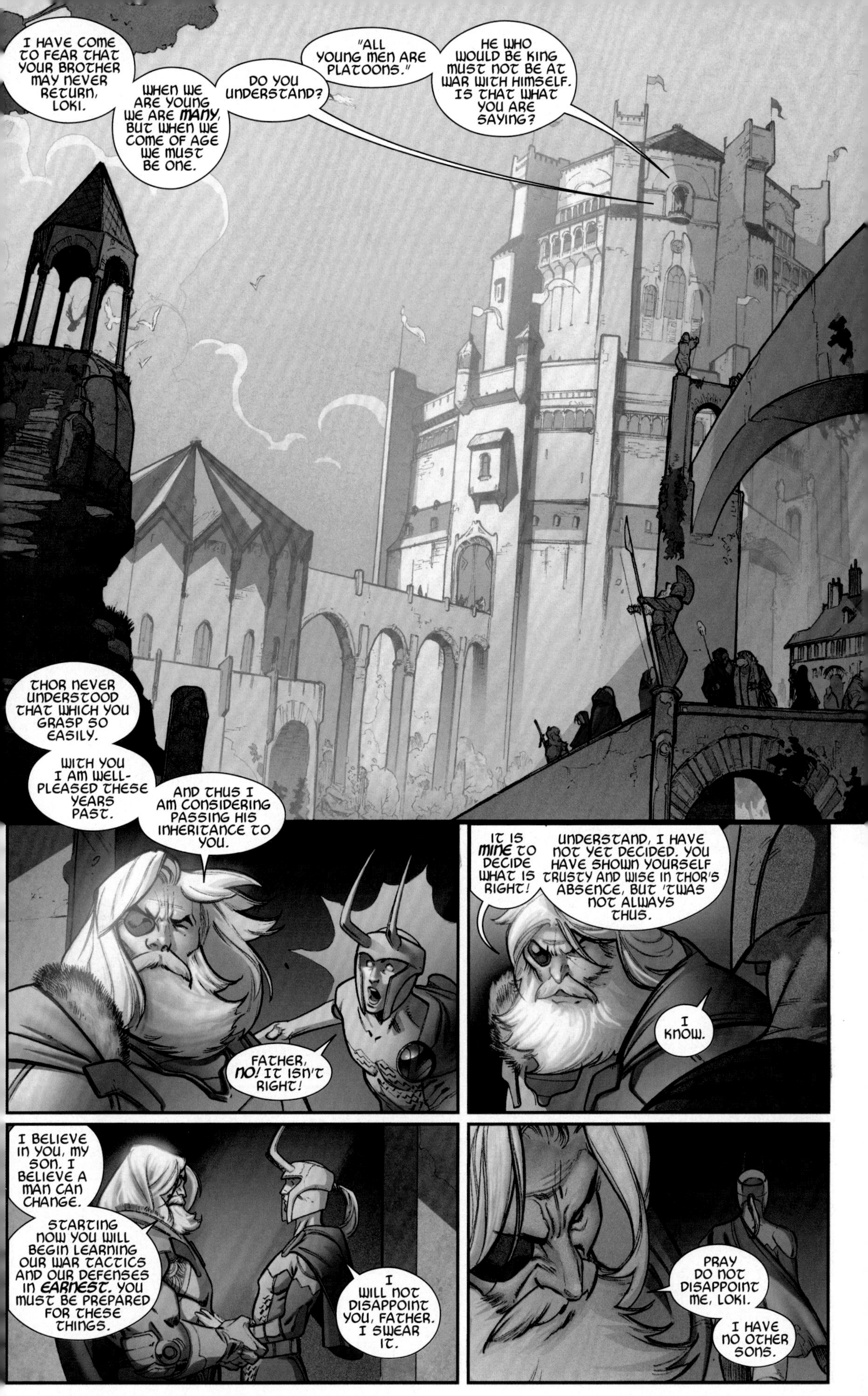
I HAVE COME TO FEAR THAT YOUR BROTHER MAY NEVER RETURN, LOKI.
WHEN WE ARE YOUNG WE ARE *MANY*, BUT WHEN WE COME OF AGE WE MUST BE ONE.
DO YOU UNDERSTAND?
"ALL YOUNG MEN ARE PLATOONS."
HE WHO WOULD BE KING MUST NOT BE AT WAR WITH HIMSELF. IS THAT WHAT YOU ARE SAYING?
THOR NEVER UNDERSTOOD THAT WHICH YOU GRASP SO EASILY.
WITH YOU I AM WELL-PLEASED THESE YEARS PAST.
AND THUS I AM CONSIDERING PASSING HIS INHERITANCE TO YOU.
FATHER, *NO!* IT ISN'T RIGHT!
IT IS *MINE* TO DECIDE WHAT IS RIGHT!
UNDERSTAND, I HAVE NOT YET DECIDED. YOU HAVE SHOWN YOURSELF TRUSTY AND WISE IN THOR'S ABSENCE, BUT 'TWAS NOT ALWAYS THUS.
I KNOW.
I BELIEVE IN YOU, MY SON. I BELIEVE A MAN CAN CHANGE.
STARTING NOW YOU WILL BEGIN LEARNING OUR WAR TACTICS AND OUR DEFENSES IN *EARNEST*. YOU MUST BE PREPARED FOR THESE THINGS.
I WILL NOT DISAPPOINT YOU, FATHER. I SWEAR IT.
PRAY DO NOT DISAPPOINT ME, LOKI.
I HAVE NO OTHER SONS.

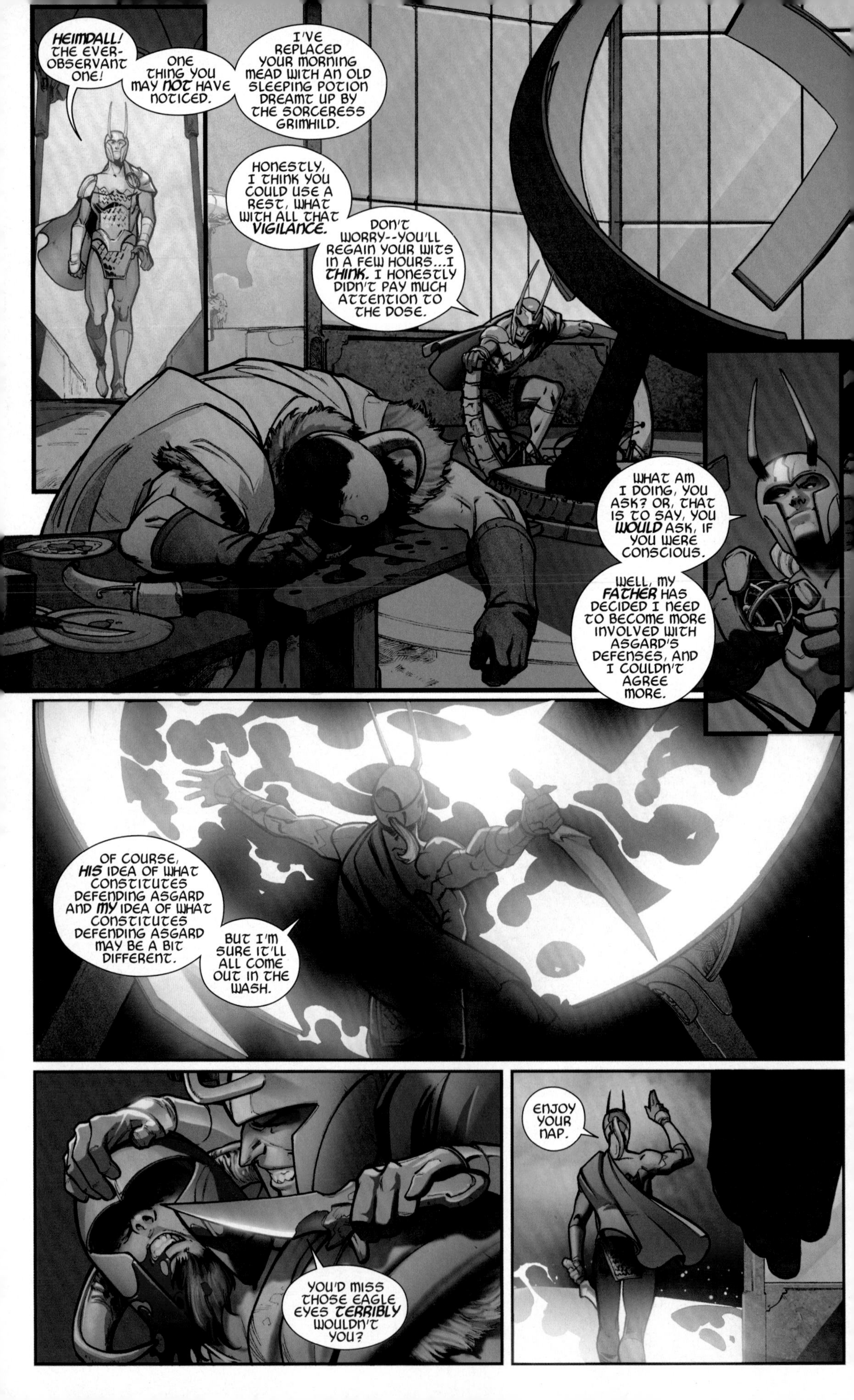
HEIMDALL! THE EVER-OBSERVANT ONE!
ONE THING YOU MAY NOT HAVE NOTICED.
I'VE REPLACED YOUR MORNING MEAD WITH AN OLD SLEEPING POTION DREAMT UP BY THE SORCERESS GRIMHILD.
HONESTLY, I THINK YOU COULD USE A REST, WHAT WITH ALL THAT VIGILANCE.
DON'T WORRY--YOU'LL REGAIN YOUR WITS IN A FEW HOURS...I THINK. I HONESTLY DIDN'T PAY MUCH ATTENTION TO THE DOSE.
WHAT AM I DOING, YOU ASK? OR, THAT IS TO SAY, YOU WOULD ASK, IF YOU WERE CONSCIOUS.
WELL, MY FATHER HAS DECIDED I NEED TO BECOME MORE INVOLVED WITH ASGARD'S DEFENSES, AND I COULDN'T AGREE MORE.
OF COURSE, HIS IDEA OF WHAT CONSTITUTES DEFENDING ASGARD AND MY IDEA OF WHAT CONSTITUTES DEFENDING ASGARD MAY BE A BIT DIFFERENT.
BUT I'M SURE IT'LL ALL COME OUT IN THE WASH.
YOU'D MISS THOSE EAGLE EYES TERRIBLY WOULDN'T YOU?
ENJOY YOUR NAP.

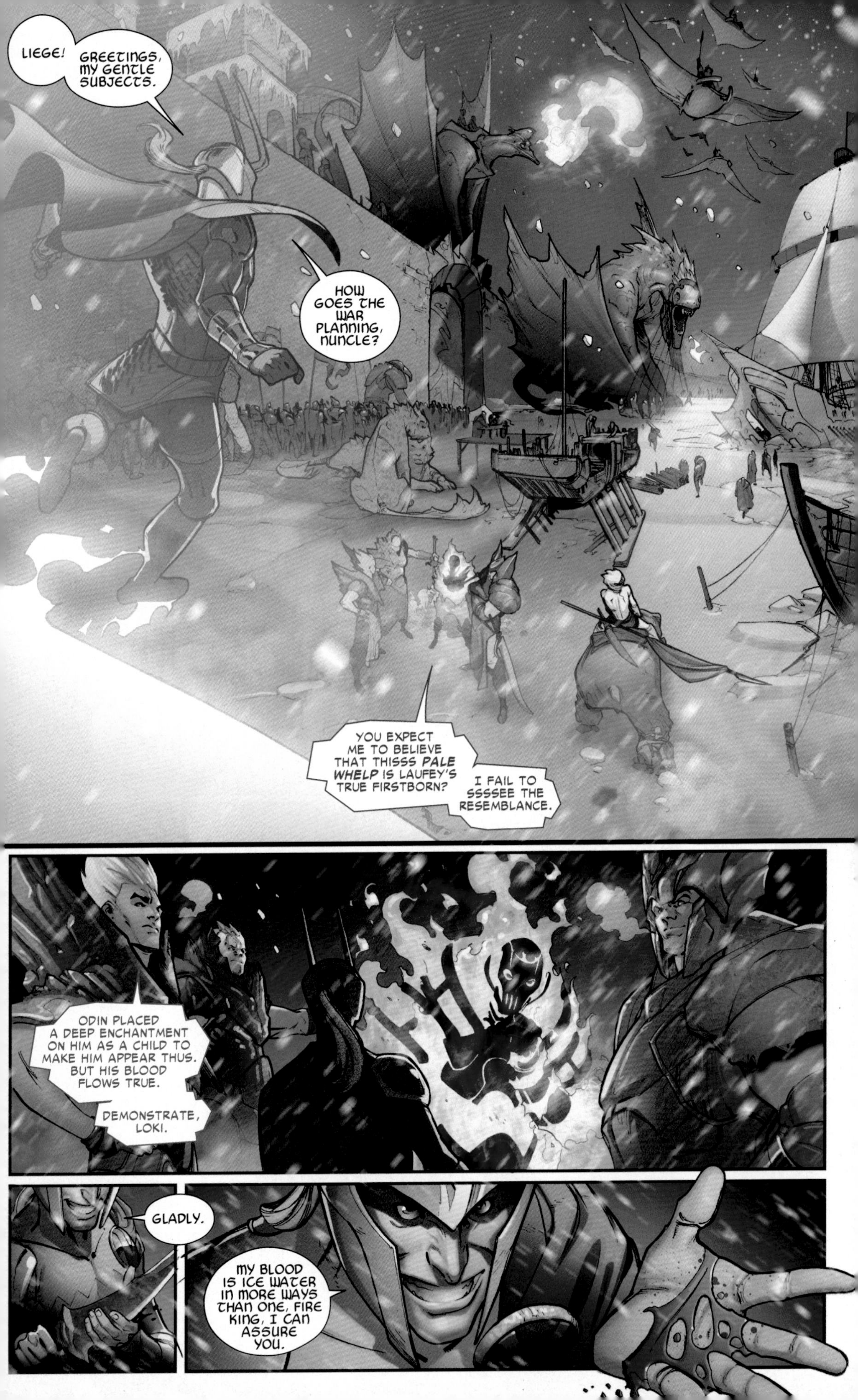
LIEGE!
GREETINGS, MY GENTLE SUBJECTS.
HOW GOES THE WAR PLANNING, NUNCLE?
YOU EXPECT ME TO BELIEVE THAT THISSS PALE WHELP IS LAUFEY'S TRUE FIRSTBORN?
I FAIL TO SSSSEE THE RESEMBLANCE.
ODIN PLACED A DEEP ENCHANTMENT ON HIM AS A CHILD TO MAKE HIM APPEAR THUS. BUT HIS BLOOD FLOWS TRUE.
DEMONSTRATE, LOKI.
GLADLY.
MY BLOOD IS ICE WATER IN MORE WAYS THAN ONE, FIRE KING, I CAN ASSURE YOU.

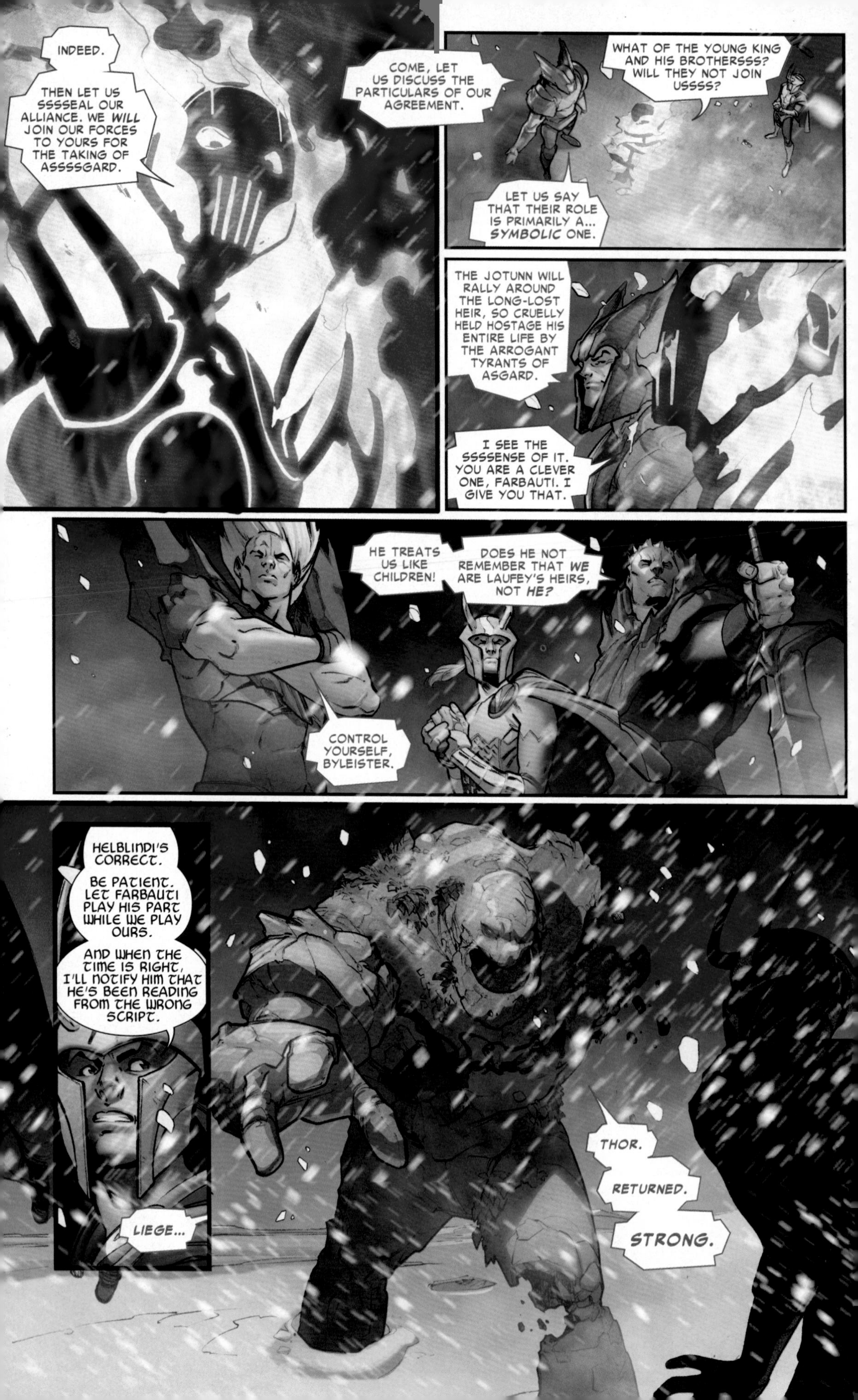
INDEED.
THEN LET US SSSSEAL OUR ALLIANCE. WE *WILL* JOIN OUR FORCES TO YOURS FOR THE TAKING OF ASSSSGARD.
COME, LET US DISCUSS THE PARTICULARS OF OUR AGREEMENT.
WHAT OF THE YOUNG KING AND HIS BROTHERSSS? WILL THEY NOT JOIN USSSS?
LET US SAY THAT THEIR ROLE IS PRIMARILY A... *SYMBOLIC* ONE.
THE JOTUNN WILL RALLY AROUND THE LONG-LOST HEIR, SO CRUELLY HELD HOSTAGE HIS ENTIRE LIFE BY THE ARROGANT TYRANTS OF ASGARD.
I SEE THE SSSSENSE OF IT. YOU ARE A CLEVER ONE, FARBAUTI. I GIVE YOU THAT.
HE TREATS US LIKE CHILDREN!
DOES HE NOT REMEMBER THAT *WE* ARE LAUFEY'S HEIRS, NOT *HE?*
CONTROL YOURSELF, BYLEISTER.
HELBLINDI'S CORRECT.
BE PATIENT. LET FARBAUTI PLAY HIS PART WHILE WE PLAY OURS.
AND WHEN THE TIME IS RIGHT, I'LL NOTIFY HIM THAT HE'S BEEN READING FROM THE WRONG SCRIPT.
LIEGE...
THOR.
RETURNED.
STRONG.

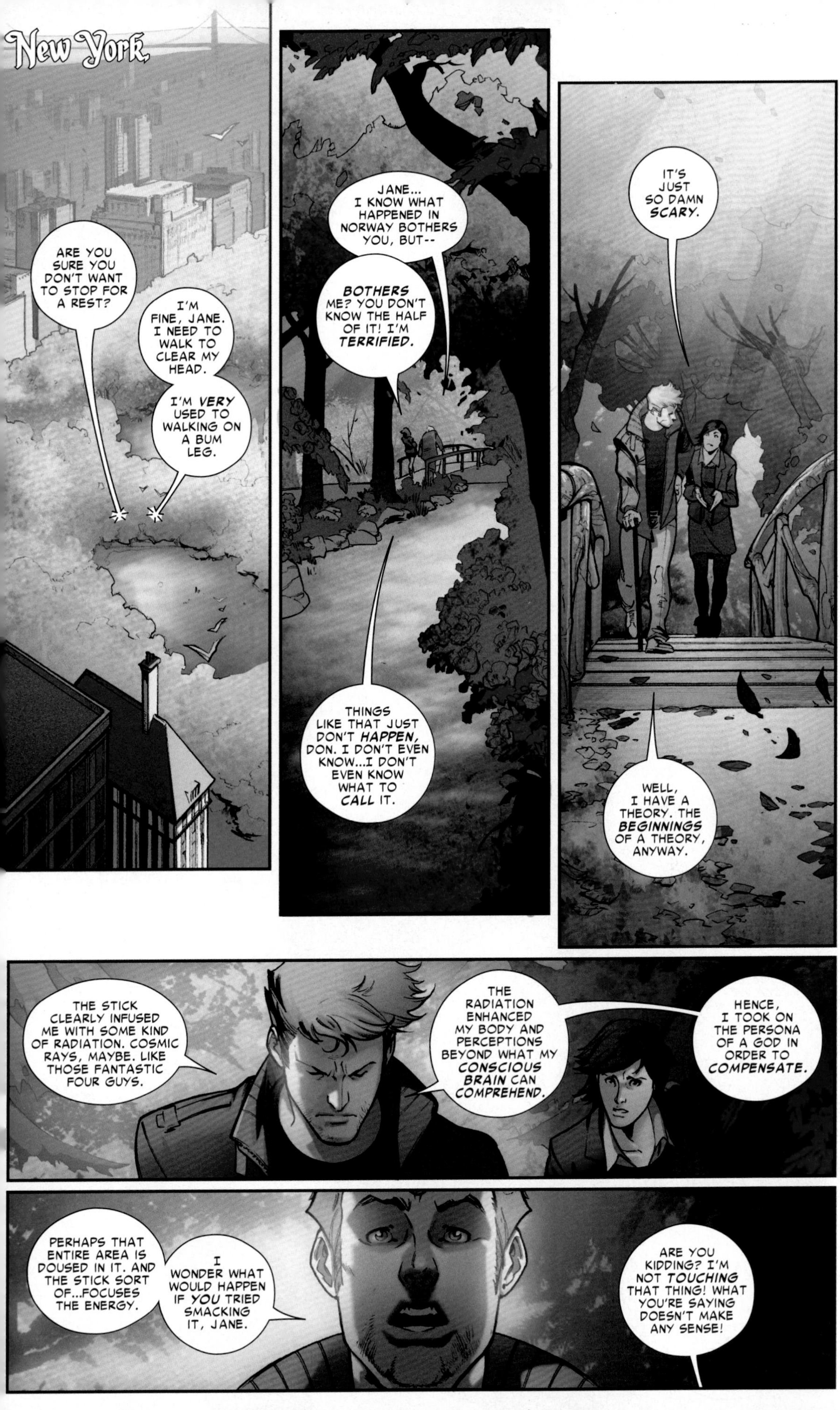
New York.
ARE YOU SURE YOU DON'T WANT TO STOP FOR A REST?
I'M FINE, JANE. I NEED TO WALK TO CLEAR MY HEAD.
I'M VERY USED TO WALKING ON A BUM LEG.
JANE... I KNOW WHAT HAPPENED IN NORWAY BOTHERS YOU, BUT--
BOTHERS ME? YOU DON'T KNOW THE HALF OF IT! I'M TERRIFIED.
THINGS LIKE THAT JUST DON'T HAPPEN, DON. I DON'T EVEN KNOW...I DON'T EVEN KNOW WHAT TO CALL IT.
IT'S JUST SO DAMN SCARY.
WELL, I HAVE A THEORY. THE BEGINNINGS OF A THEORY, ANYWAY.
THE STICK CLEARLY INFUSED ME WITH SOME KIND OF RADIATION. COSMIC RAYS, MAYBE. LIKE THOSE FANTASTIC FOUR GUYS.
THE RADIATION ENHANCED MY BODY AND PERCEPTIONS BEYOND WHAT MY CONSCIOUS BRAIN CAN COMPREHEND.
HENCE, I TOOK ON THE PERSONA OF A GOD IN ORDER TO COMPENSATE.
PERHAPS THAT ENTIRE AREA IS DOUSED IN IT. AND THE STICK SORT OF...FOCUSES THE ENERGY.
I WONDER WHAT WOULD HAPPEN IF YOU TRIED SMACKING IT, JANE.
ARE YOU KIDDING? I'M NOT TOUCHING THAT THING! WHAT YOU'RE SAYING DOESN'T MAKE ANY SENSE!

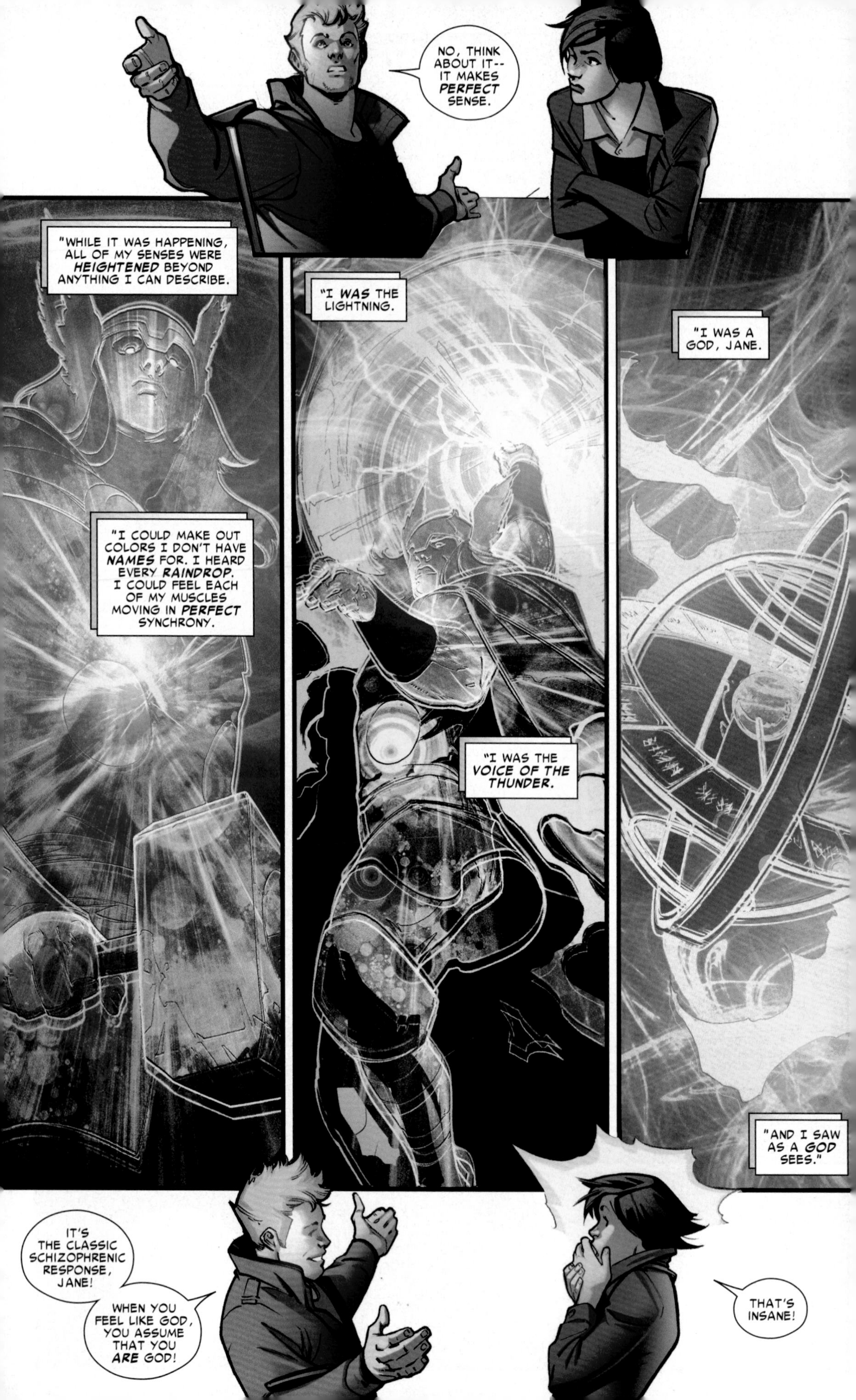
NO, THINK ABOUT IT-- IT MAKES PERFECT SENSE.
"WHILE IT WAS HAPPENING, ALL OF MY SENSES WERE HEIGHTENED BEYOND ANYTHING I CAN DESCRIBE.
"I COULD MAKE OUT COLORS I DON'T HAVE NAMES FOR. I HEARD EVERY RAINDROP. I COULD FEEL EACH OF MY MUSCLES MOVING IN PERFECT SYNCHRONY.
"I WAS THE LIGHTNING.
"I WAS THE VOICE OF THE THUNDER.
"I WAS A GOD, JANE.
"AND I SAW AS A GOD SEES."
IT'S THE CLASSIC SCHIZOPHRENIC RESPONSE, JANE!
WHEN YOU FEEL LIKE GOD, YOU ASSUME THAT YOU ARE GOD!
THAT'S INSANE!

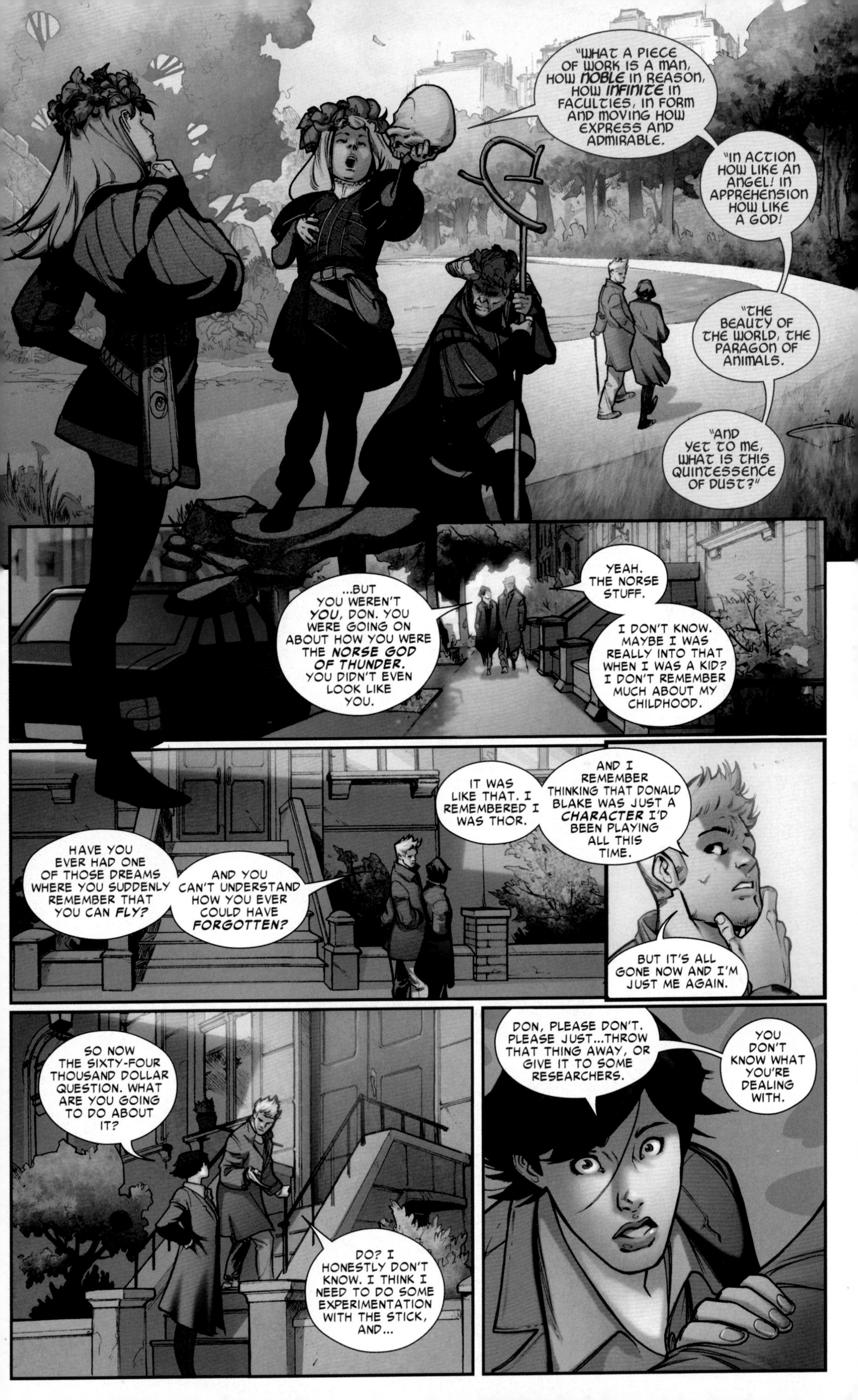
"WHAT A PIECE OF WORK IS A MAN, HOW NOBLE IN REASON, HOW INFINITE IN FACULTIES, IN FORM AND MOVING HOW EXPRESS AND ADMIRABLE.
"IN ACTION HOW LIKE AN ANGEL! IN APPREHENSION HOW LIKE A GOD!
"THE BEAUTY OF THE WORLD, THE PARAGON OF ANIMALS.
"AND YET TO ME, WHAT IS THIS QUINTESSENCE OF DUST?"
...BUT YOU WEREN'T YOU, DON. YOU WERE GOING ON ABOUT HOW YOU WERE THE NORSE GOD OF THUNDER. YOU DIDN'T EVEN LOOK LIKE YOU.
YEAH. THE NORSE STUFF.
I DON'T KNOW. MAYBE I WAS REALLY INTO THAT WHEN I WAS A KID? I DON'T REMEMBER MUCH ABOUT MY CHILDHOOD.
HAVE YOU EVER HAD ONE OF THOSE DREAMS WHERE YOU SUDDENLY REMEMBER THAT YOU CAN FLY?
AND YOU CAN'T UNDERSTAND HOW YOU EVER COULD HAVE FORGOTTEN?
IT WAS LIKE THAT. I REMEMBERED I WAS THOR.
AND I REMEMBER THINKING THAT DONALD BLAKE WAS JUST A CHARACTER I'D BEEN PLAYING ALL THIS TIME.
BUT IT'S ALL GONE NOW AND I'M JUST ME AGAIN.
SO NOW THE SIXTY-FOUR THOUSAND DOLLAR QUESTION. WHAT ARE YOU GOING TO DO ABOUT IT?
DO? I HONESTLY DON'T KNOW. I THINK I NEED TO DO SOME EXPERIMENTATION WITH THE STICK, AND...
DON, PLEASE DON'T. PLEASE JUST...THROW THAT THING AWAY, OR GIVE IT TO SOME RESEARCHERS.
YOU DON'T KNOW WHAT YOU'RE DEALING WITH.

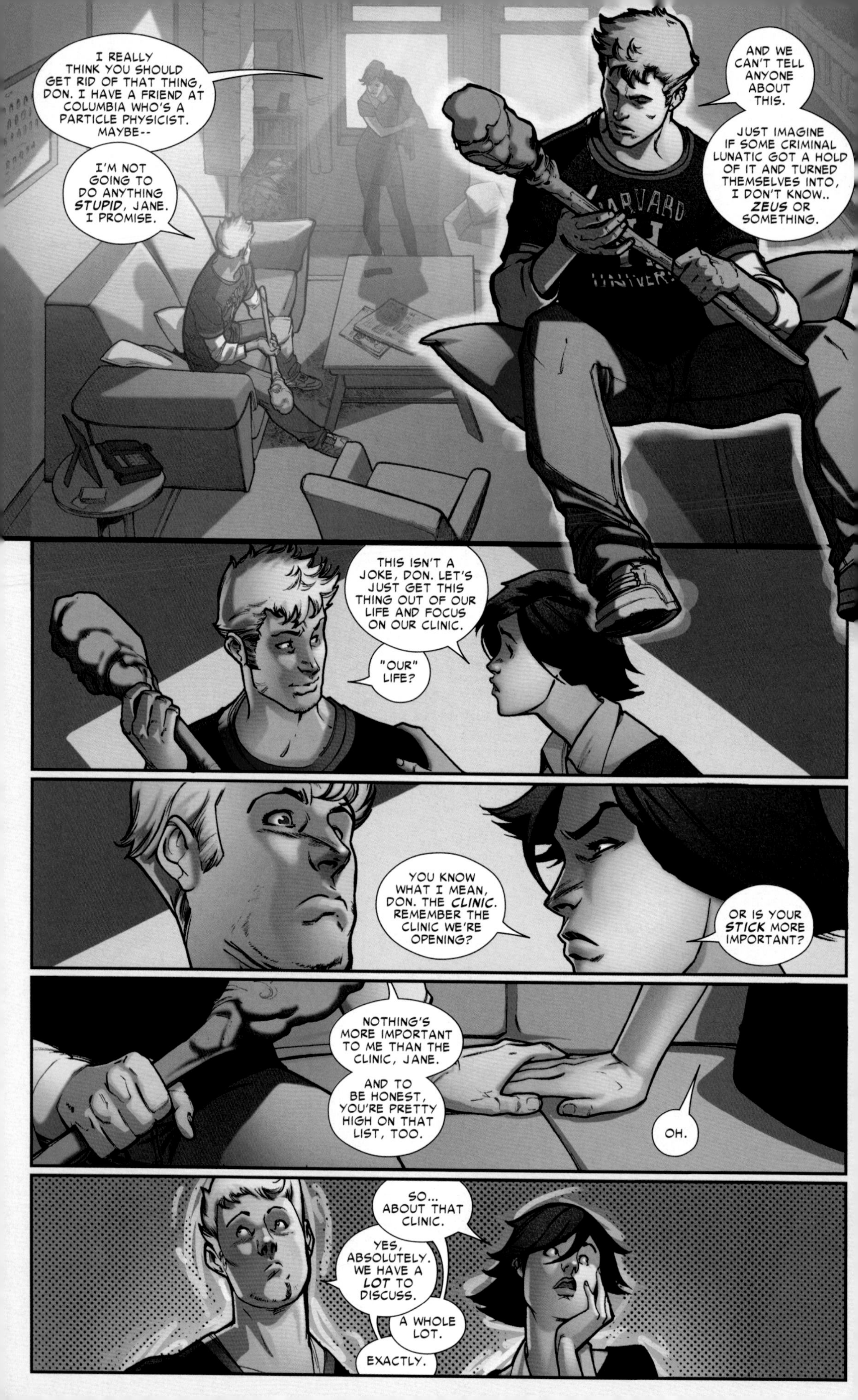

I REALLY THINK YOU SHOULD GET RID OF THAT THING, DON. I HAVE A FRIEND AT COLUMBIA WHO'S A PARTICLE PHYSICIST. MAYBE--
I'M NOT GOING TO DO ANYTHING STUPID, JANE. I PROMISE.
AND WE CAN'T TELL ANYONE ABOUT THIS.
JUST IMAGINE IF SOME CRIMINAL LUNATIC GOT A HOLD OF IT AND TURNED THEMSELVES INTO, I DON'T KNOW.. ZEUS OR SOMETHING.
THIS ISN'T A JOKE, DON. LET'S JUST GET THIS THING OUT OF OUR LIFE AND FOCUS ON OUR CLINIC.
"OUR" LIFE?
YOU KNOW WHAT I MEAN, DON. THE CLINIC. REMEMBER THE CLINIC WE'RE OPENING?
OR IS YOUR STICK MORE IMPORTANT?
NOTHING'S MORE IMPORTANT TO ME THAN THE CLINIC, JANE.
AND TO BE HONEST, YOU'RE PRETTY HIGH ON THAT LIST, TOO.
OH.
SO... ABOUT THAT CLINIC.
YES, ABSOLUTELY. WE HAVE A LOT TO DISCUSS.
A WHOLE LOT.
EXACTLY.

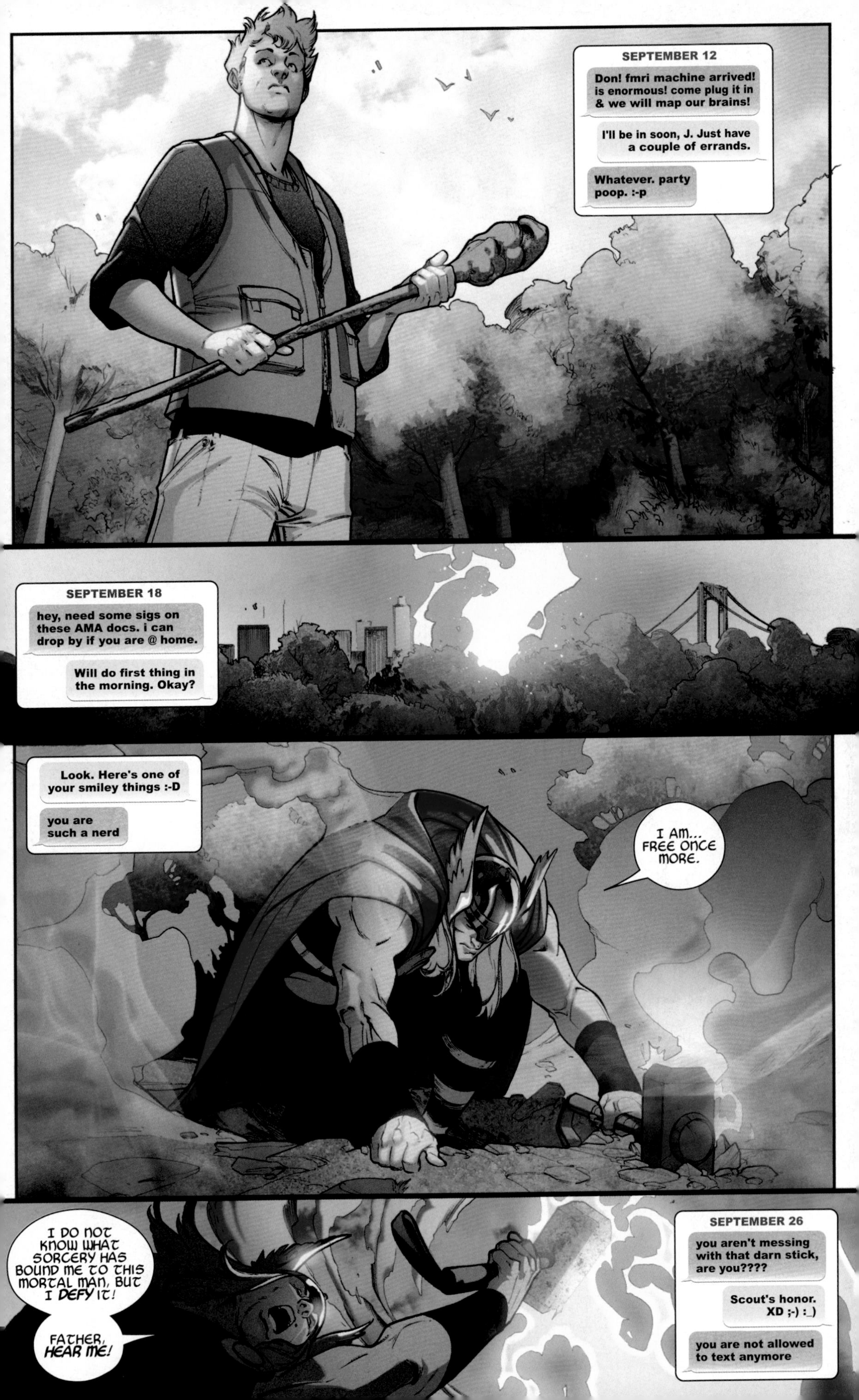
SEPTEMBER 12
Don! fmri machine arrived! is enormous! come plug it in & we will map our brains!
I'll be in soon, J. Just have a couple of errands.
Whatever. party poop. :-p
SEPTEMBER 18
hey, need some sigs on these AMA docs. i can drop by if you are @ home.
Will do first thing in the morning. Okay?
Look. Here's one of your smiley things :-D
you are such a nerd
I AM... FREE ONCE MORE.
I DO NOT KNOW WHAT SORCERY HAS BOUND ME TO THIS MORTAL MAN, BUT I DEFY IT!
FATHER, HEAR ME!
SEPTEMBER 26
you aren't messing with that darn stick, are you????
Scout's honor. XD ;-) :_)
you are not allowed to text anymore

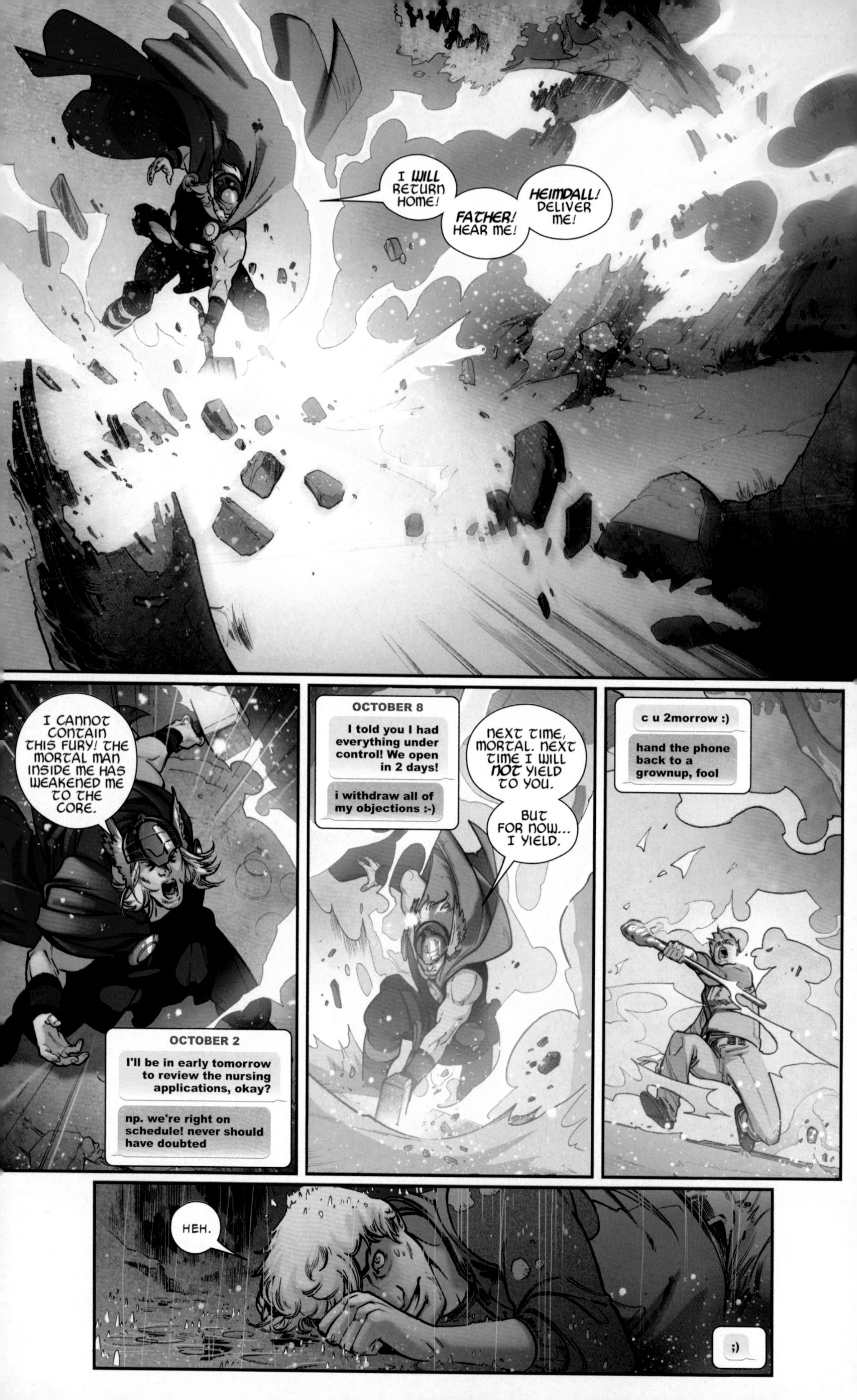
I WILL RETURN HOME!
FATHER! HEAR ME!
HEIMDALL! DELIVER ME!
I CANNOT CONTAIN THIS FURY! THE MORTAL MAN INSIDE ME HAS WEAKENED ME TO THE CORE.
OCTOBER 2
I'll be in early tomorrow to review the nursing applications, okay?
np. we're right on schedule! never should have doubted
OCTOBER 8
I told you I had everything under control! We open in 2 days!
i withdraw all of my objections :-)
NEXT TIME, MORTAL. NEXT TIME I WILL NOT YIELD TO YOU.
BUT FOR NOW... I YIELD.
c u 2morrow :)
hand the phone back to a grownup, fool
HEH.
;)

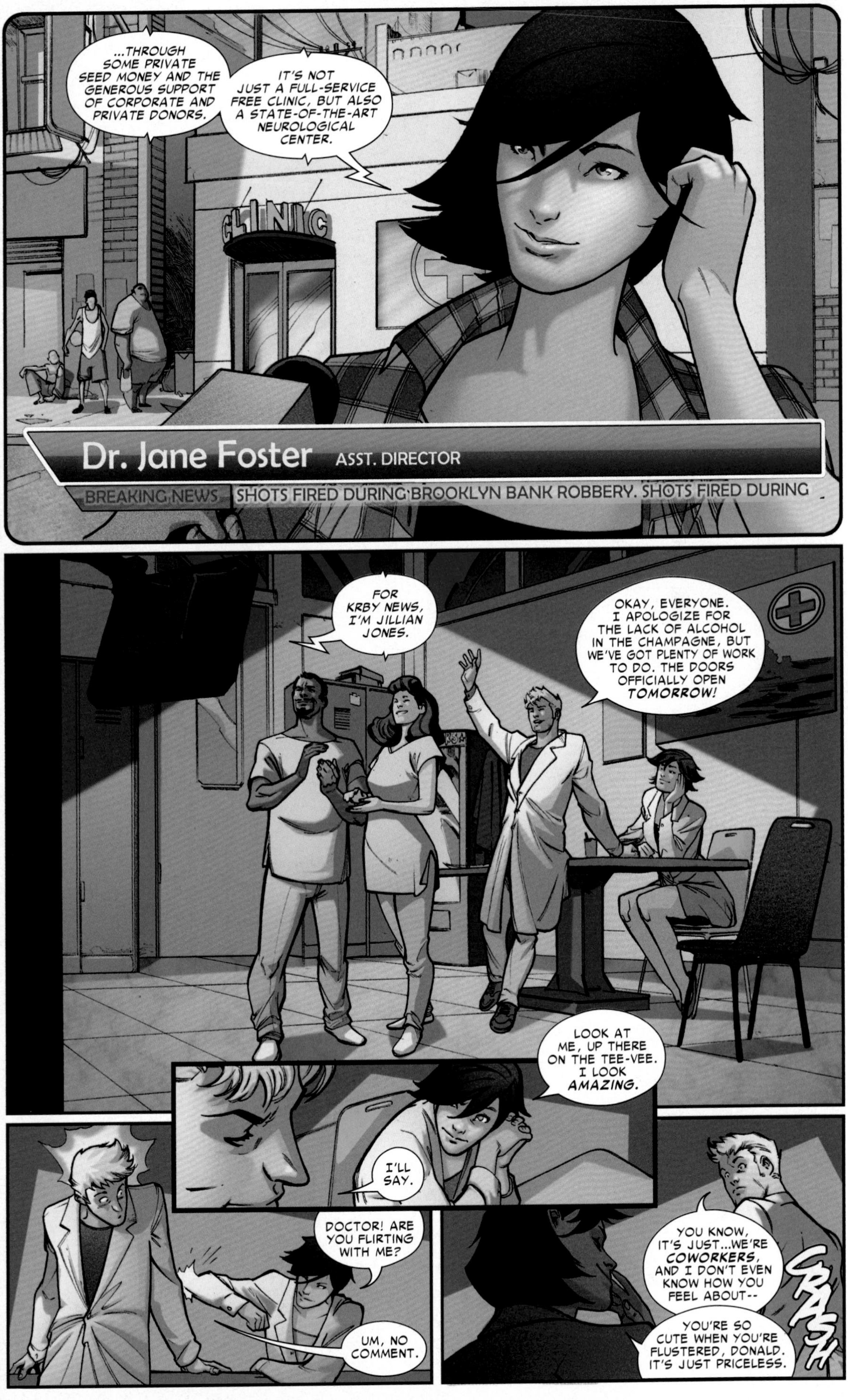
...THROUGH SOME PRIVATE SEED MONEY AND THE GENEROUS SUPPORT OF CORPORATE AND PRIVATE DONORS.
IT'S NOT JUST A FULL-SERVICE FREE CLINIC, BUT ALSO A STATE-OF-THE-ART NEUROLOGICAL CENTER.
CLINIC
Dr. Jane Foster ASST. DIRECTOR
BREAKING NEWS SHOTS FIRED DURING BROOKLYN BANK ROBBERY. SHOTS FIRED DURING
FOR KRBY NEWS, I'M JILLIAN JONES.
OKAY, EVERYONE. I APOLOGIZE FOR THE LACK OF ALCOHOL IN THE CHAMPAGNE, BUT WE'VE GOT PLENTY OF WORK TO DO. THE DOORS OFFICIALLY OPEN *TOMORROW!*
LOOK AT ME, UP THERE ON THE TEE-VEE. I LOOK *AMAZING.*
I'LL SAY.
DOCTOR! ARE YOU FLIRTING WITH ME?
UM, NO COMMENT.
YOU KNOW, IT'S JUST...WE'RE *COWORKERS,* AND I DON'T EVEN KNOW HOW YOU FEEL ABOUT--
YOU'RE SO CUTE WHEN YOU'RE FLUSTERED, DONALD. IT'S JUST PRICELESS.
CRASH

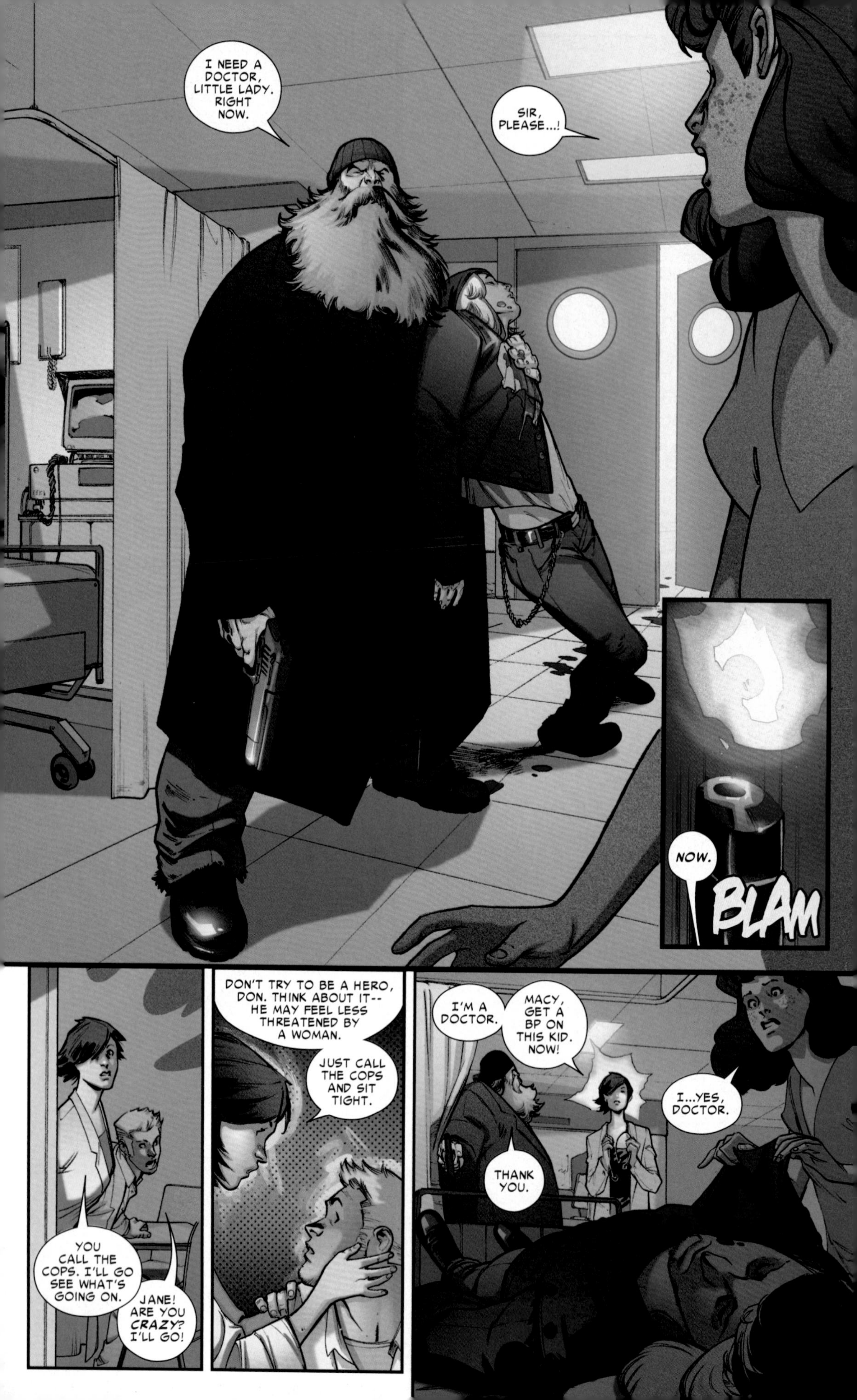
I NEED A DOCTOR, LITTLE LADY. RIGHT NOW.
SIR, PLEASE...!
NOW.
BLAM
YOU CALL THE COPS. I'LL GO SEE WHAT'S GOING ON.
JANE! ARE YOU CRAZY? I'LL GO!
DON'T TRY TO BE A HERO, DON. THINK ABOUT IT-- HE MAY FEEL LESS THREATENED BY A WOMAN.
JUST CALL THE COPS AND SIT TIGHT.
I'M A DOCTOR.
MACY, GET A BP ON THIS KID. NOW!
THANK YOU.
I...YES, DOCTOR.

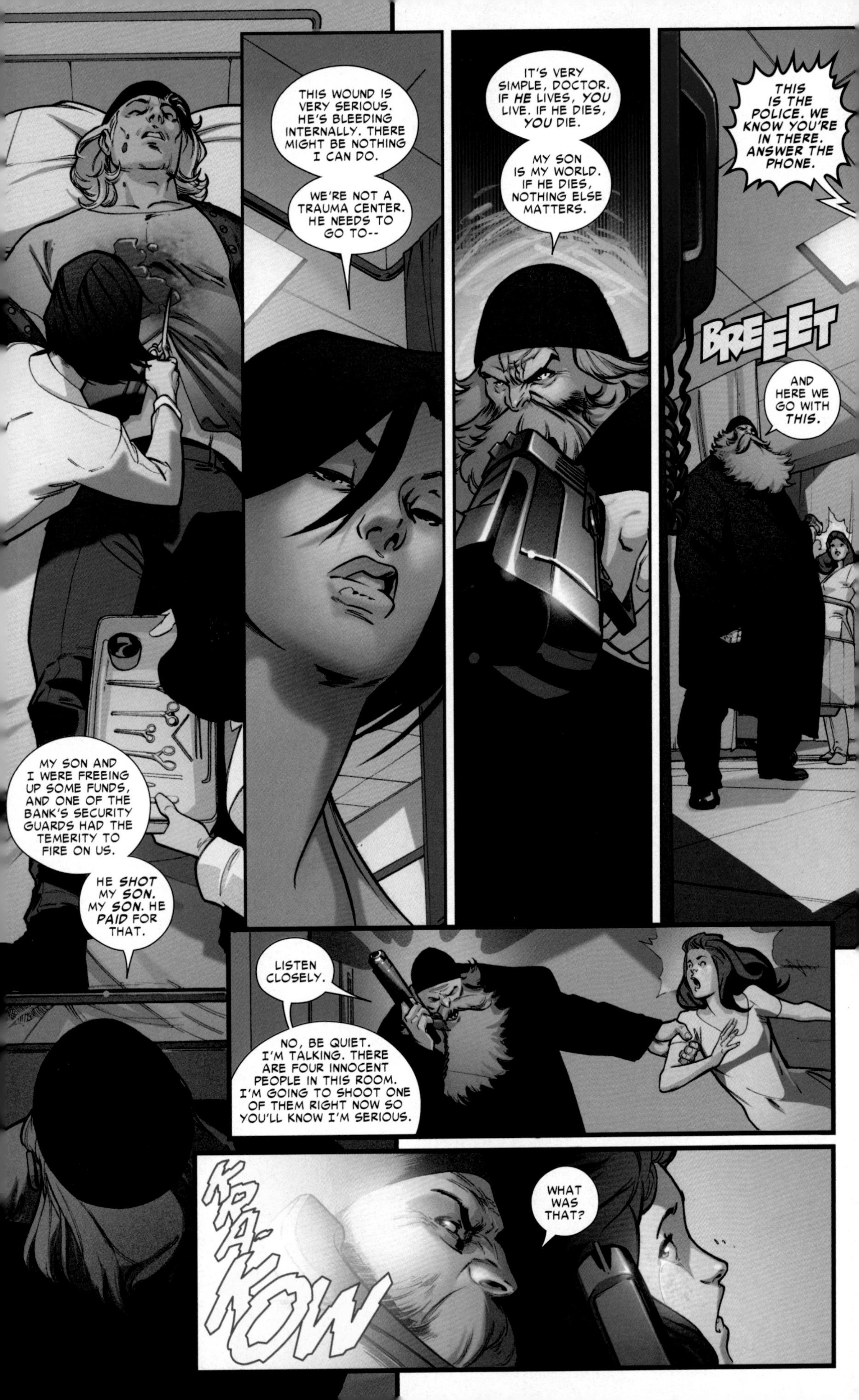
THIS WOUND IS VERY SERIOUS. HE'S BLEEDING INTERNALLY. THERE MIGHT BE NOTHING I CAN DO.
WE'RE NOT A TRAUMA CENTER. HE NEEDS TO GO TO--
IT'S VERY SIMPLE, DOCTOR. IF HE LIVES, YOU LIVE. IF HE DIES, YOU DIE.
MY SON IS MY WORLD. IF HE DIES, NOTHING ELSE MATTERS.
THIS IS THE POLICE. WE KNOW YOU'RE IN THERE. ANSWER THE PHONE.
BREEET
AND HERE WE GO WITH THIS.
MY SON AND I WERE FREEING UP SOME FUNDS, AND ONE OF THE BANK'S SECURITY GUARDS HAD THE TEMERITY TO FIRE ON US.
HE SHOT MY SON. MY SON. HE PAID FOR THAT.
LISTEN CLOSELY.
NO, BE QUIET. I'M TALKING. THERE ARE FOUR INNOCENT PEOPLE IN THIS ROOM. I'M GOING TO SHOOT ONE OF THEM RIGHT NOW SO YOU'LL KNOW I'M SERIOUS.
KA-KOW
WHAT WAS THAT?

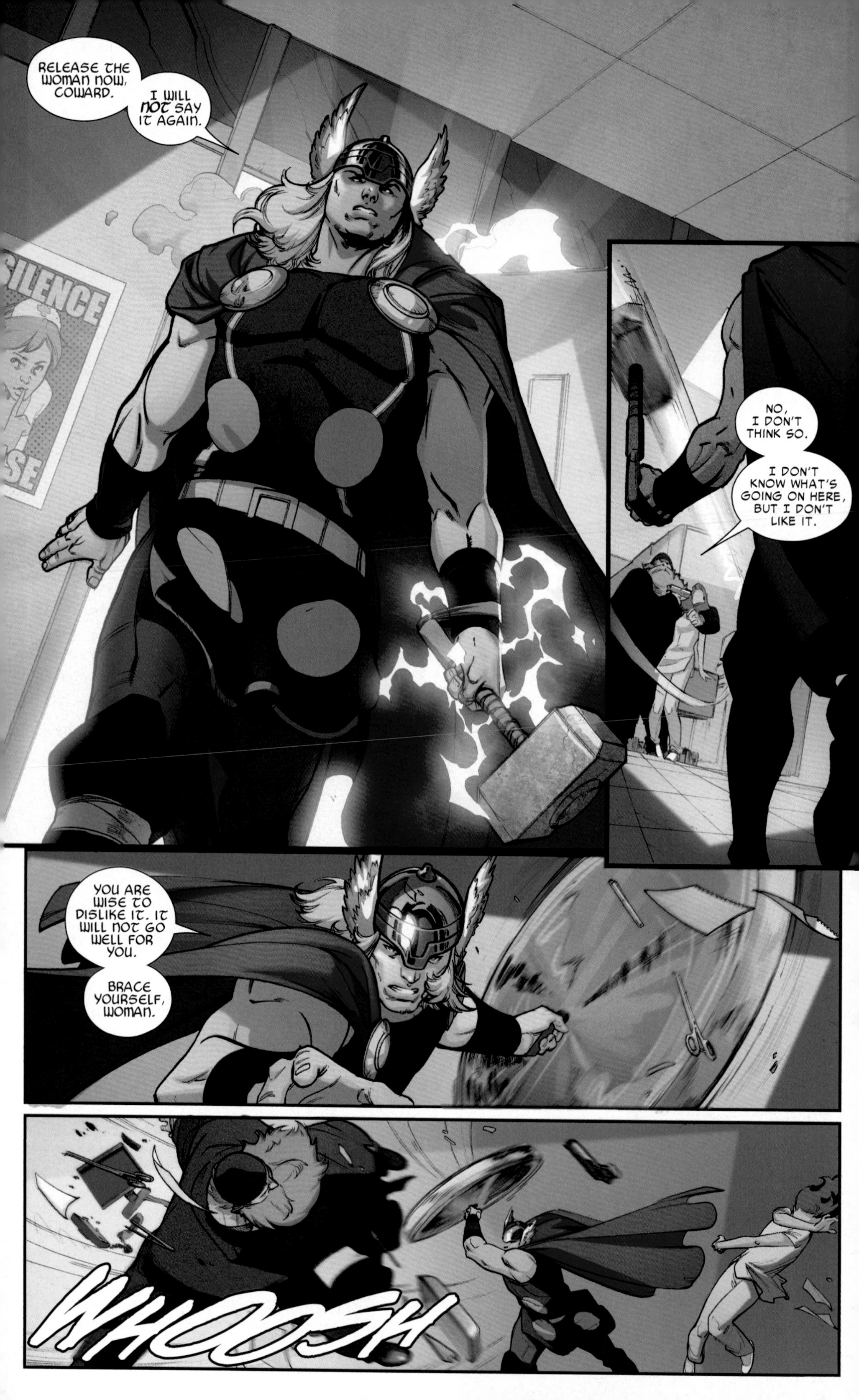
RELEASE THE WOMAN NOW, COWARD.
I WILL NOT SAY IT AGAIN.
SILENCE
NO, I DON'T THINK SO.
I DON'T KNOW WHAT'S GOING ON HERE, BUT I DON'T LIKE IT.
YOU ARE WISE TO DISLIKE IT. IT WILL NOT GO WELL FOR YOU.
BRACE YOURSELF, WOMAN.
WHOOSH

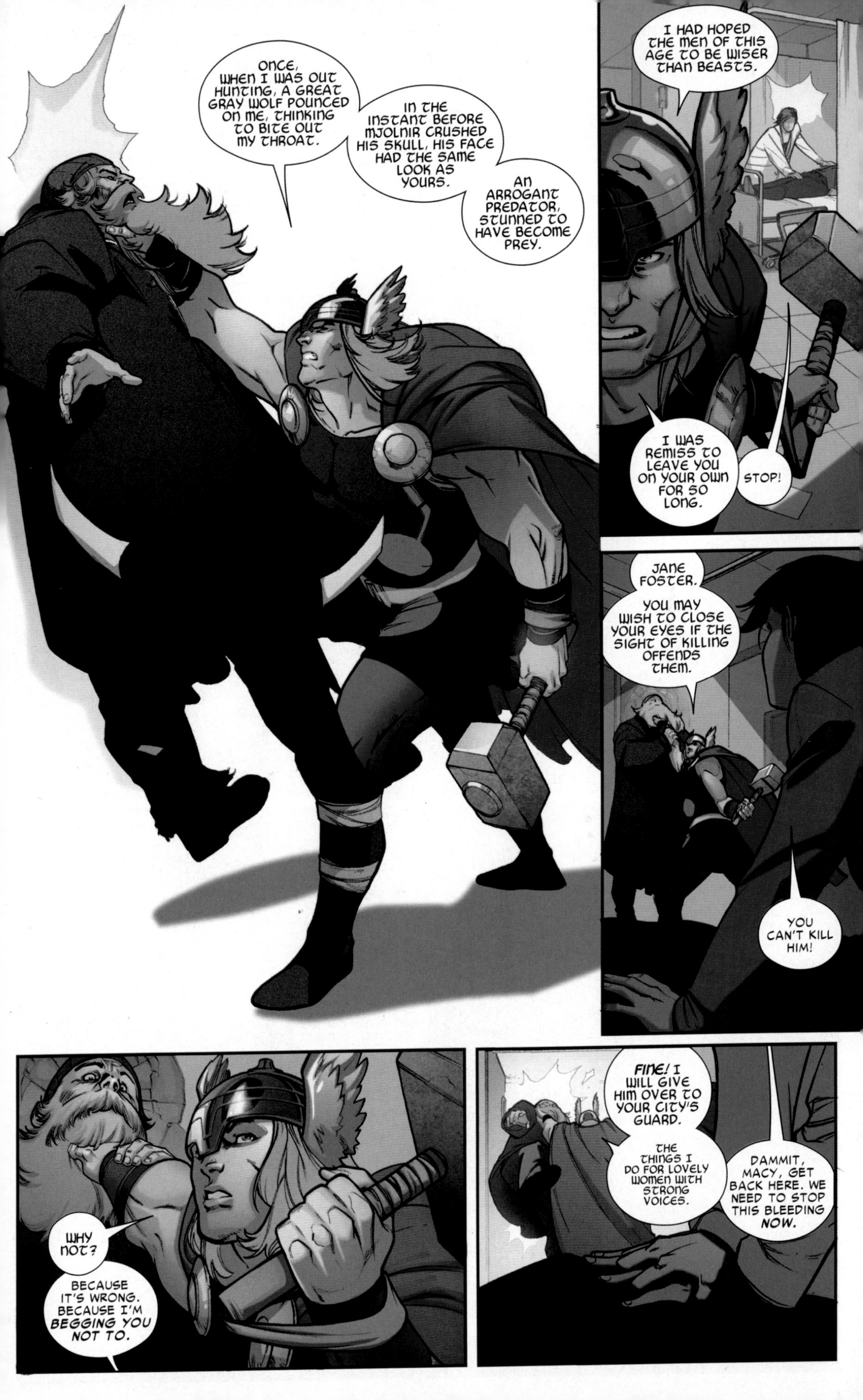
ONCE, WHEN I WAS OUT HUNTING, A GREAT GRAY WOLF POUNCED ON ME, THINKING TO BITE OUT MY THROAT.
IN THE INSTANT BEFORE MJOLNIR CRUSHED HIS SKULL, HIS FACE HAD THE SAME LOOK AS YOURS.
AN ARROGANT PREDATOR, STUNNED TO HAVE BECOME PREY.
I HAD HOPED THE MEN OF THIS AGE TO BE WISER THAN BEASTS.
I WAS REMISS TO LEAVE YOU ON YOUR OWN FOR SO LONG.
STOP!
JANE FOSTER.
YOU MAY WISH TO CLOSE YOUR EYES IF THE SIGHT OF KILLING OFFENDS THEM.
YOU CAN'T KILL HIM!
WHY NOT?
BECAUSE IT'S WRONG. BECAUSE I'M *BEGGING YOU* NOT TO.
FINE! I WILL GIVE HIM OVER TO YOUR CITY'S GUARD.
THE THINGS I DO FOR LOVELY WOMEN WITH STRONG VOICES.
DAMMIT, MACY, GET BACK HERE. WE NEED TO STOP THIS BLEEDING *NOW.*

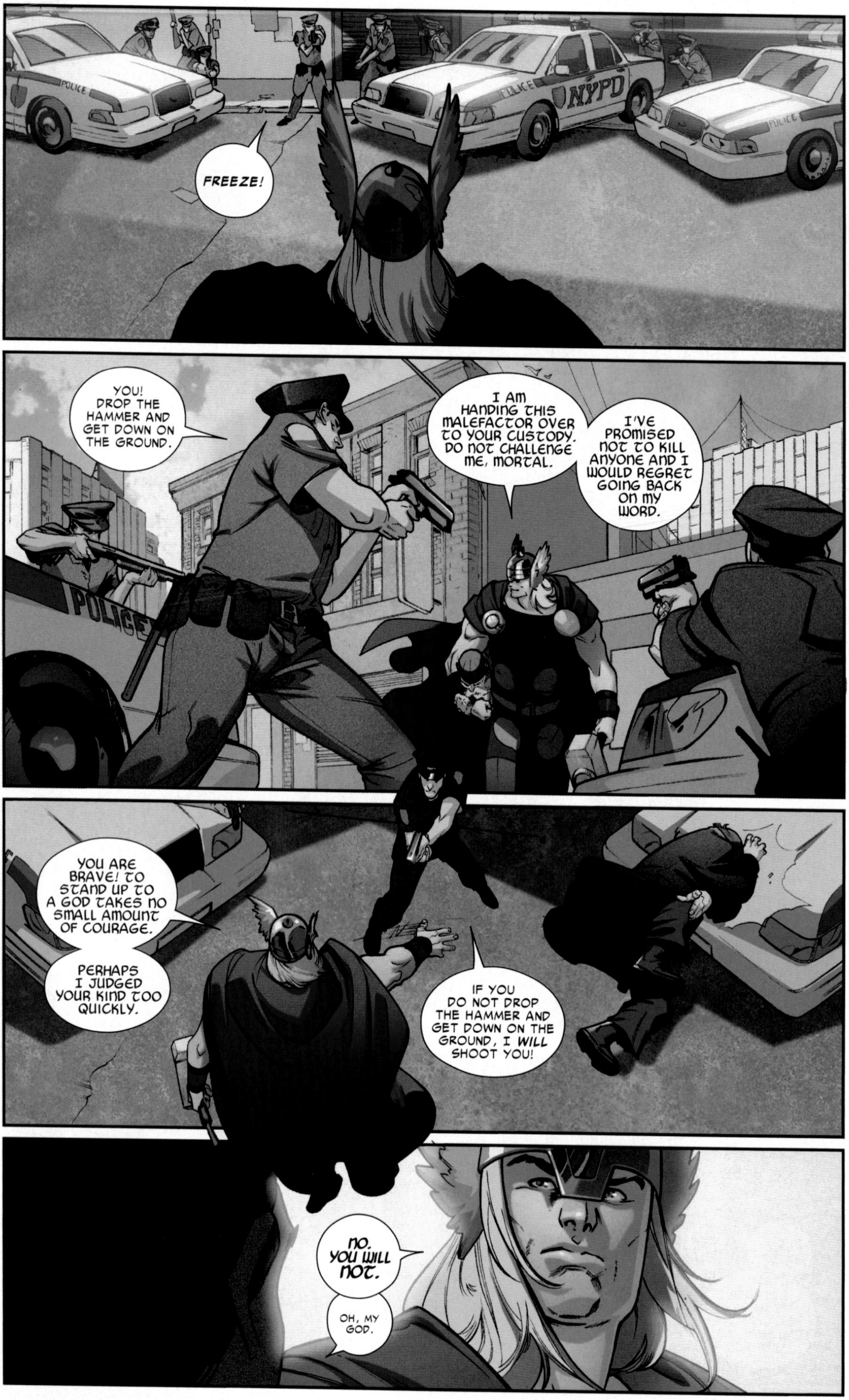
FREEZE!
YOU! DROP THE HAMMER AND GET DOWN ON THE GROUND.
I AM HANDING THIS MALEFACTOR OVER TO YOUR CUSTODY. DO NOT CHALLENGE ME, MORTAL.
I'VE PROMISED NOT TO KILL ANYONE AND I WOULD REGRET GOING BACK ON MY WORD.
YOU ARE BRAVE! TO STAND UP TO A GOD TAKES NO SMALL AMOUNT OF COURAGE.
PERHAPS I JUDGED YOUR KIND TOO QUICKLY.
IF YOU DO NOT DROP THE HAMMER AND GET DOWN ON THE GROUND, I WILL SHOOT YOU!
NO. YOU WILL NOT.
OH, MY GOD.

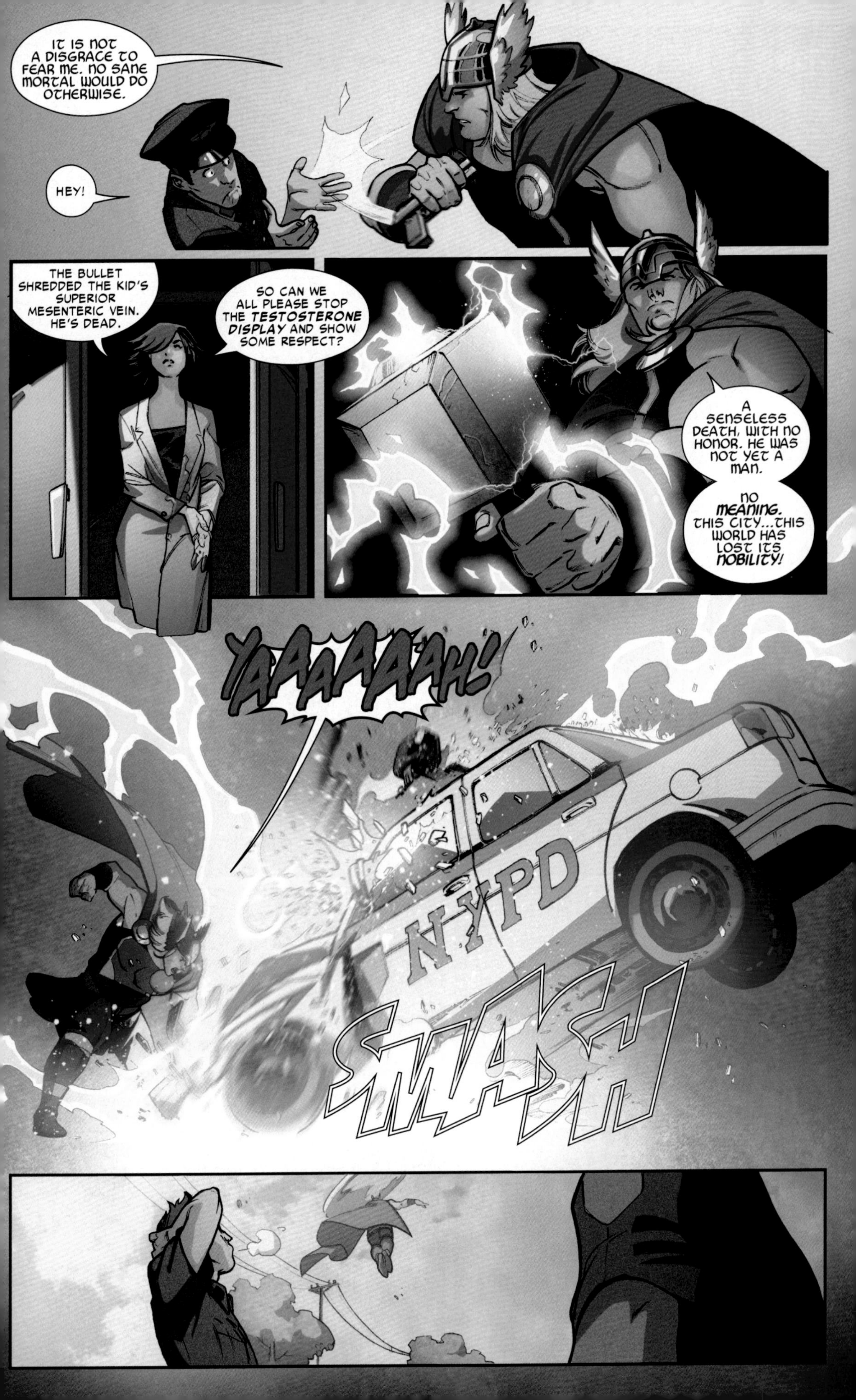
IT IS NOT A DISGRACE TO FEAR ME. NO SANE MORTAL WOULD DO OTHERWISE.
HEY!
THE BULLET SHREDDED THE KID'S SUPERIOR MESENTERIC VEIN. HE'S DEAD.
SO CAN WE ALL PLEASE STOP THE *TESTOSTERONE DISPLAY* AND SHOW SOME RESPECT?
A SENSELESS DEATH, WITH NO HONOR. HE WAS NOT YET A MAN.
NO *MEANING.* THIS CITY...THIS WORLD HAS LOST ITS *NOBILITY!*
YAAAAAAH!
NYPD
SMASH

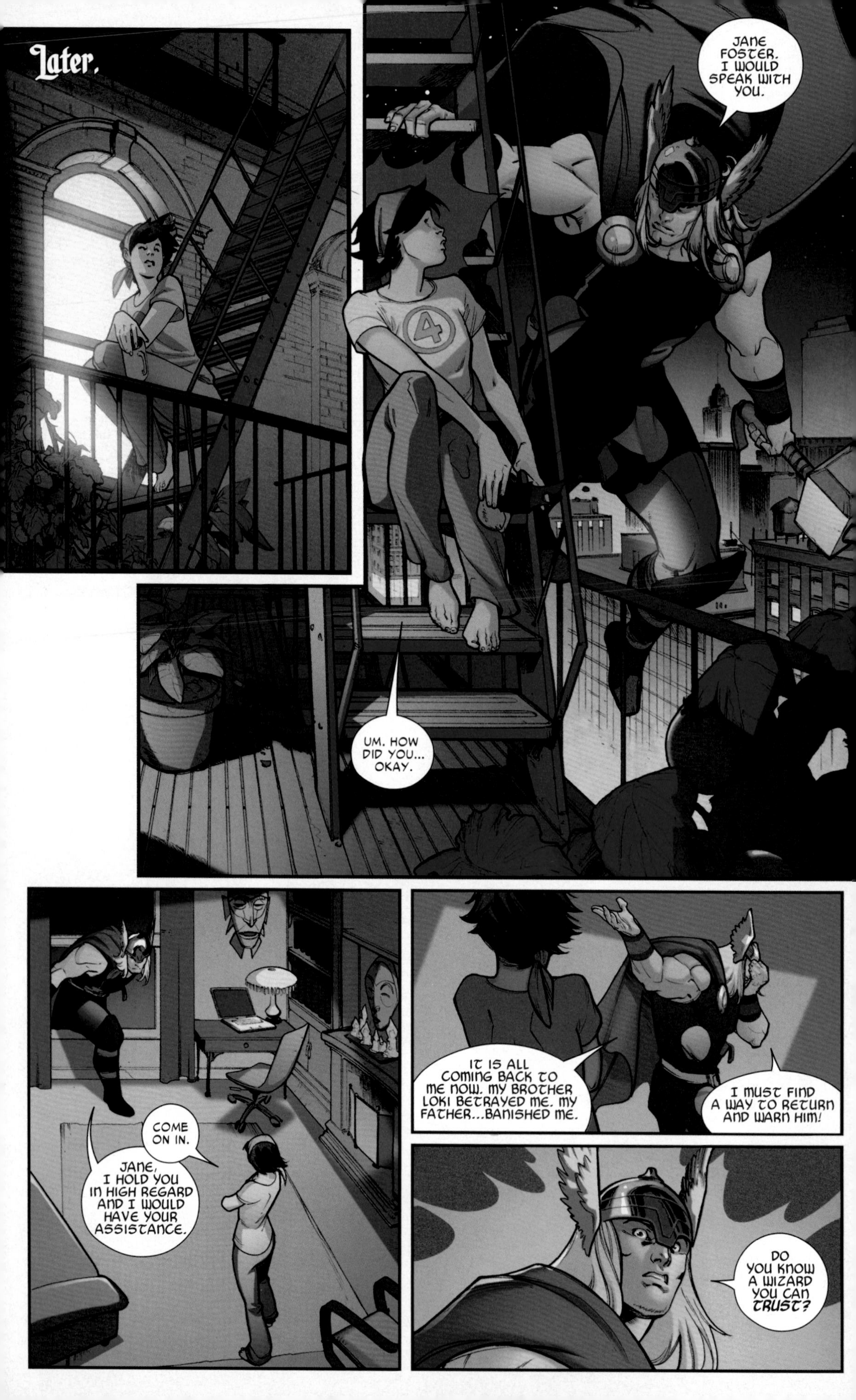
Later.
JANE FOSTER. I WOULD SPEAK WITH YOU.
UM. HOW DID YOU... OKAY.
COME ON IN.
JANE, I HOLD YOU IN HIGH REGARD AND I WOULD HAVE YOUR ASSISTANCE.
IT IS ALL COMING BACK TO ME NOW. MY BROTHER LOKI BETRAYED ME. MY FATHER...BANISHED ME.
I MUST FIND A WAY TO RETURN AND WARN HIM!
DO YOU KNOW A WIZARD YOU CAN TRUST?

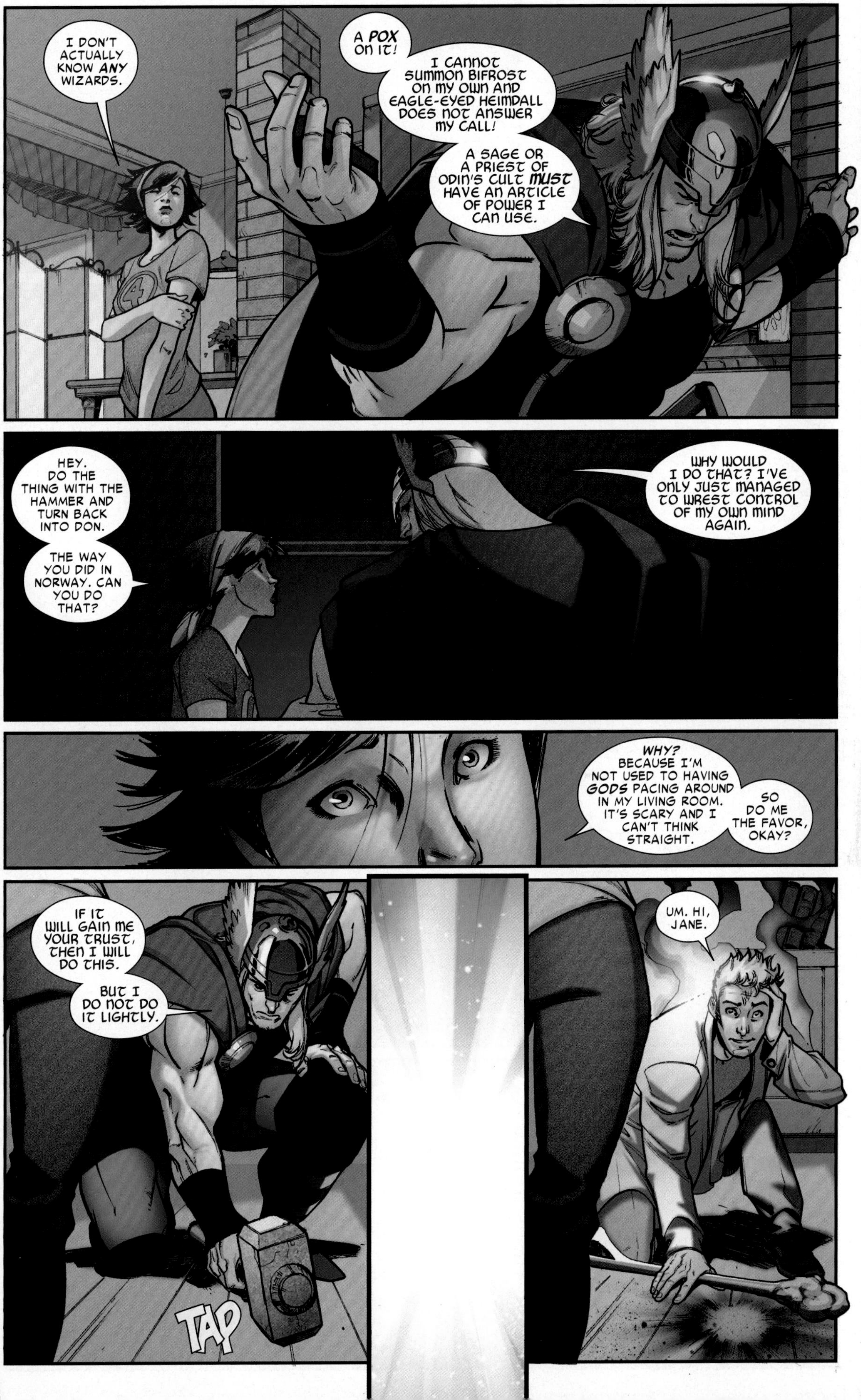
I DON'T ACTUALLY KNOW ANY WIZARDS.
A POX ON IT!
I CANNOT SUMMON BIFROST ON MY OWN AND EAGLE-EYED HEIMDALL DOES NOT ANSWER MY CALL!
A SAGE OR A PRIEST OF ODIN'S CULT MUST HAVE AN ARTICLE OF POWER I CAN USE.
HEY. DO THE THING WITH THE HAMMER AND TURN BACK INTO DON.
THE WAY YOU DID IN NORWAY. CAN YOU DO THAT?
WHY WOULD I DO THAT? I'VE ONLY JUST MANAGED TO WREST CONTROL OF MY OWN MIND AGAIN.
WHY? BECAUSE I'M NOT USED TO HAVING GODS PACING AROUND IN MY LIVING ROOM. IT'S SCARY AND I CAN'T THINK STRAIGHT.
SO DO ME THE FAVOR, OKAY?
IF IT WILL GAIN ME YOUR TRUST, THEN I WILL DO THIS.
BUT I DO NOT DO IT LIGHTLY.
TAP
UM. HI, JANE.

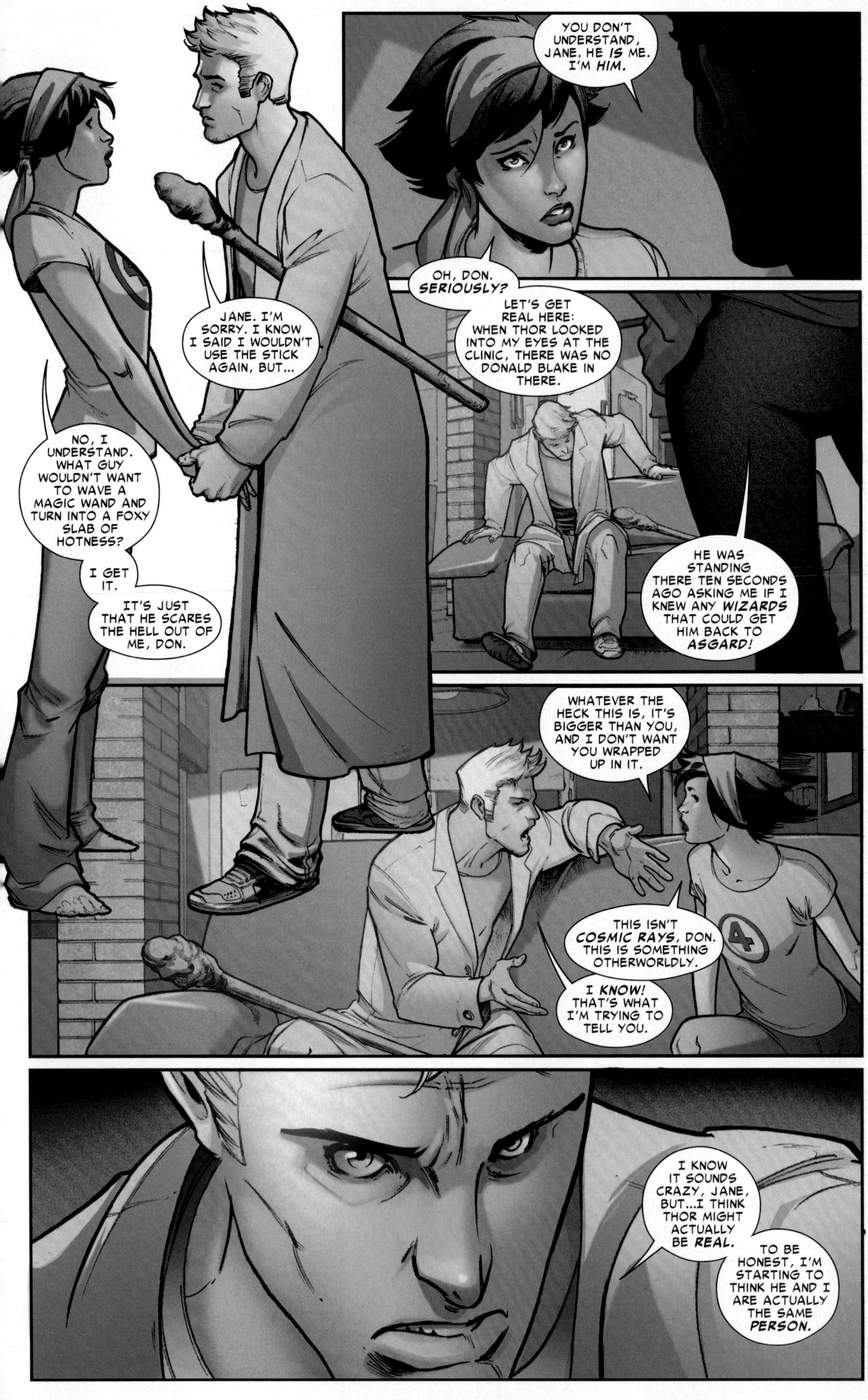
YOU DON'T UNDERSTAND, JANE. HE *IS* ME. I'M *HIM*.
JANE. I'M SORRY. I KNOW I SAID I WOULDN'T USE THE STICK AGAIN, BUT...
NO, I UNDERSTAND. WHAT GUY WOULDN'T WANT TO WAVE A MAGIC WAND AND TURN INTO A FOXY SLAB OF HOTNESS?
I GET IT.
IT'S JUST THAT HE SCARES THE HELL OUT OF ME, DON.
OH, DON. ***SERIOUSLY?***
LET'S GET REAL HERE: WHEN THOR LOOKED INTO MY EYES AT THE CLINIC, THERE WAS NO DONALD BLAKE IN THERE.
HE WAS STANDING THERE TEN SECONDS AGO ASKING ME IF I KNEW ANY ***WIZARDS*** THAT COULD GET HIM BACK TO ***ASGARD!***
WHATEVER THE HECK THIS IS, IT'S BIGGER THAN YOU, AND I DON'T WANT YOU WRAPPED UP IN IT.
THIS ISN'T ***COSMIC RAYS***, DON. THIS IS SOMETHING OTHERWORLDLY.
I ***KNOW!*** THAT'S WHAT I'M TRYING TO TELL YOU.
I KNOW IT SOUNDS CRAZY, JANE, BUT...I THINK THOR MIGHT ACTUALLY BE ***REAL***.
TO BE HONEST, I'M STARTING TO THINK HE AND I ARE ACTUALLY THE SAME ***PERSON***.

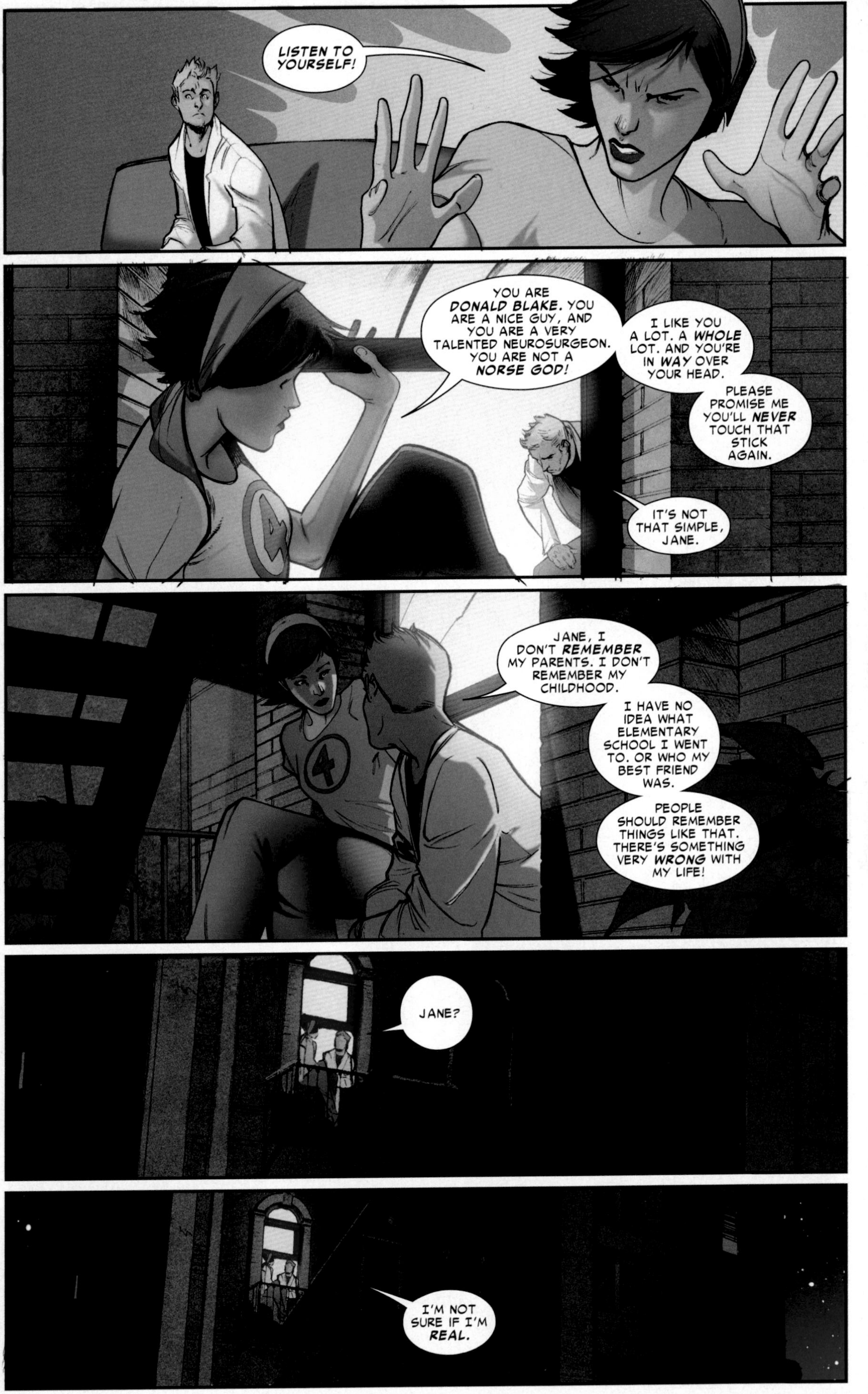
LISTEN TO YOURSELF!
YOU ARE DONALD BLAKE. YOU ARE A NICE GUY, AND YOU ARE A VERY TALENTED NEUROSURGEON. YOU ARE NOT A NORSE GOD!
I LIKE YOU A LOT. A WHOLE LOT. AND YOU'RE IN WAY OVER YOUR HEAD.
PLEASE PROMISE ME YOU'LL NEVER TOUCH THAT STICK AGAIN.
IT'S NOT THAT SIMPLE, JANE.
JANE, I DON'T REMEMBER MY PARENTS. I DON'T REMEMBER MY CHILDHOOD.
I HAVE NO IDEA WHAT ELEMENTARY SCHOOL I WENT TO. OR WHO MY BEST FRIEND WAS.
PEOPLE SHOULD REMEMBER THINGS LIKE THAT. THERE'S SOMETHING VERY WRONG WITH MY LIFE!
JANE?
I'M NOT SURE IF I'M REAL.

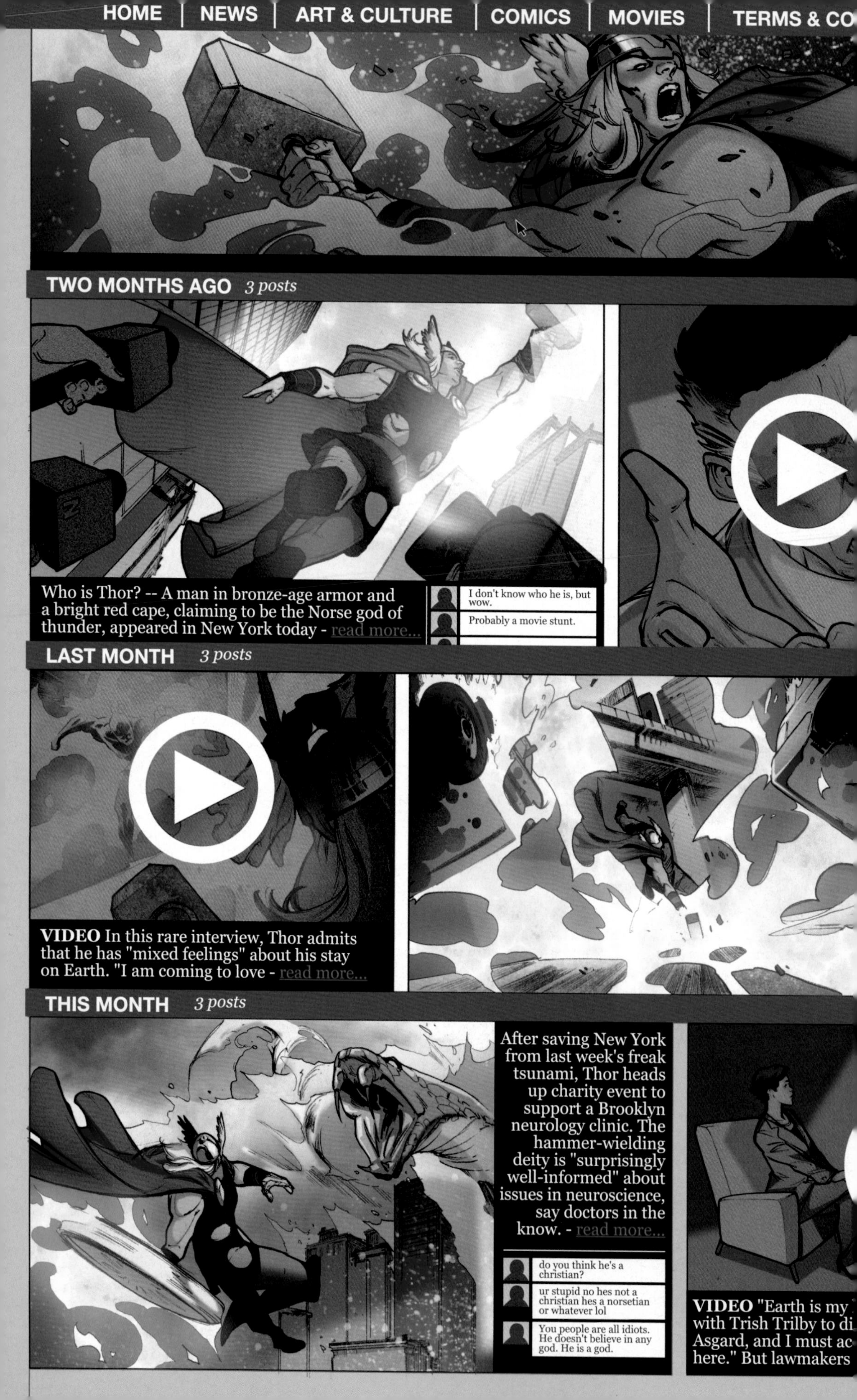

HOME | NEWS | ART & CULTURE | COMICS | MOVIES | TERMS & CO
TWO MONTHS AGO 3 posts
Who is Thor? -- A man in bronze-age armor and a bright red cape, claiming to be the Norse god of thunder, appeared in New York today - read more...
I don't know who he is, but wow.
Probably a movie stunt.
LAST MONTH 3 posts
VIDEO In this rare interview, Thor admits that he has "mixed feelings" about his stay on Earth. "I am coming to love - read more...
THIS MONTH 3 posts
After saving New York from last week's freak tsunami, Thor heads up charity event to support a Brooklyn neurology clinic. The hammer-wielding deity is "surprisingly well-informed" about issues in neuroscience, say doctors in the know. - read more...
do you think he's a christian?
ur stupid no hes not a christian hes a norsetian or whatever lol
You people are all idiots. He doesn't believe in any god. He is a god.
VIDEO "Earth is my
with Trish Trilby to di
Asgard, and I must ac
here." But lawmakers

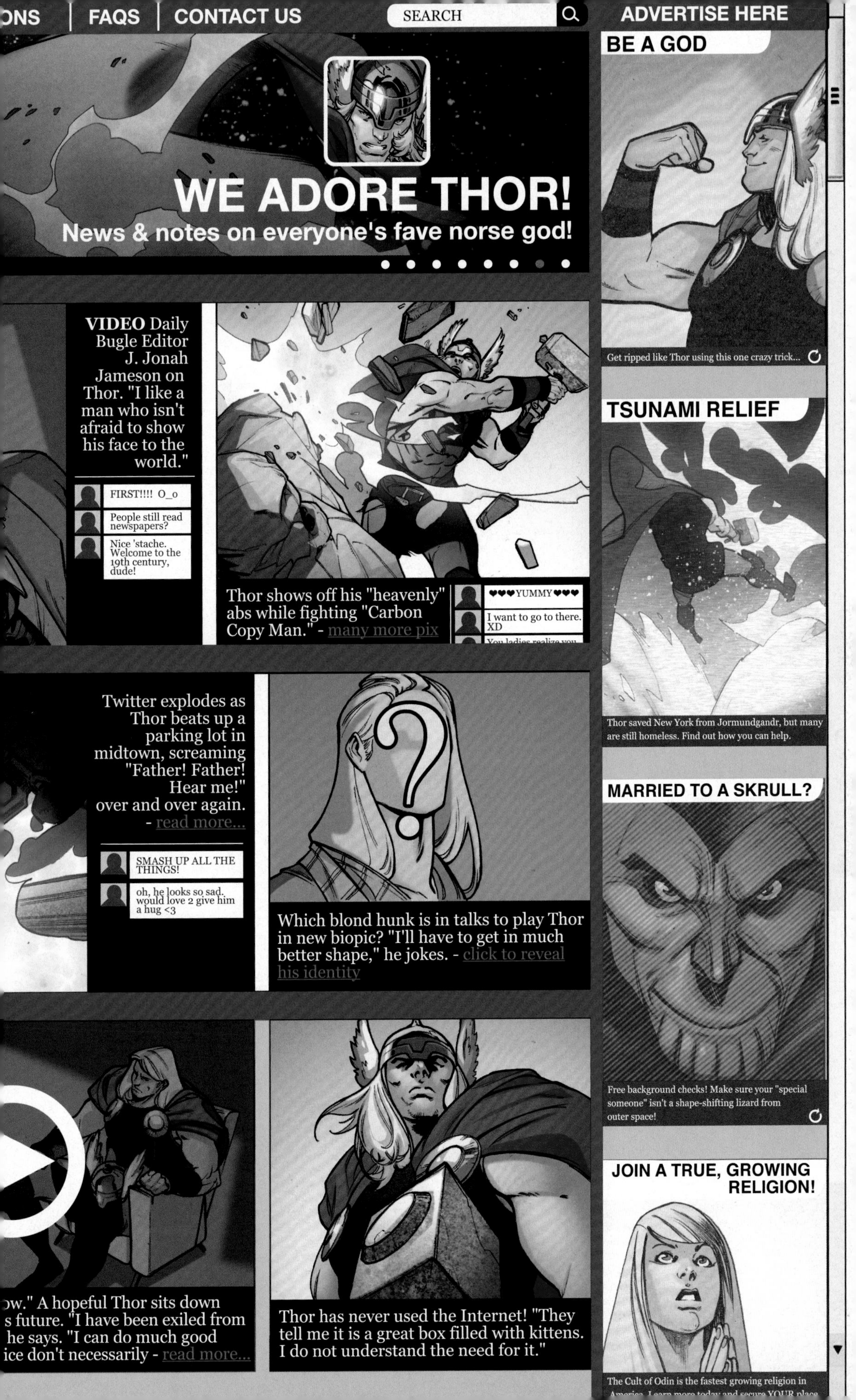

ONS
FAQS
CONTACT US
SEARCH
ADVERTISE HERE
WE ADORE THOR!
News & notes on everyone's fave norse god!
VIDEO Daily Bugle Editor J. Jonah Jameson on Thor. "I like a man who isn't afraid to show his face to the world."
FIRST!!!! O_o
People still read newspapers?
Nice 'stache. Welcome to the 19th century, dude!
Thor shows off his "heavenly" abs while fighting "Carbon Copy Man." - many more pix
❤❤❤YUMMY❤❤❤
I want to go to there. XD
Twitter explodes as Thor beats up a parking lot in midtown, screaming "Father! Father! Hear me!" over and over again. - read more...
SMASH UP ALL THE THINGS!
oh, he looks so sad. would love 2 give him a hug <3
Which blond hunk is in talks to play Thor in new biopic? "I'll have to get in much better shape," he jokes. - click to reveal his identity
ow." A hopeful Thor sits down
s future. "I have been exiled from
he says. "I can do much good
ice don't necessarily - read more...
Thor has never used the Internet! "They tell me it is a great box filled with kittens. I do not understand the need for it."
BE A GOD
Get ripped like Thor using this one crazy trick...
TSUNAMI RELIEF
Thor saved New York from Jormundgandr, but many are still homeless. Find out how you can help.
MARRIED TO A SKRULL?
Free background checks! Make sure your "special someone" isn't a shape-shifting lizard from outer space!
JOIN A TRUE, GROWING RELIGION!
The Cult of Odin is the fastest growing religion in

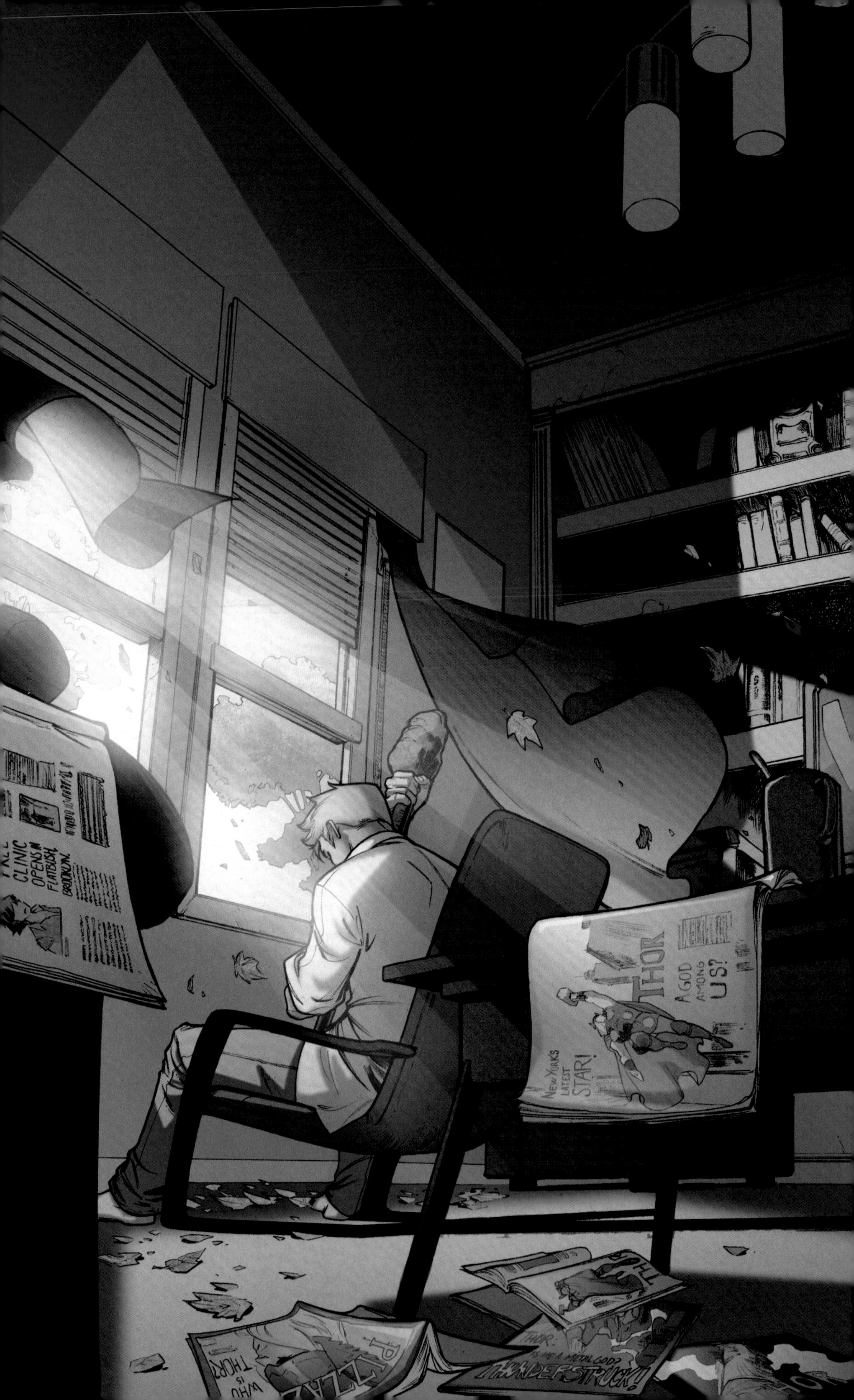

CLINIC OPENS IN FLATBUSH, BROOKLYN.
THOR
A GOD AMONG US?
NEW YORK'S LATEST STAR!
WHO IS THOR?
THOR:
IS HE A METAL GOD?
THUNDERSTRUCK!

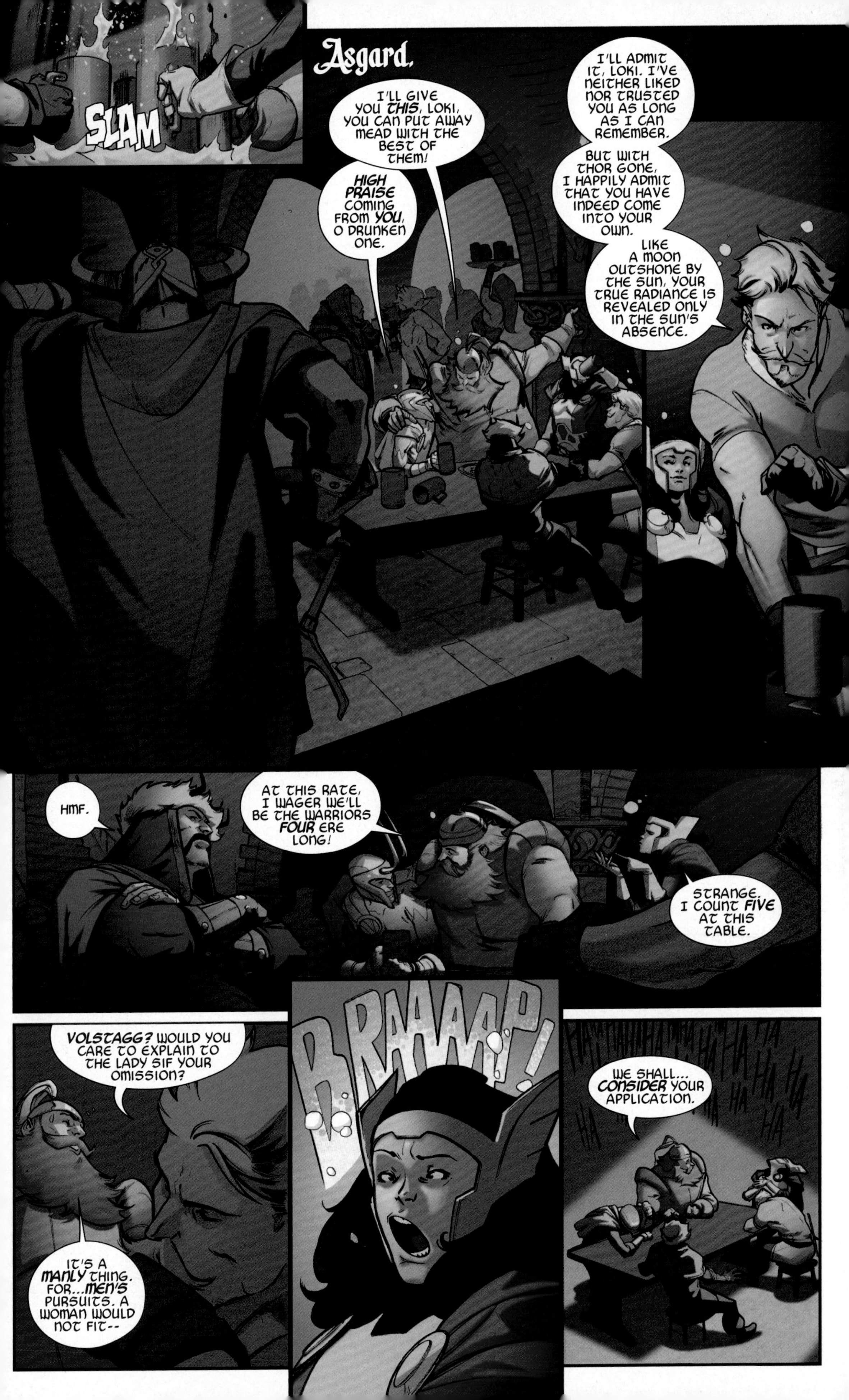
SLAM
Asgard.
I'LL GIVE YOU THIS, LOKI, YOU CAN PUT AWAY MEAD WITH THE BEST OF THEM!
HIGH PRAISE COMING FROM YOU, O DRUNKEN ONE.
I'LL ADMIT IT, LOKI. I'VE NEITHER LIKED NOR TRUSTED YOU AS LONG AS I CAN REMEMBER.
BUT WITH THOR GONE, I HAPPILY ADMIT THAT YOU HAVE INDEED COME INTO YOUR OWN.
LIKE A MOON OUTSHONE BY THE SUN, YOUR TRUE RADIANCE IS REVEALED ONLY IN THE SUN'S ABSENCE.
HMF.
AT THIS RATE, I WAGER WE'LL BE THE WARRIORS FOUR ERE LONG!
STRANGE. I COUNT FIVE AT THIS TABLE.
VOLSTAGG? WOULD YOU CARE TO EXPLAIN TO THE LADY SIF YOUR OMISSION?
IT'S A MANLY THING. FOR...MEN'S PURSUITS. A WOMAN WOULD NOT FIT--
BRAAAAP!
WE SHALL... CONSIDER YOUR APPLICATION.
HA HA HA HA HA HA HA HA HA HA HA HA HA HA HA

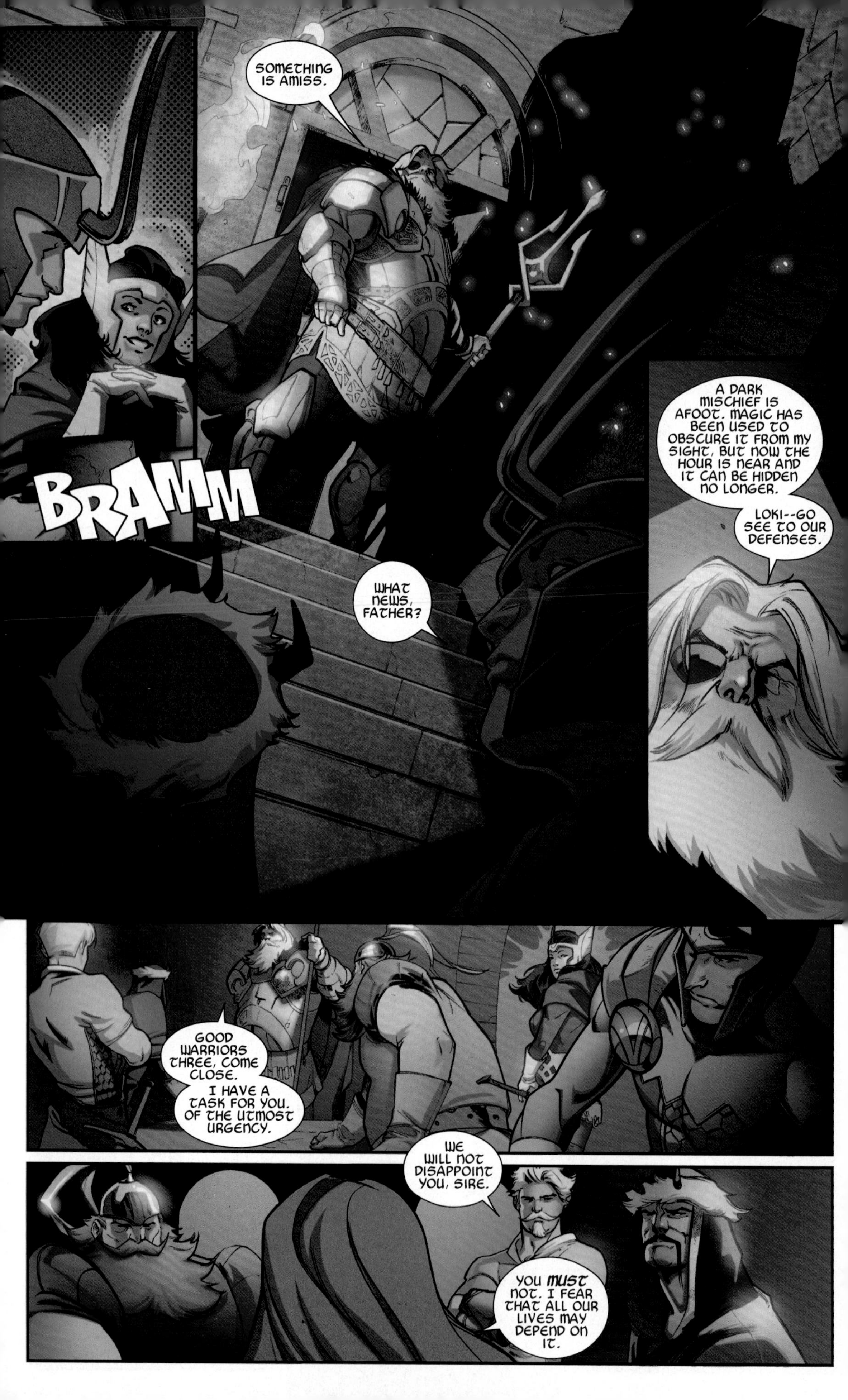
SOMETHING IS AMISS.
BRAMM
WHAT NEWS, FATHER?
A DARK MISCHIEF IS AFOOT. MAGIC HAS BEEN USED TO OBSCURE IT FROM MY SIGHT, BUT NOW THE HOUR IS NEAR AND IT CAN BE HIDDEN NO LONGER.
LOKI--GO SEE TO OUR DEFENSES.
GOOD WARRIORS THREE, COME CLOSE.
I HAVE A TASK FOR YOU. OF THE UTMOST URGENCY.
WE WILL NOT DISAPPOINT YOU, SIRE.
YOU MUST NOT. I FEAR THAT ALL OUR LIVES MAY DEPEND ON IT.

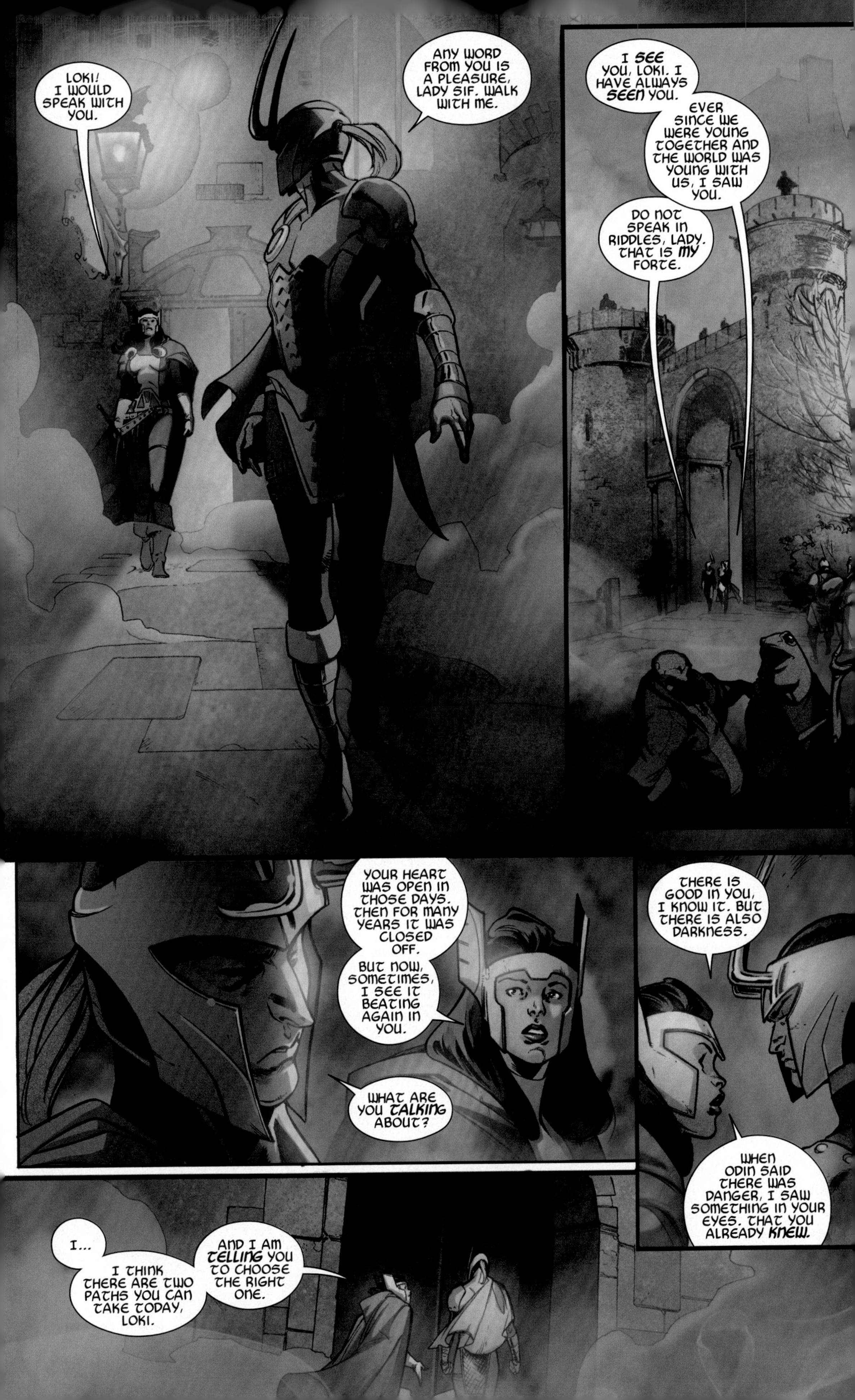
LOKI! I WOULD SPEAK WITH YOU.
ANY WORD FROM YOU IS A PLEASURE, LADY SIF. WALK WITH ME.
I SEE YOU, LOKI. I HAVE ALWAYS SEEN YOU.
EVER SINCE WE WERE YOUNG TOGETHER AND THE WORLD WAS YOUNG WITH US, I SAW YOU.
DO NOT SPEAK IN RIDDLES, LADY. THAT IS MY FORTE.
YOUR HEART WAS OPEN IN THOSE DAYS. THEN FOR MANY YEARS IT WAS CLOSED OFF.
BUT NOW, SOMETIMES, I SEE IT BEATING AGAIN IN YOU.
WHAT ARE YOU TALKING ABOUT?
THERE IS GOOD IN YOU, I KNOW IT. BUT THERE IS ALSO DARKNESS.
WHEN ODIN SAID THERE WAS DANGER, I SAW SOMETHING IN YOUR EYES. THAT YOU ALREADY KNEW.
I...
I THINK THERE ARE TWO PATHS YOU CAN TAKE TODAY, LOKI.
AND I AM TELLING YOU TO CHOOSE THE RIGHT ONE.

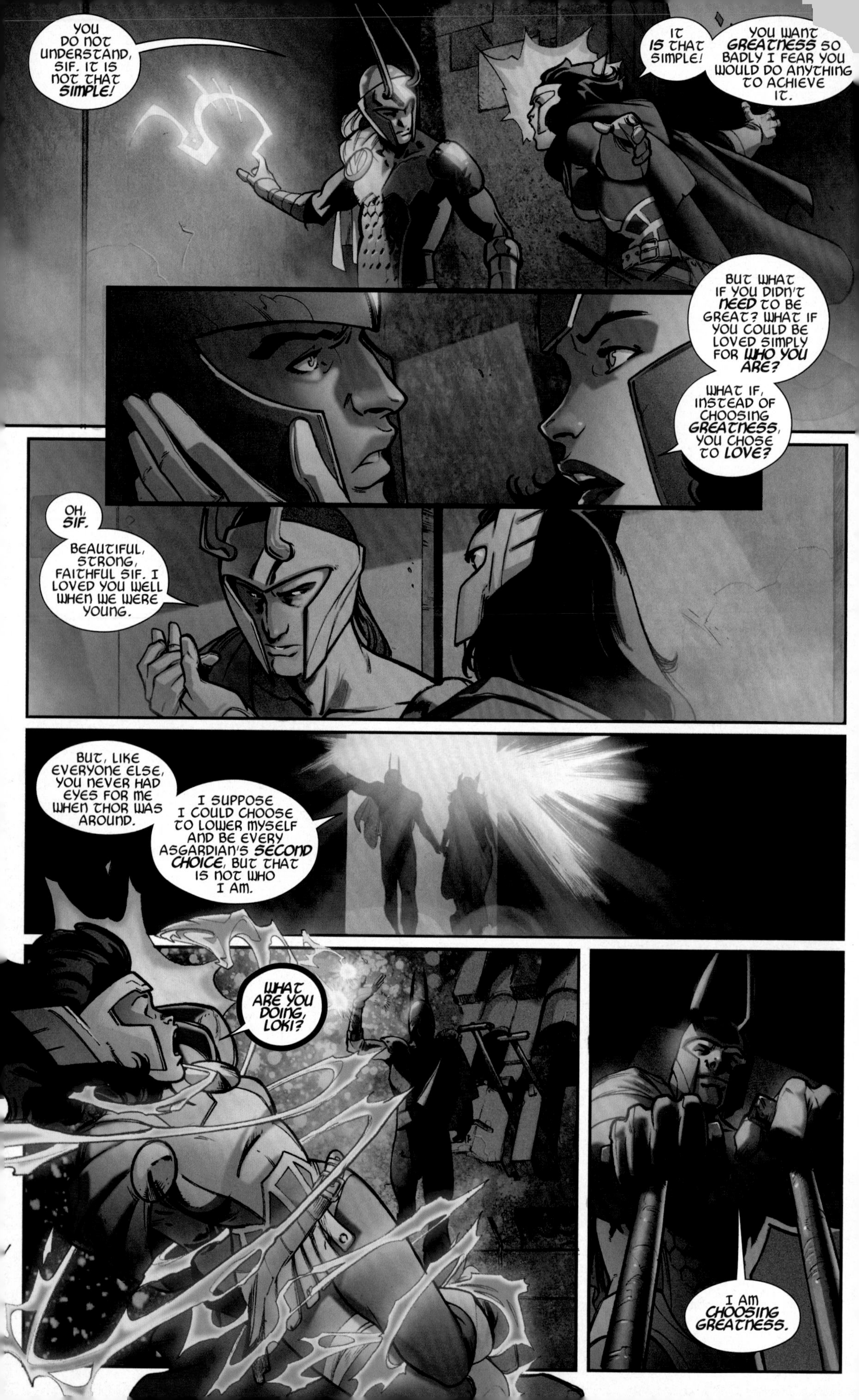
YOU DO NOT UNDERSTAND, SIF. IT IS NOT THAT SIMPLE!
IT IS THAT SIMPLE!
YOU WANT GREATNESS SO BADLY I FEAR YOU WOULD DO ANYTHING TO ACHIEVE IT.
BUT WHAT IF YOU DIDN'T NEED TO BE GREAT? WHAT IF YOU COULD BE LOVED SIMPLY FOR WHO YOU ARE?
WHAT IF, INSTEAD OF CHOOSING GREATNESS, YOU CHOSE TO LOVE?
OH, SIF.
BEAUTIFUL, STRONG, FAITHFUL SIF. I LOVED YOU WELL WHEN WE WERE YOUNG.
BUT, LIKE EVERYONE ELSE, YOU NEVER HAD EYES FOR ME WHEN THOR WAS AROUND.
I SUPPOSE I COULD CHOOSE TO LOWER MYSELF AND BE EVERY ASGARDIAN'S SECOND CHOICE, BUT THAT IS NOT WHO I AM.
WHAT ARE YOU DOING, LOKI?
I AM CHOOSING GREATNESS.

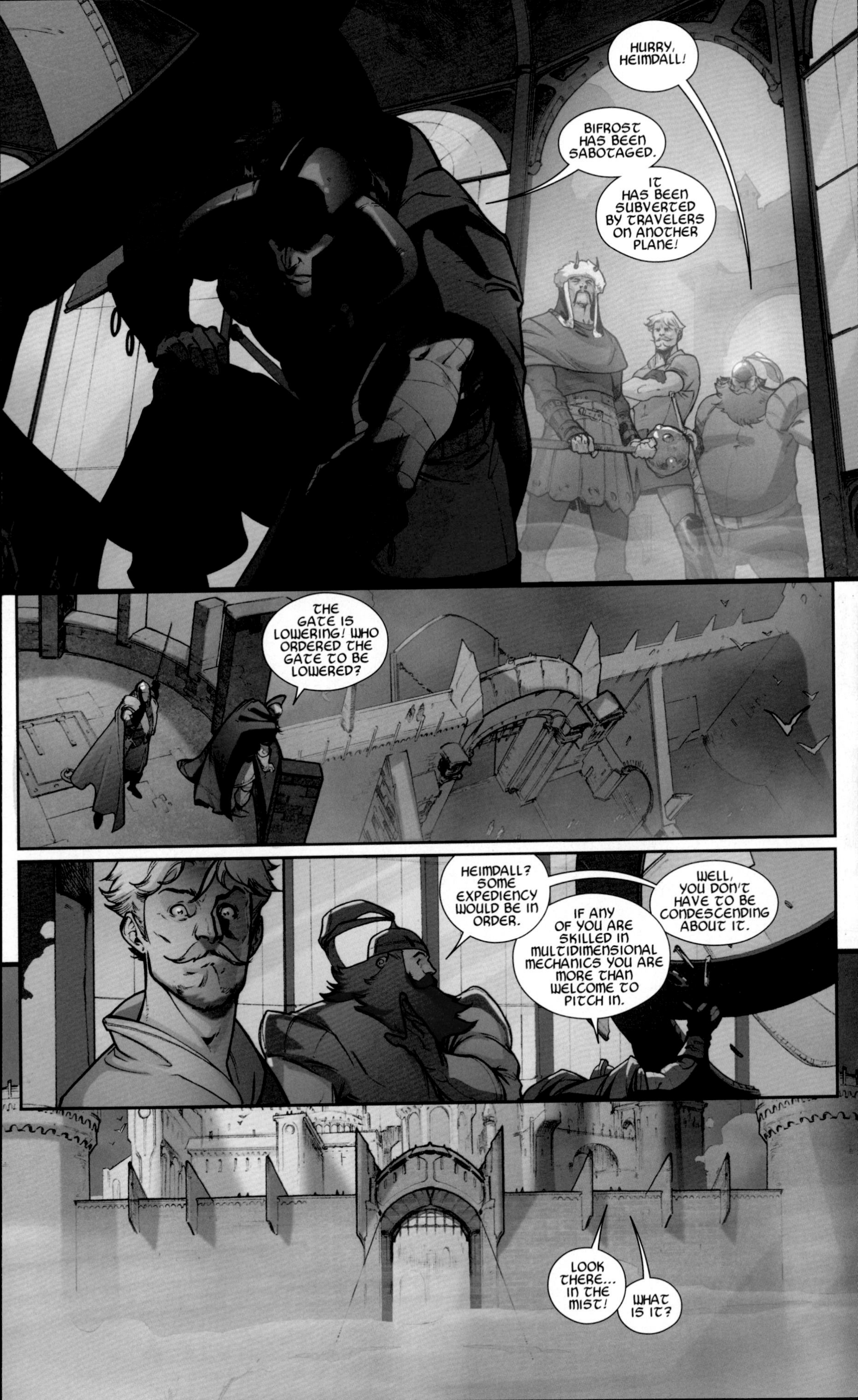
HURRY, HEIMDALL!
BIFROST HAS BEEN SABOTAGED.
IT HAS BEEN SUBVERTED BY TRAVELERS ON ANOTHER PLANE!
THE GATE IS LOWERING! WHO ORDERED THE GATE TO BE LOWERED?
HEIMDALL? SOME EXPEDIENCY WOULD BE IN ORDER.
IF ANY OF YOU ARE SKILLED IN MULTIDIMENSIONAL MECHANICS YOU ARE MORE THAN WELCOME TO PITCH IN.
WELL, YOU DON'T HAVE TO BE CONDESCENDING ABOUT IT.
LOOK THERE... IN THE MIST!
WHAT IS IT?

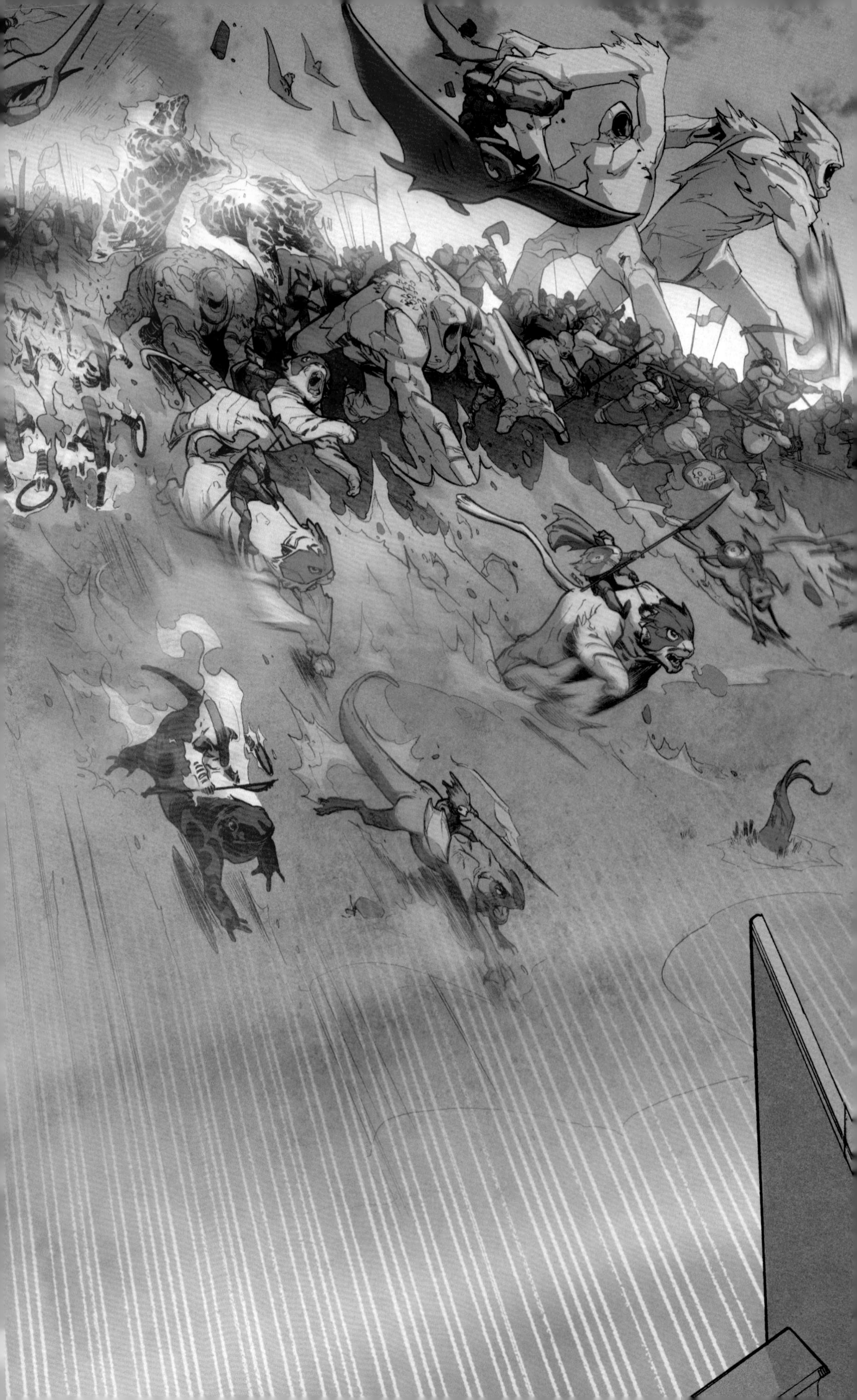

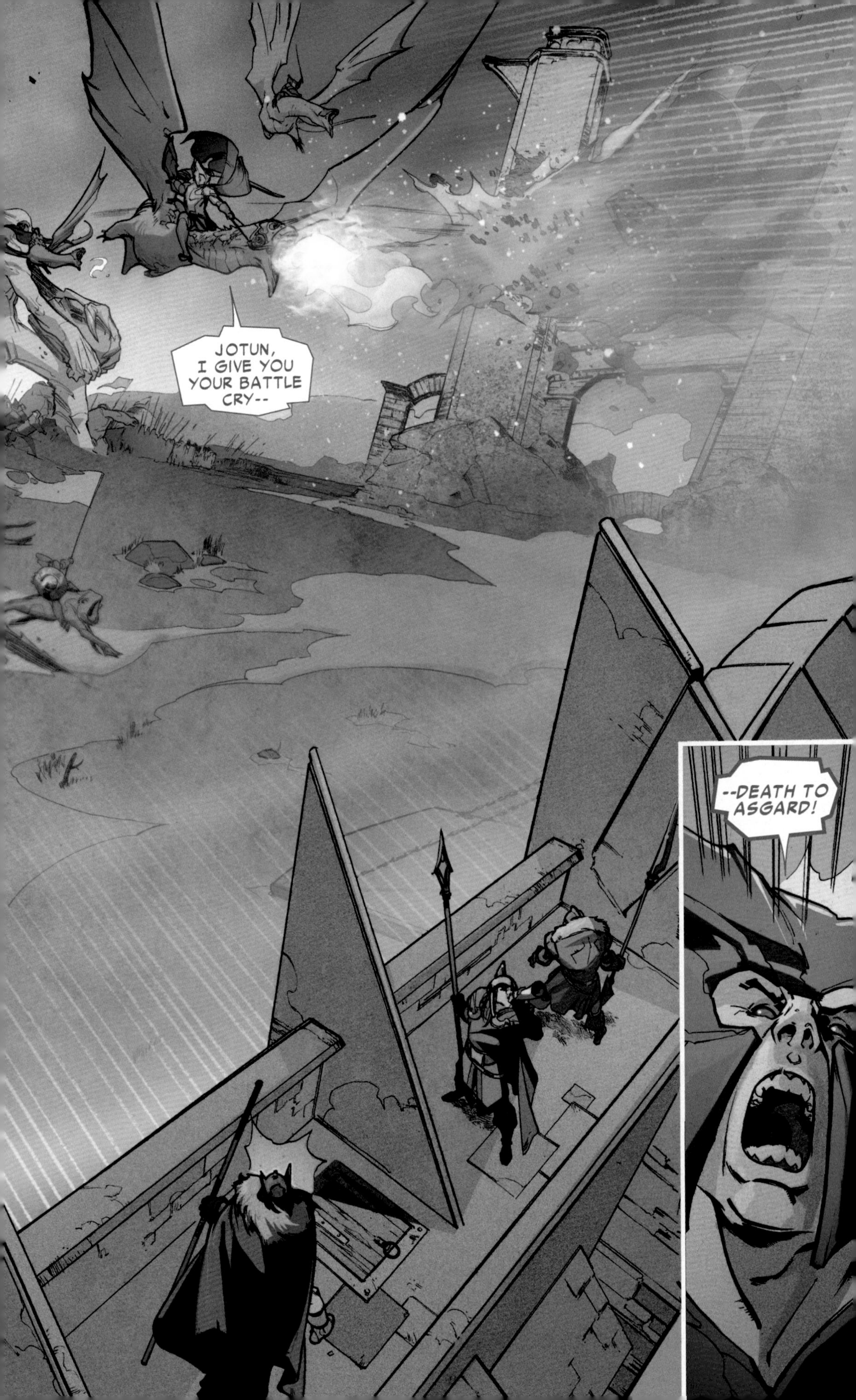
JOTUN, I GIVE YOU YOUR BATTLE CRY--
--DEATH TO ASGARD!

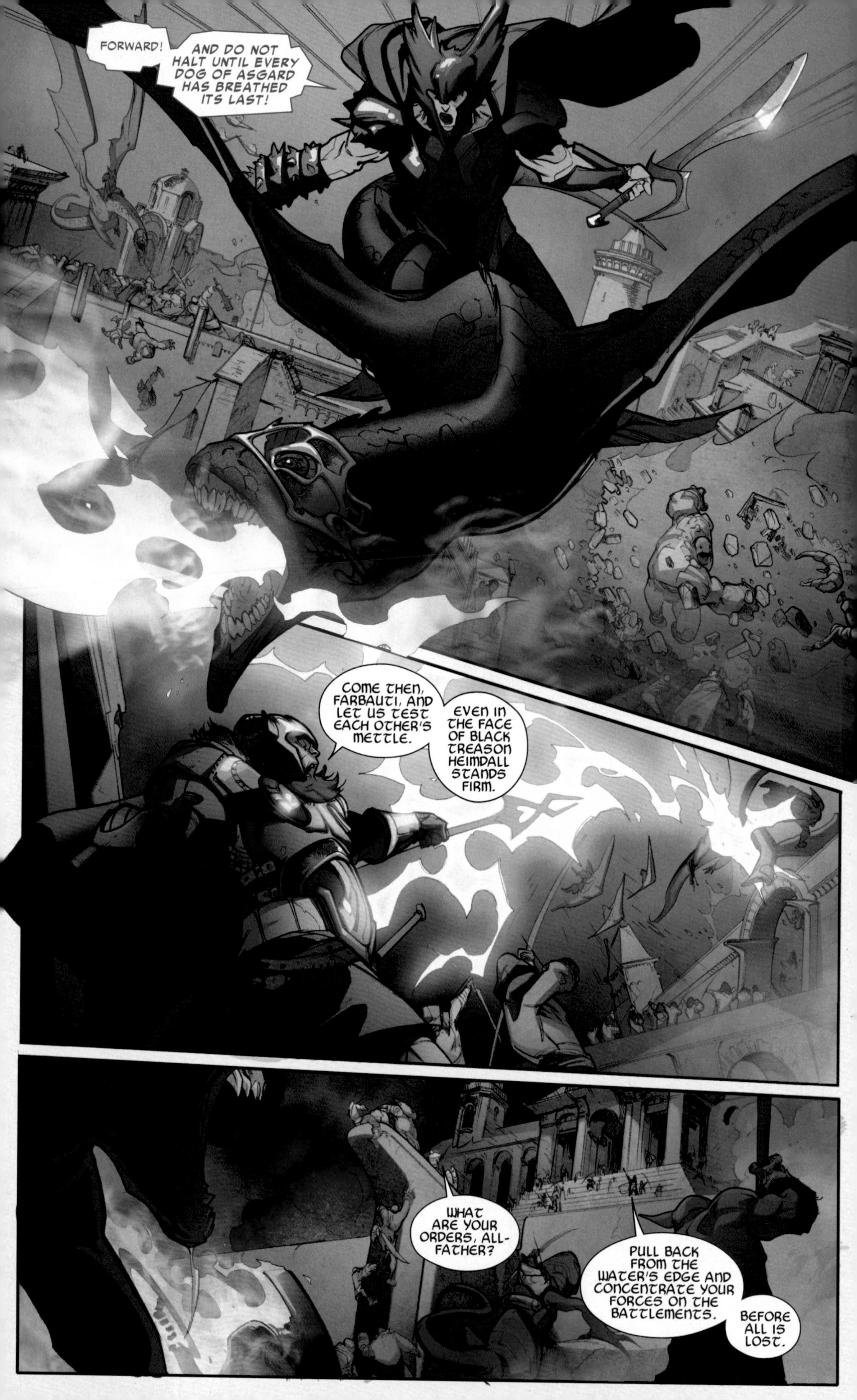
FORWARD!
AND DO NOT HALT UNTIL EVERY DOG OF ASGARD HAS BREATHED ITS LAST!
COME THEN, FARBAUTI, AND LET US TEST EACH OTHER'S METTLE.
EVEN IN THE FACE OF BLACK TREASON HEIMDALL STANDS FIRM.
WHAT ARE YOUR ORDERS, ALL-FATHER?
PULL BACK FROM THE WATER'S EDGE AND CONCENTRATE YOUR FORCES ON THE BATTLEMENTS.
BEFORE ALL IS LOST.

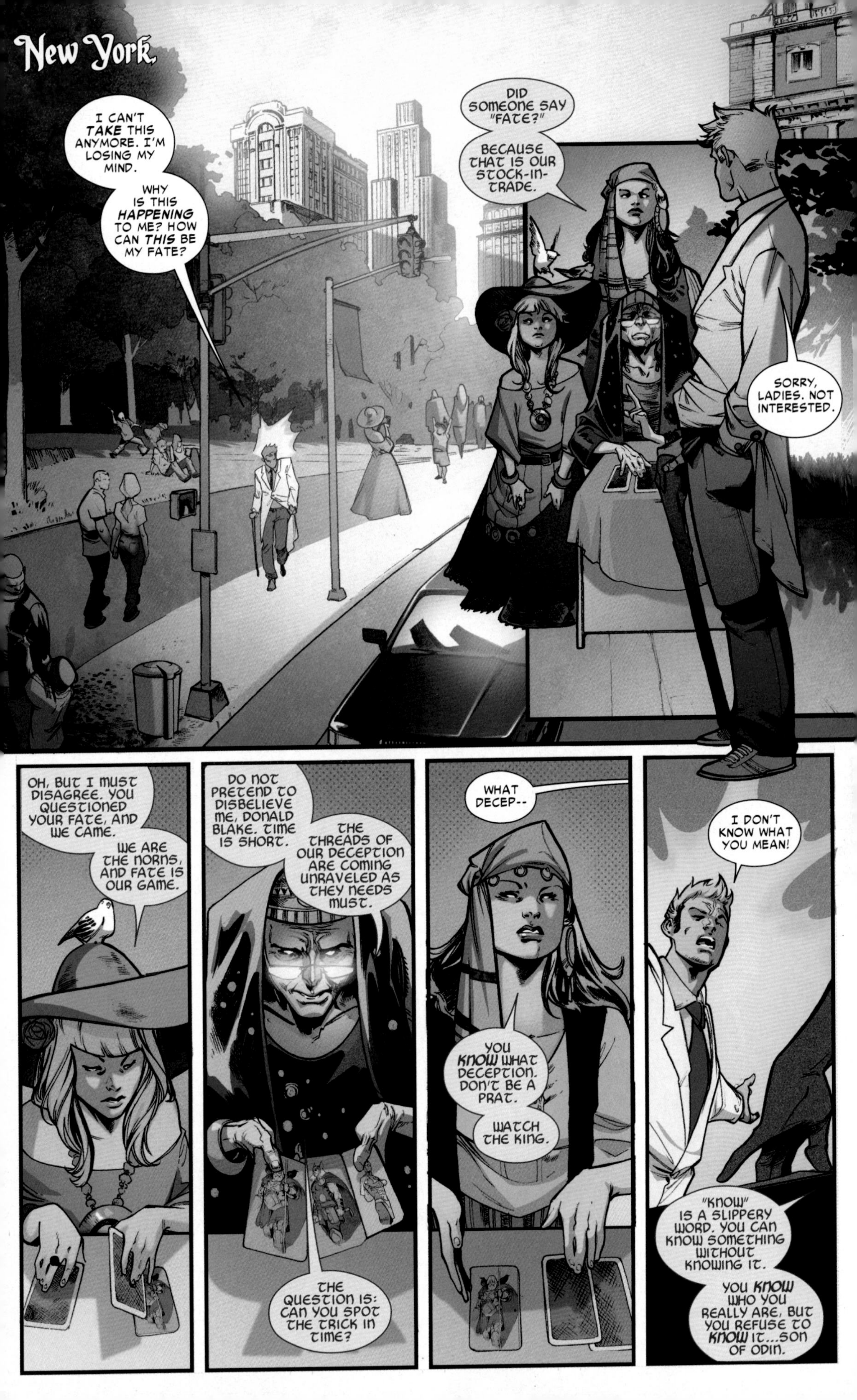
New York.
I CAN'T TAKE THIS ANYMORE. I'M LOSING MY MIND.
WHY IS THIS HAPPENING TO ME? HOW CAN THIS BE MY FATE?
DID SOMEONE SAY "FATE?"
BECAUSE THAT IS OUR STOCK-IN-TRADE.
SORRY, LADIES. NOT INTERESTED.
OH, BUT I MUST DISAGREE. YOU QUESTIONED YOUR FATE, AND WE CAME.
WE ARE THE NORNS, AND FATE IS OUR GAME.
DO NOT PRETEND TO DISBELIEVE ME, DONALD BLAKE. TIME IS SHORT.
THE THREADS OF OUR DECEPTION ARE COMING UNRAVELED AS THEY NEEDS MUST.
THE QUESTION IS: CAN YOU SPOT THE TRICK IN TIME?
WHAT DECEP--
YOU KNOW WHAT DECEPTION. DON'T BE A PRAT.
WATCH THE KING.
I DON'T KNOW WHAT YOU MEAN!
"KNOW" IS A SLIPPERY WORD. YOU CAN KNOW SOMETHING WITHOUT KNOWING IT.
YOU KNOW WHO YOU REALLY ARE, BUT YOU REFUSE TO KNOW IT...SON OF ODIN.

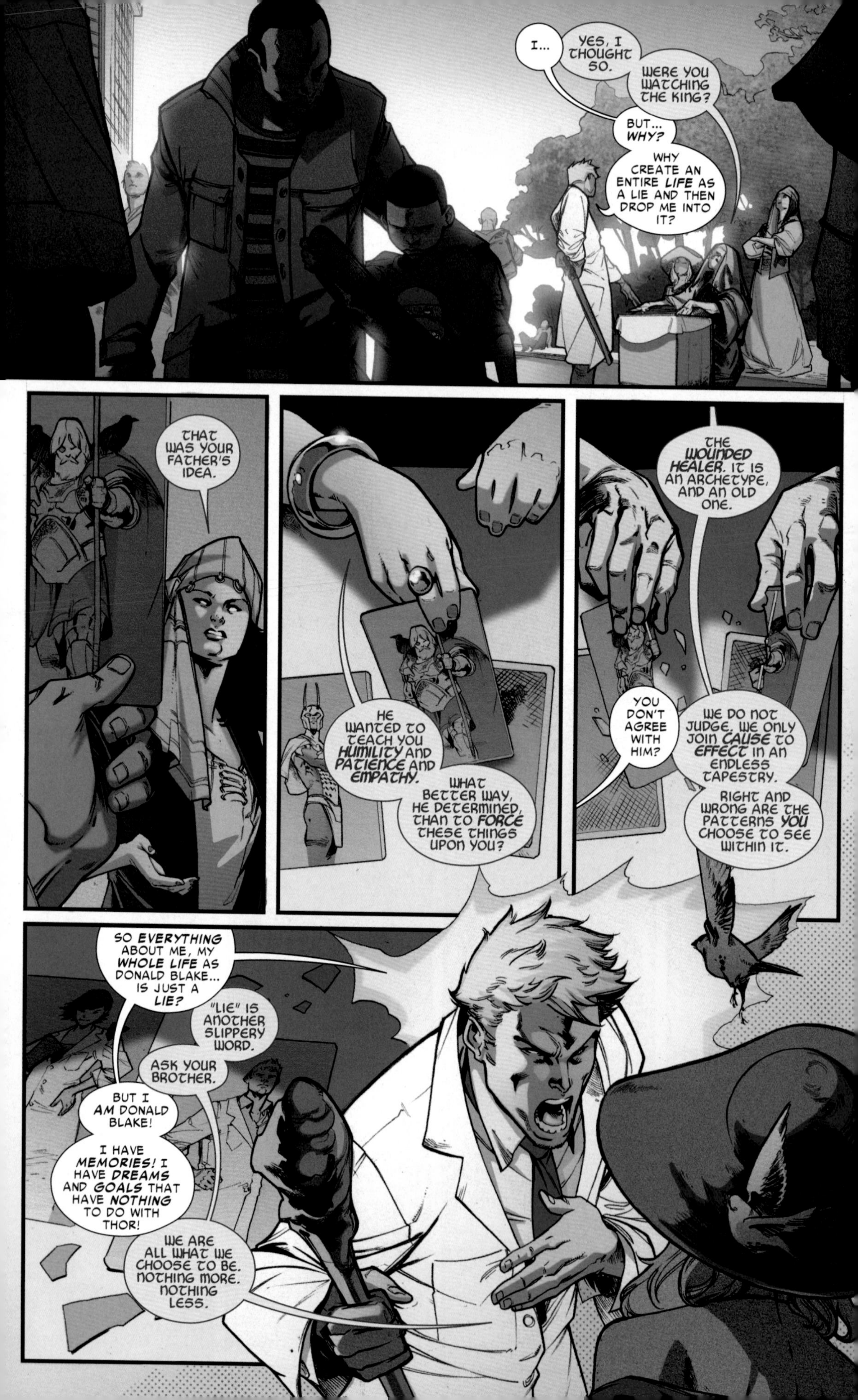
I...
YES, I THOUGHT SO.
WERE YOU WATCHING THE KING?
BUT... WHY?
WHY CREATE AN ENTIRE LIFE AS A LIE AND THEN DROP ME INTO IT?
THAT WAS YOUR FATHER'S IDEA.
HE WANTED TO TEACH YOU HUMILITY AND PATIENCE AND EMPATHY.
WHAT BETTER WAY, HE DETERMINED, THAN TO FORCE THESE THINGS UPON YOU?
THE WOUNDED HEALER. IT IS AN ARCHETYPE, AND AN OLD ONE.
YOU DON'T AGREE WITH HIM?
WE DO NOT JUDGE. WE ONLY JOIN CAUSE TO EFFECT IN AN ENDLESS TAPESTRY.
RIGHT AND WRONG ARE THE PATTERNS YOU CHOOSE TO SEE WITHIN IT.
SO EVERYTHING ABOUT ME, MY WHOLE LIFE AS DONALD BLAKE... IS JUST A LIE?
"LIE" IS ANOTHER SLIPPERY WORD.
ASK YOUR BROTHER.
BUT I AM DONALD BLAKE!
I HAVE MEMORIES! I HAVE DREAMS AND GOALS THAT HAVE NOTHING TO DO WITH THOR!
WE ARE ALL WHAT WE CHOOSE TO BE. NOTHING MORE. NOTHING LESS.

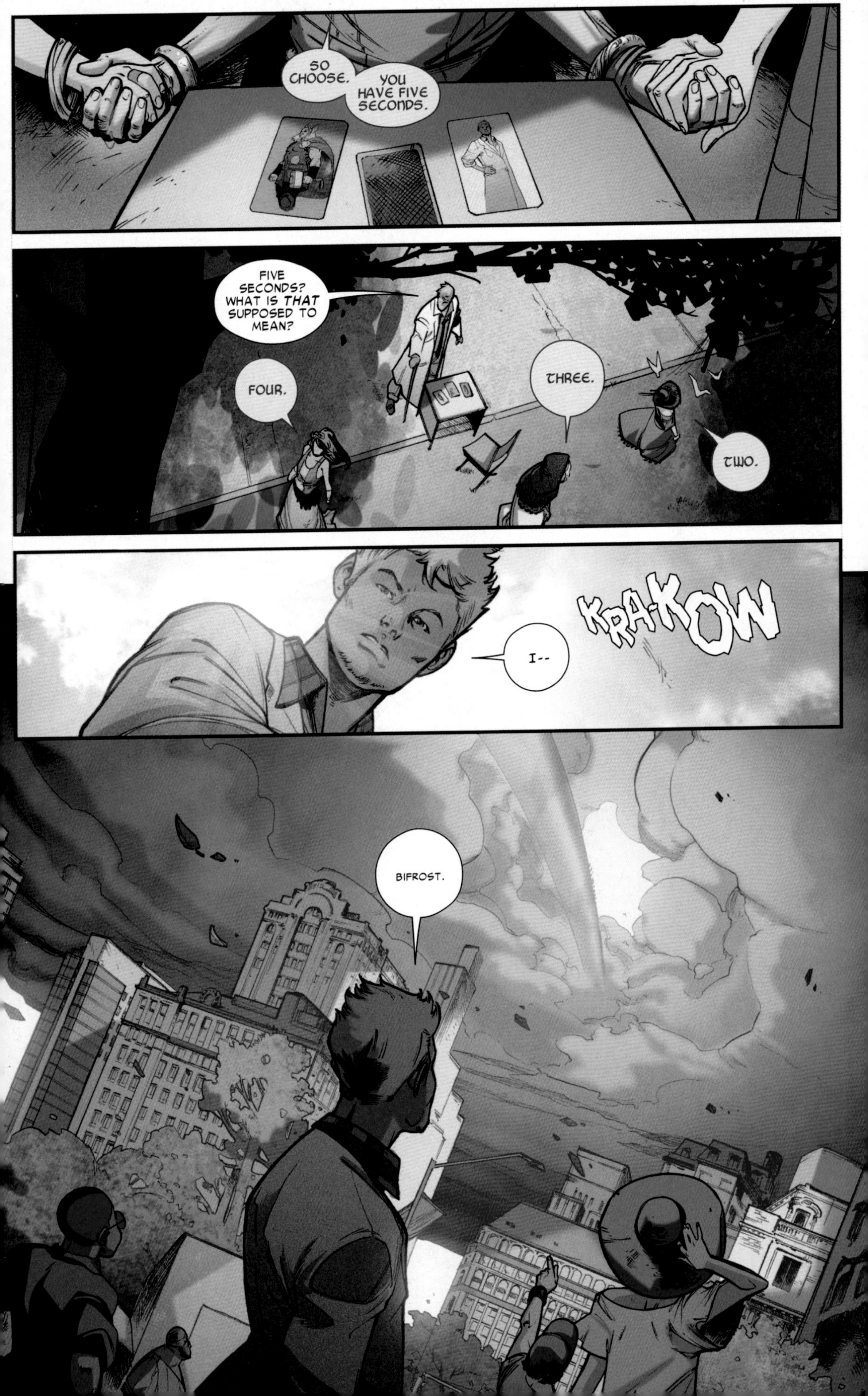
SO CHOOSE.
YOU HAVE FIVE SECONDS.
FIVE SECONDS? WHAT IS *THAT* SUPPOSED TO MEAN?
FOUR.
THREE.
TWO.
I--
KRA-KOW
BIFROST.

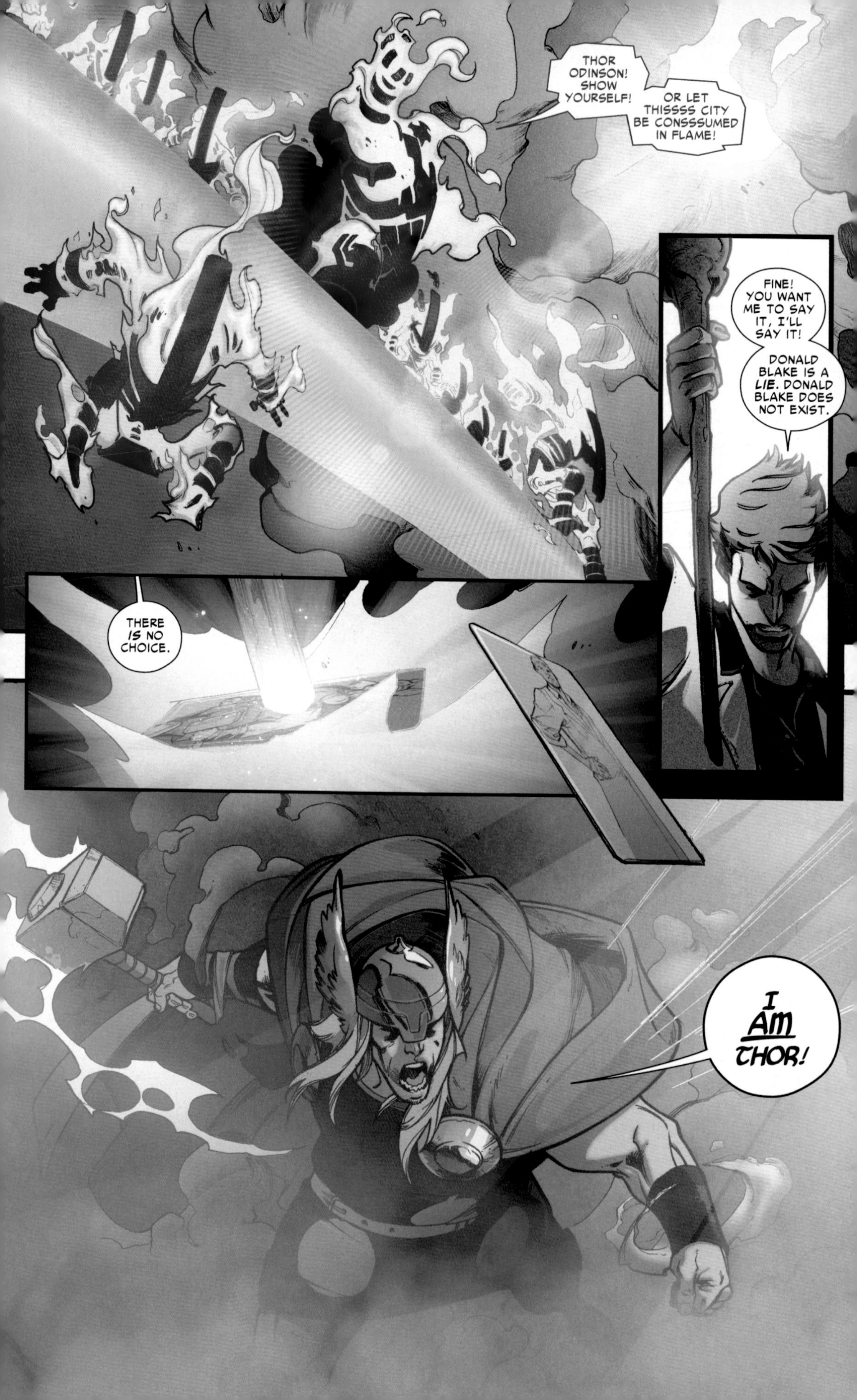
THOR ODINSON! SHOW YOURSELF!
OR LET THISSSS CITY BE CONSSSUMED IN FLAME!
FINE! YOU WANT ME TO SAY IT, I'LL SAY IT!
DONALD BLAKE IS A *LIE*. DONALD BLAKE DOES NOT EXIST.
THERE *IS* NO CHOICE.
I AM THOR!

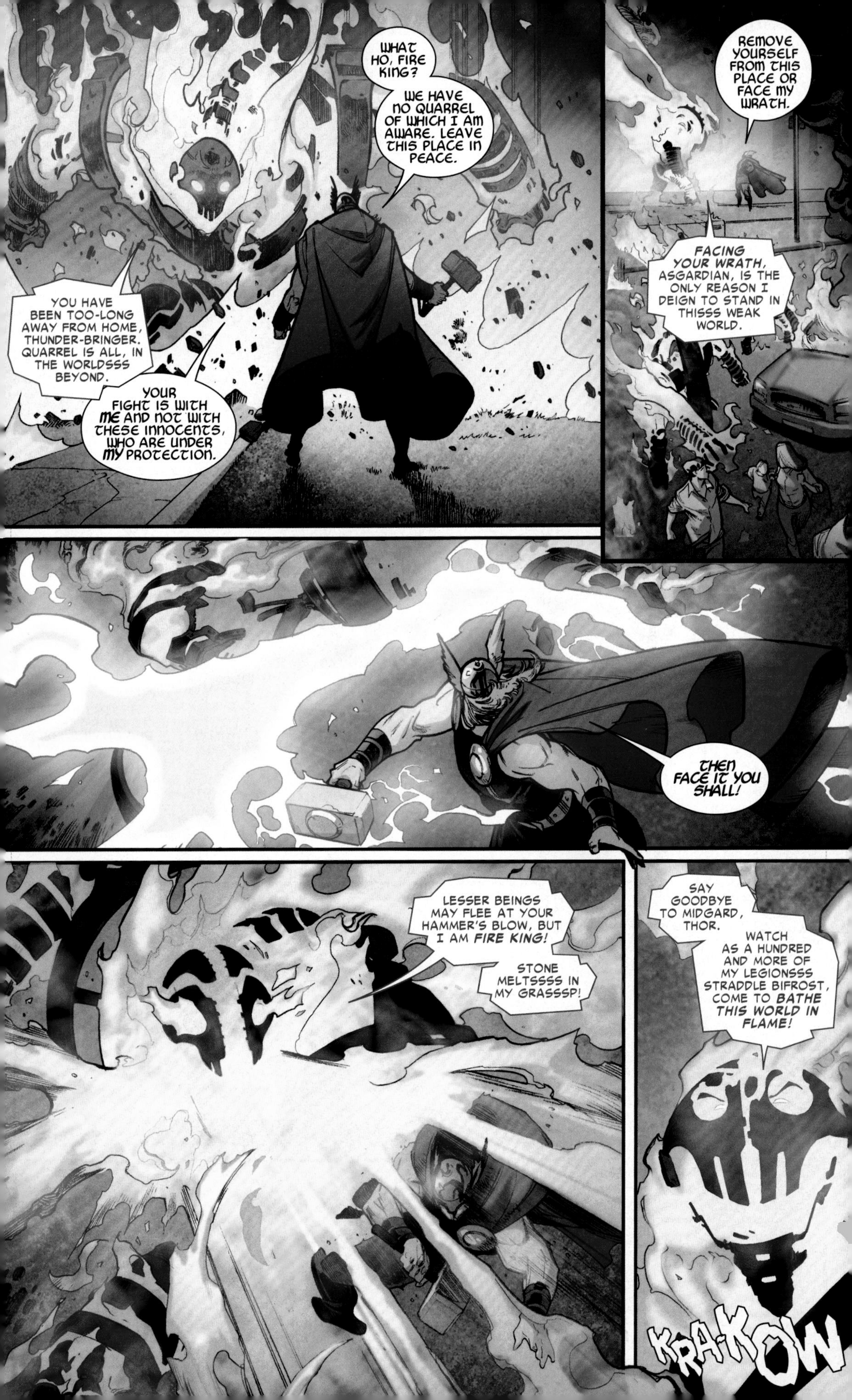
WHAT HO, FIRE KING?
WE HAVE NO QUARREL OF WHICH I AM AWARE. LEAVE THIS PLACE IN PEACE.
YOU HAVE BEEN TOO-LONG AWAY FROM HOME, THUNDER-BRINGER. QUARREL IS ALL, IN THE WORLDSSS BEYOND.
YOUR FIGHT IS WITH ME AND NOT WITH THESE INNOCENTS, WHO ARE UNDER MY PROTECTION.
REMOVE YOURSELF FROM THIS PLACE OR FACE MY WRATH.
FACING YOUR WRATH, ASGARDIAN, IS THE ONLY REASON I DEIGN TO STAND IN THISSS WEAK WORLD.
THEN FACE IT YOU SHALL!
LESSER BEINGS MAY FLEE AT YOUR HAMMER'S BLOW, BUT I AM FIRE KING!
STONE MELTSSSS IN MY GRASSSP!
SAY GOODBYE TO MIDGARD, THOR.
WATCH AS A HUNDRED AND MORE OF MY LEGIONSSS STRADDLE BIFROST, COME TO BATHE THIS WORLD IN FLAME!
KRA-KOW

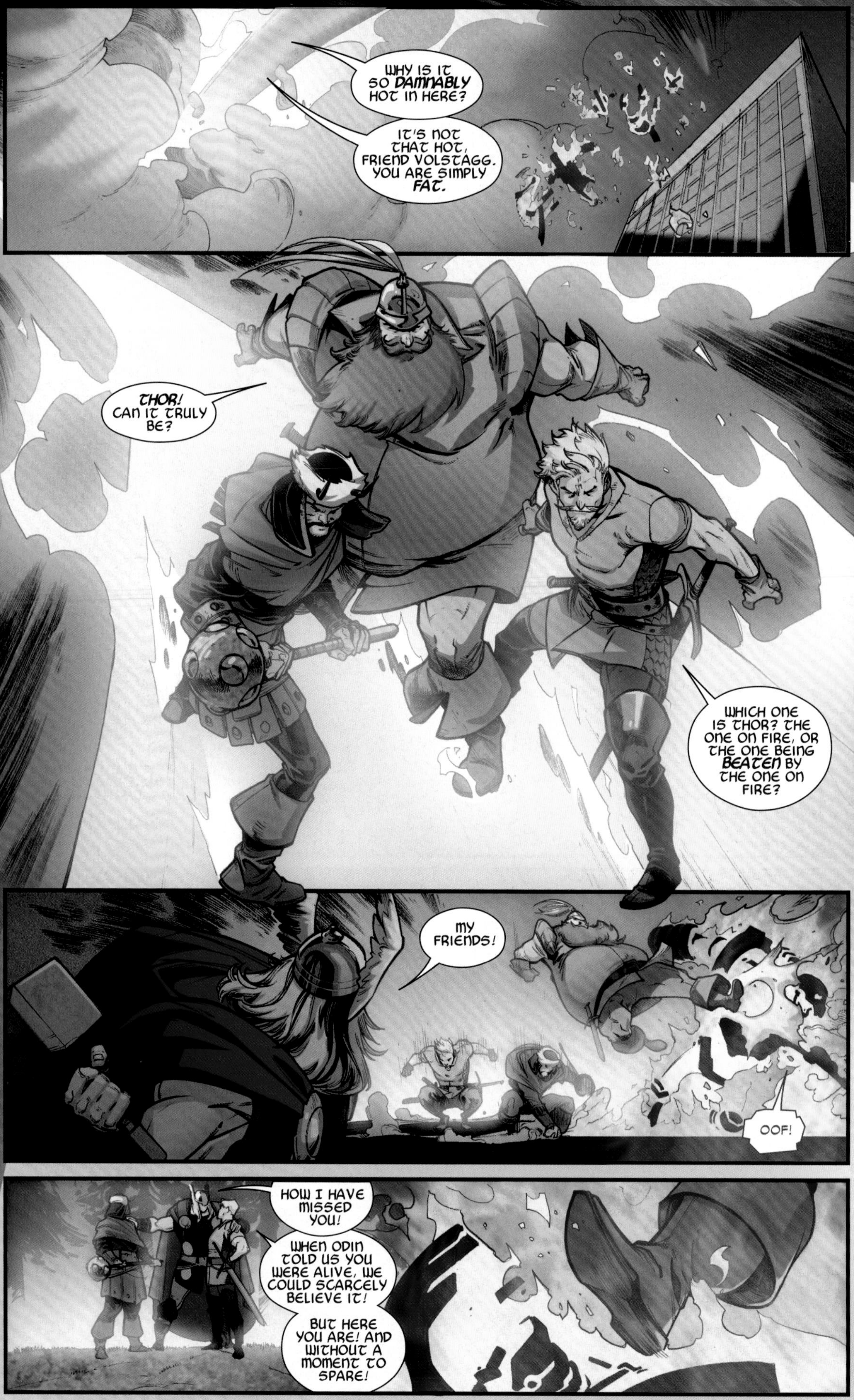

WHY IS IT SO DAMNABLY HOT IN HERE?
IT'S NOT THAT HOT, FRIEND VOLSTAGG. YOU ARE SIMPLY FAT.
THOR! CAN IT TRULY BE?
WHICH ONE IS THOR? THE ONE ON FIRE, OR THE ONE BEING BEATEN BY THE ONE ON FIRE?
MY FRIENDS!
OOF!
HOW I HAVE MISSED YOU!
WHEN ODIN TOLD US YOU WERE ALIVE, WE COULD SCARCELY BELIEVE IT!
BUT HERE YOU ARE! AND WITHOUT A MOMENT TO SPARE!

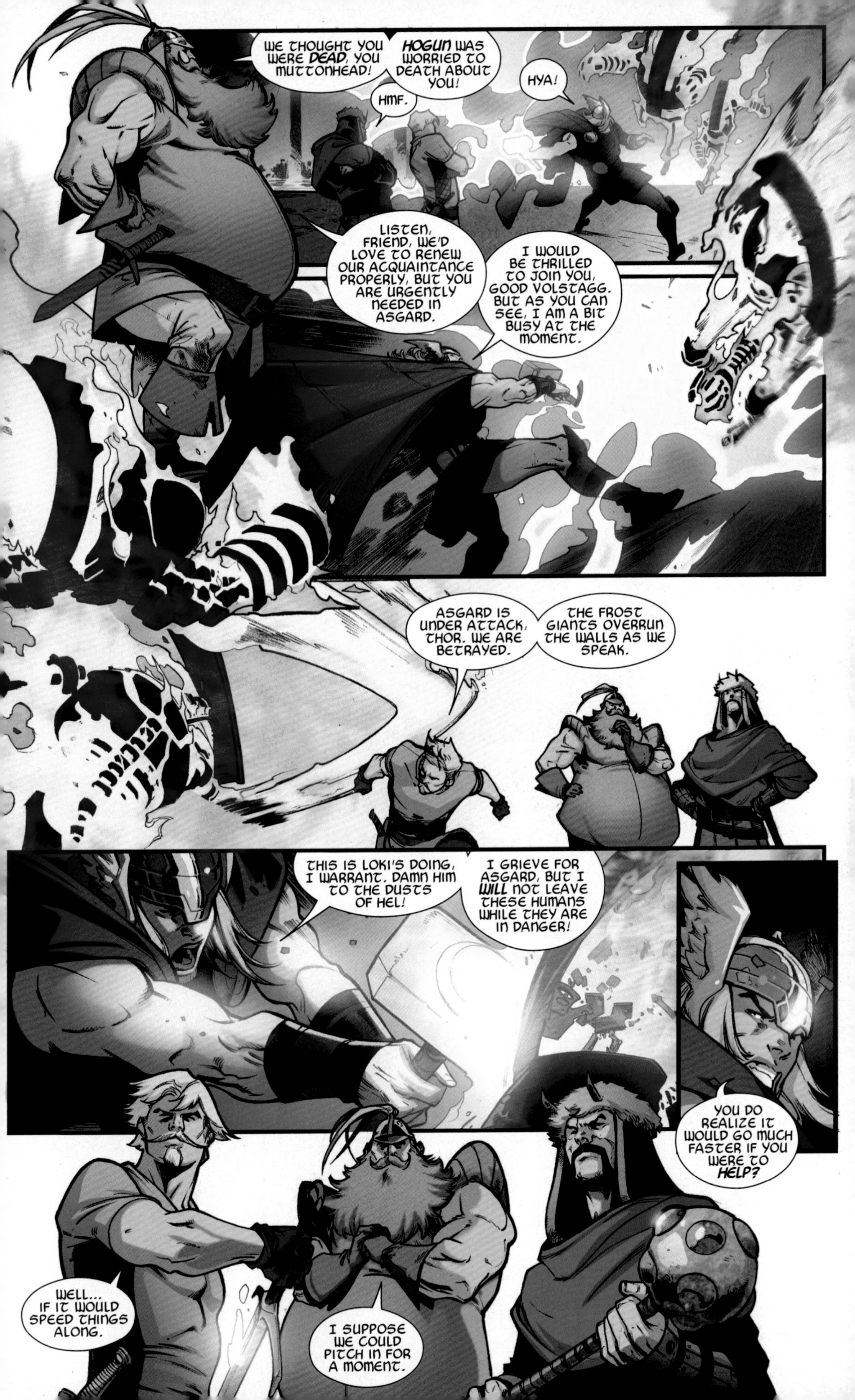
WE THOUGHT YOU WERE DEAD, YOU MUTTONHEAD!
HOGUN WAS WORRIED TO DEATH ABOUT YOU!
HMF.
HYA!
LISTEN, FRIEND, WE'D LOVE TO RENEW OUR ACQUAINTANCE PROPERLY, BUT YOU ARE URGENTLY NEEDED IN ASGARD.
I WOULD BE THRILLED TO JOIN YOU, GOOD VOLSTAGG. BUT AS YOU CAN SEE, I AM A BIT BUSY AT THE MOMENT.
ASGARD IS UNDER ATTACK, THOR. WE ARE BETRAYED.
THE FROST GIANTS OVERRUN THE WALLS AS WE SPEAK.
THIS IS LOKI'S DOING, I WARRANT. DAMN HIM TO THE DUSTS OF HEL!
I GRIEVE FOR ASGARD, BUT I WILL NOT LEAVE THESE HUMANS WHILE THEY ARE IN DANGER!
YOU DO REALIZE IT WOULD GO MUCH FASTER IF YOU WERE TO HELP?
WELL... IF IT WOULD SPEED THINGS ALONG.
I SUPPOSE WE COULD PITCH IN FOR A MOMENT.

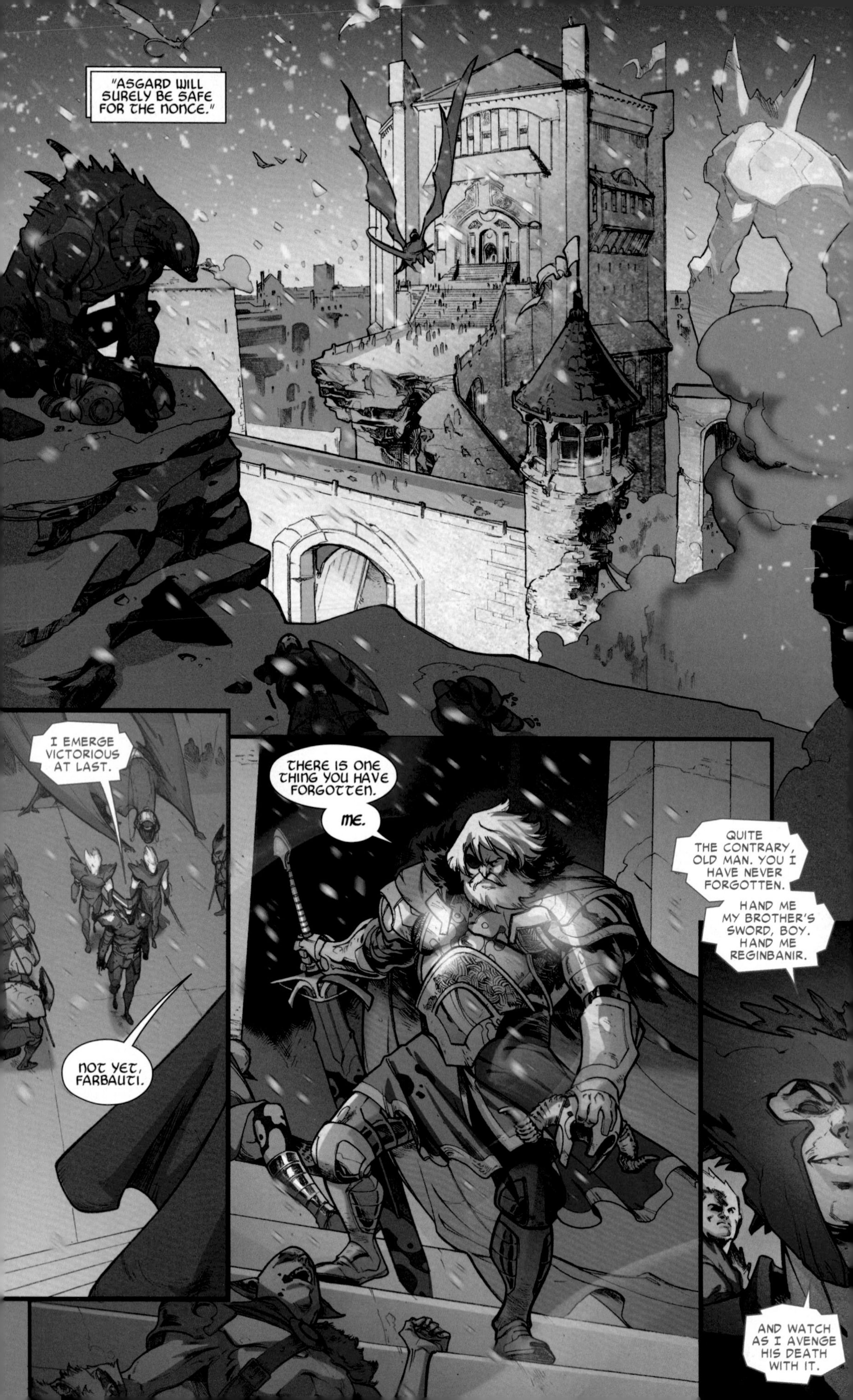
"ASGARD WILL SURELY BE SAFE FOR THE NONCE."
I EMERGE VICTORIOUS AT LAST.
NOT YET, FARBAUTI.
THERE IS ONE THING YOU HAVE FORGOTTEN.
ME.
QUITE THE CONTRARY, OLD MAN. YOU I HAVE NEVER FORGOTTEN.
HAND ME MY BROTHER'S SWORD, BOY. HAND ME REGINBANIR.
AND WATCH AS I AVENGE HIS DEATH WITH IT.

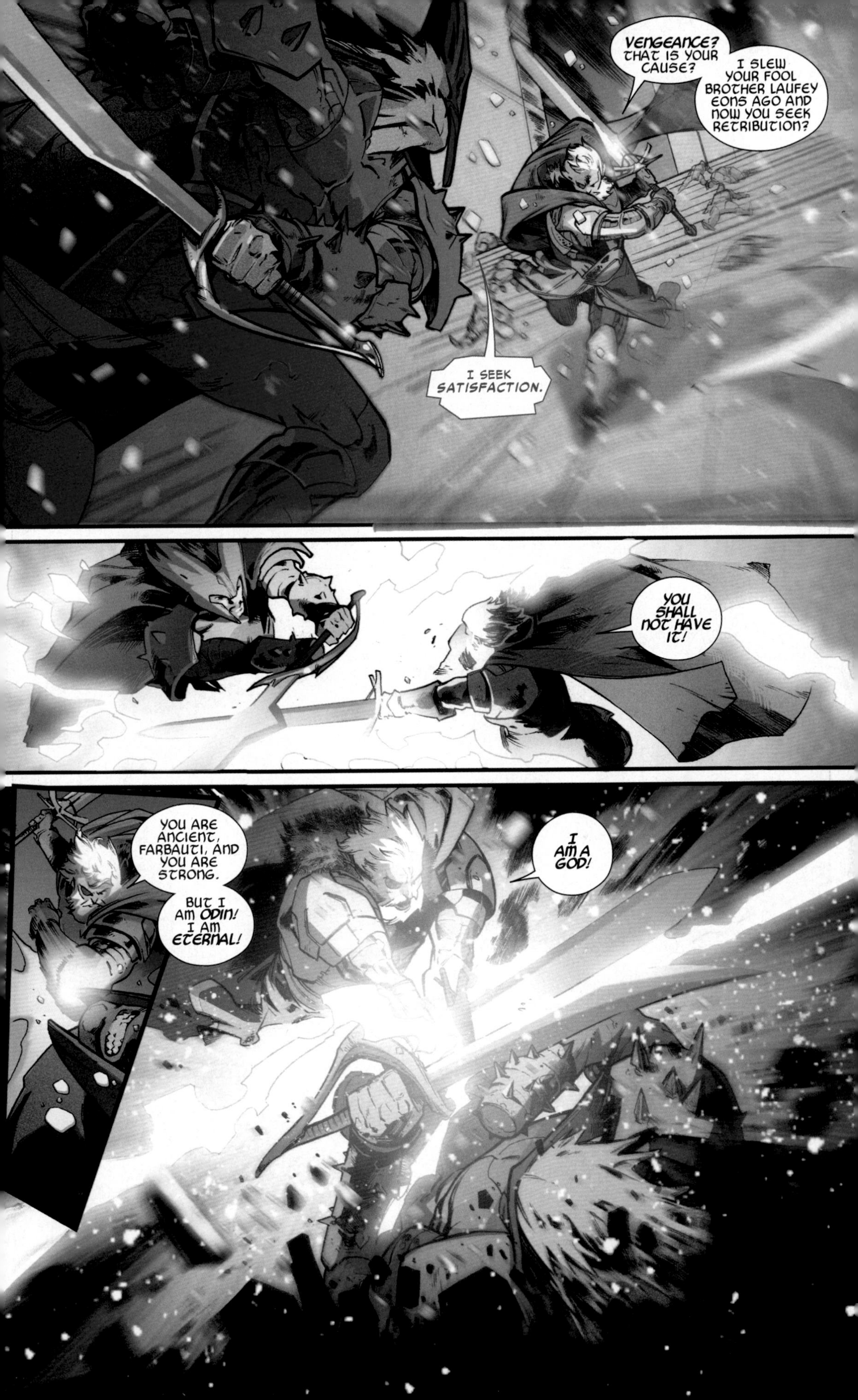
VENGEANCE? THAT IS YOUR CAUSE?
I SLEW YOUR FOOL BROTHER LAUFEY EONS AGO AND NOW YOU SEEK RETRIBUTION?
I SEEK SATISFACTION.
YOU SHALL NOT HAVE IT!
YOU ARE ANCIENT, FARBAUTI, AND YOU ARE STRONG.
BUT I AM ODIN! I AM ETERNAL!
I AM A GOD!

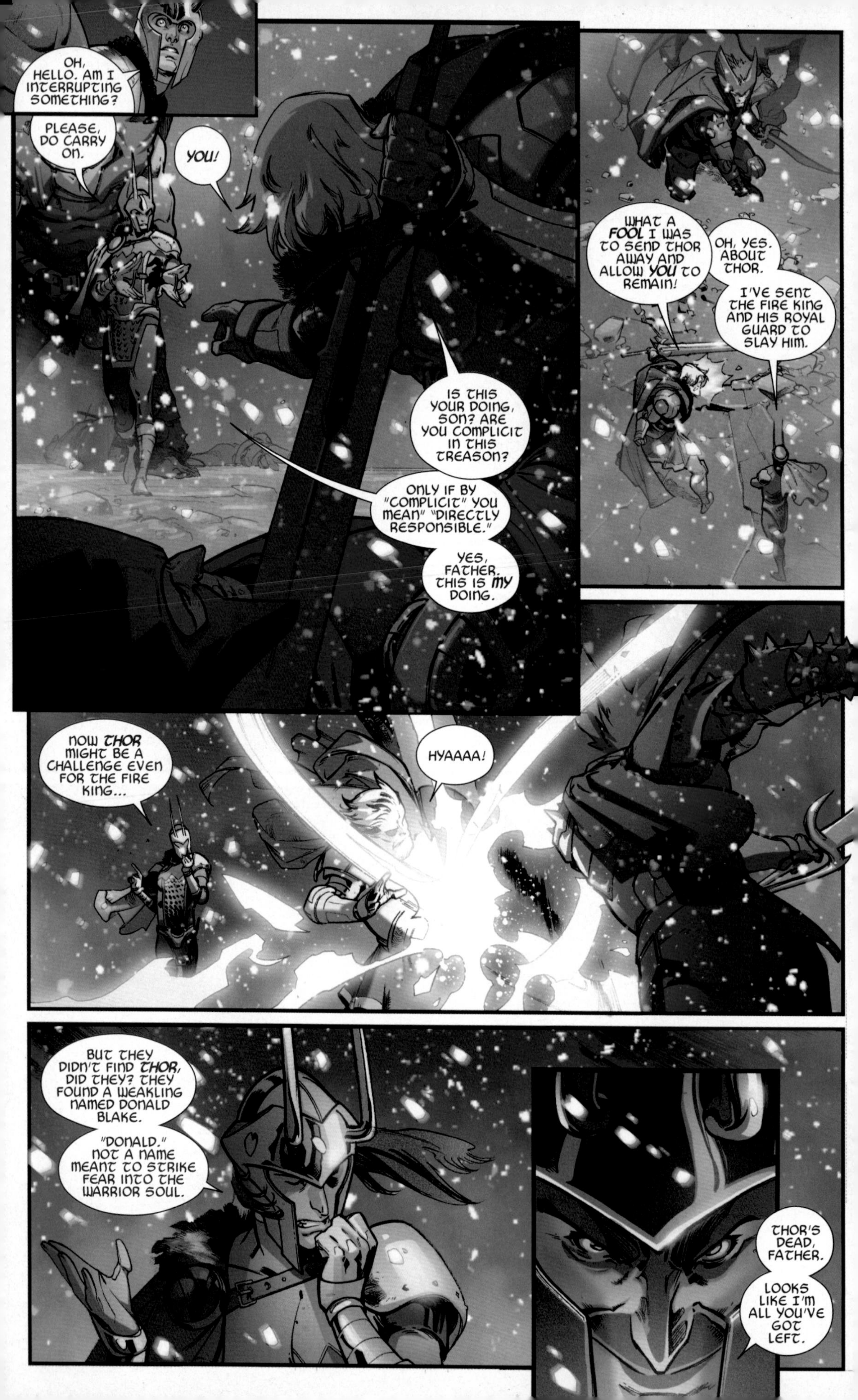
OH, HELLO. AM I INTERRUPTING SOMETHING?
PLEASE, DO CARRY ON.
YOU!
IS THIS YOUR DOING, SON? ARE YOU COMPLICIT IN THIS TREASON?
ONLY IF BY "COMPLICIT" YOU MEAN" "DIRECTLY RESPONSIBLE."
YES, FATHER. THIS IS MY DOING.
WHAT A FOOL I WAS TO SEND THOR AWAY AND ALLOW YOU TO REMAIN!
OH, YES. ABOUT THOR.
I'VE SENT THE FIRE KING AND HIS ROYAL GUARD TO SLAY HIM.
NOW THOR MIGHT BE A CHALLENGE EVEN FOR THE FIRE KING...
HYAAAA!
BUT THEY DIDN'T FIND THOR, DID THEY? THEY FOUND A WEAKLING NAMED DONALD BLAKE.
"DONALD." NOT A NAME MEANT TO STRIKE FEAR INTO THE WARRIOR SOUL.
THOR'S DEAD, FATHER.
LOOKS LIKE I'M ALL YOU'VE GOT LEFT.

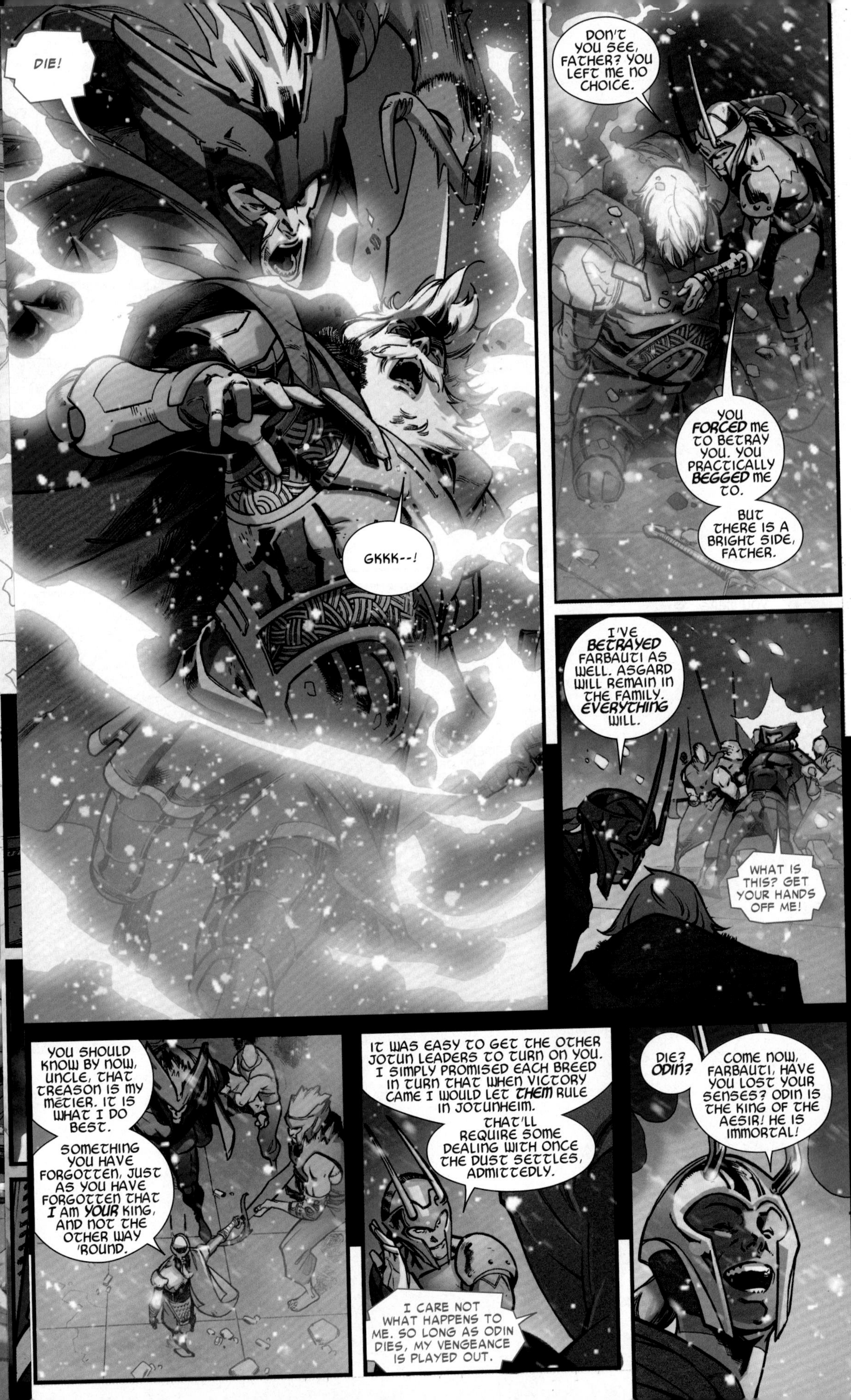
DIE!
GKKK--!
DON'T YOU SEE, FATHER? YOU LEFT ME NO CHOICE.
YOU FORCED ME TO BETRAY YOU. YOU PRACTICALLY BEGGED ME TO.
BUT THERE IS A BRIGHT SIDE, FATHER.
I'VE BETRAYED FARBAUTI AS WELL. ASGARD WILL REMAIN IN THE FAMILY. EVERYTHING WILL.
WHAT IS THIS? GET YOUR HANDS OFF ME!
YOU SHOULD KNOW BY NOW, UNCLE, THAT TREASON IS MY MÉTIER. IT IS WHAT I DO BEST.
SOMETHING YOU HAVE FORGOTTEN, JUST AS YOU HAVE FORGOTTEN THAT I AM YOUR KING, AND NOT THE OTHER WAY 'ROUND.
IT WAS EASY TO GET THE OTHER JOTUN LEADERS TO TURN ON YOU. I SIMPLY PROMISED EACH BREED IN TURN THAT WHEN VICTORY CAME I WOULD LET THEM RULE IN JOTUNHEIM.
THAT'LL REQUIRE SOME DEALING WITH ONCE THE DUST SETTLES, ADMITTEDLY.
I CARE NOT WHAT HAPPENS TO ME. SO LONG AS ODIN DIES, MY VENGEANCE IS PLAYED OUT.
DIE? ODIN?
COME NOW, FARBAUTI, HAVE YOU LOST YOUR SENSES? ODIN IS THE KING OF THE AESIR! HE IS IMMORTAL!

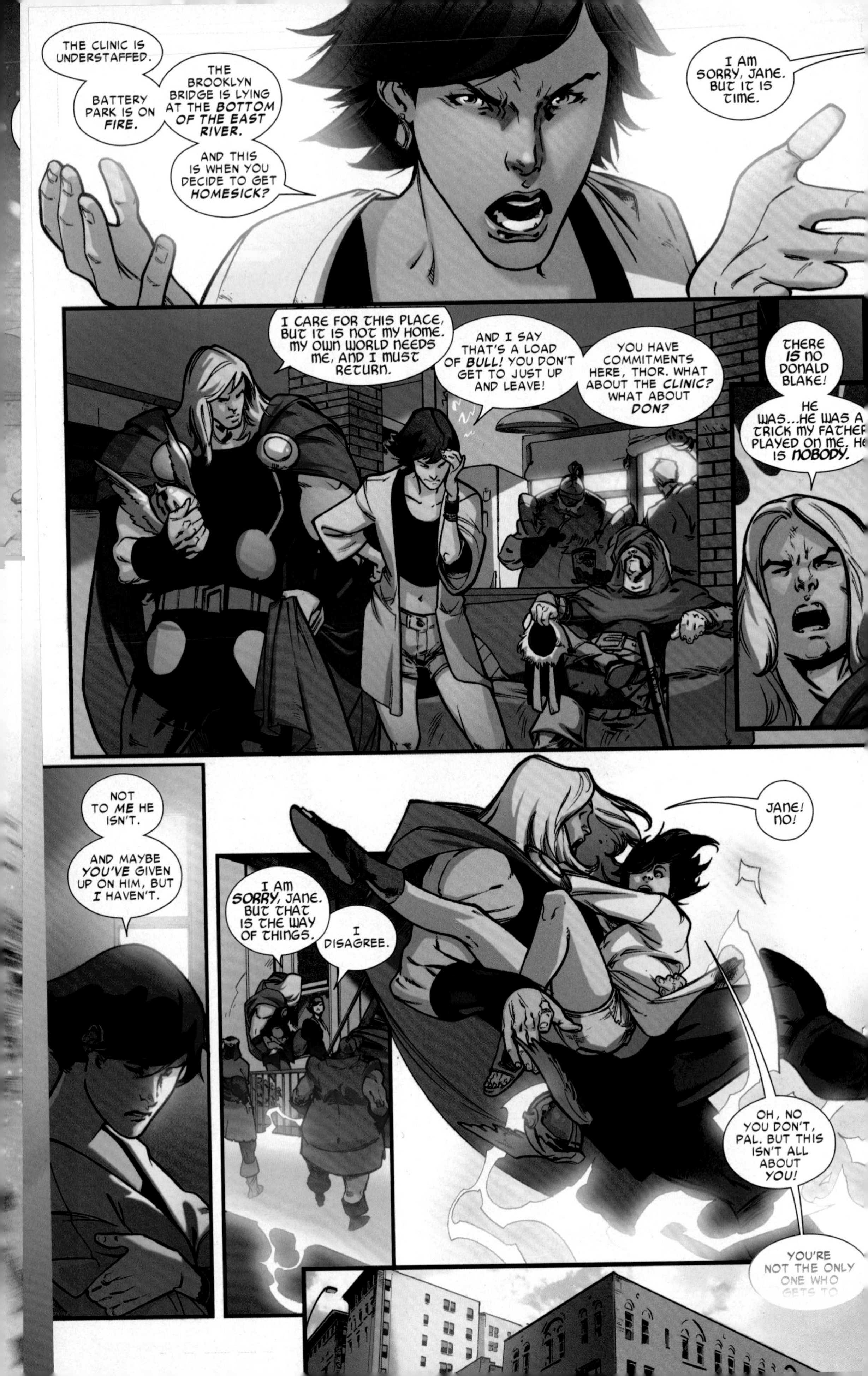
THE CLINIC IS UNDERSTAFFED.
BATTERY PARK IS ON FIRE.
THE BROOKLYN BRIDGE IS LYING AT THE BOTTOM OF THE EAST RIVER.
AND THIS IS WHEN YOU DECIDE TO GET HOMESICK?
I AM SORRY, JANE. BUT IT IS TIME.
I CARE FOR THIS PLACE, BUT IT IS NOT MY HOME. MY OWN WORLD NEEDS ME, AND I MUST RETURN.
AND I SAY THAT'S A LOAD OF BULL! YOU DON'T GET TO JUST UP AND LEAVE!
YOU HAVE COMMITMENTS HERE, THOR. WHAT ABOUT THE CLINIC? WHAT ABOUT DON?
THERE IS NO DONALD BLAKE!
HE WAS...HE WAS A TRICK MY FATHER PLAYED ON ME. HE IS NOBODY.
NOT TO ME HE ISN'T.
AND MAYBE YOU'VE GIVEN UP ON HIM, BUT I HAVEN'T.
I AM SORRY, JANE. BUT THAT IS THE WAY OF THINGS.
I DISAGREE.
JANE! NO!
OH, NO YOU DON'T, PAL. BUT THIS ISN'T ALL ABOUT YOU!
YOU'RE NOT THE ONLY ONE WHO GETS TO

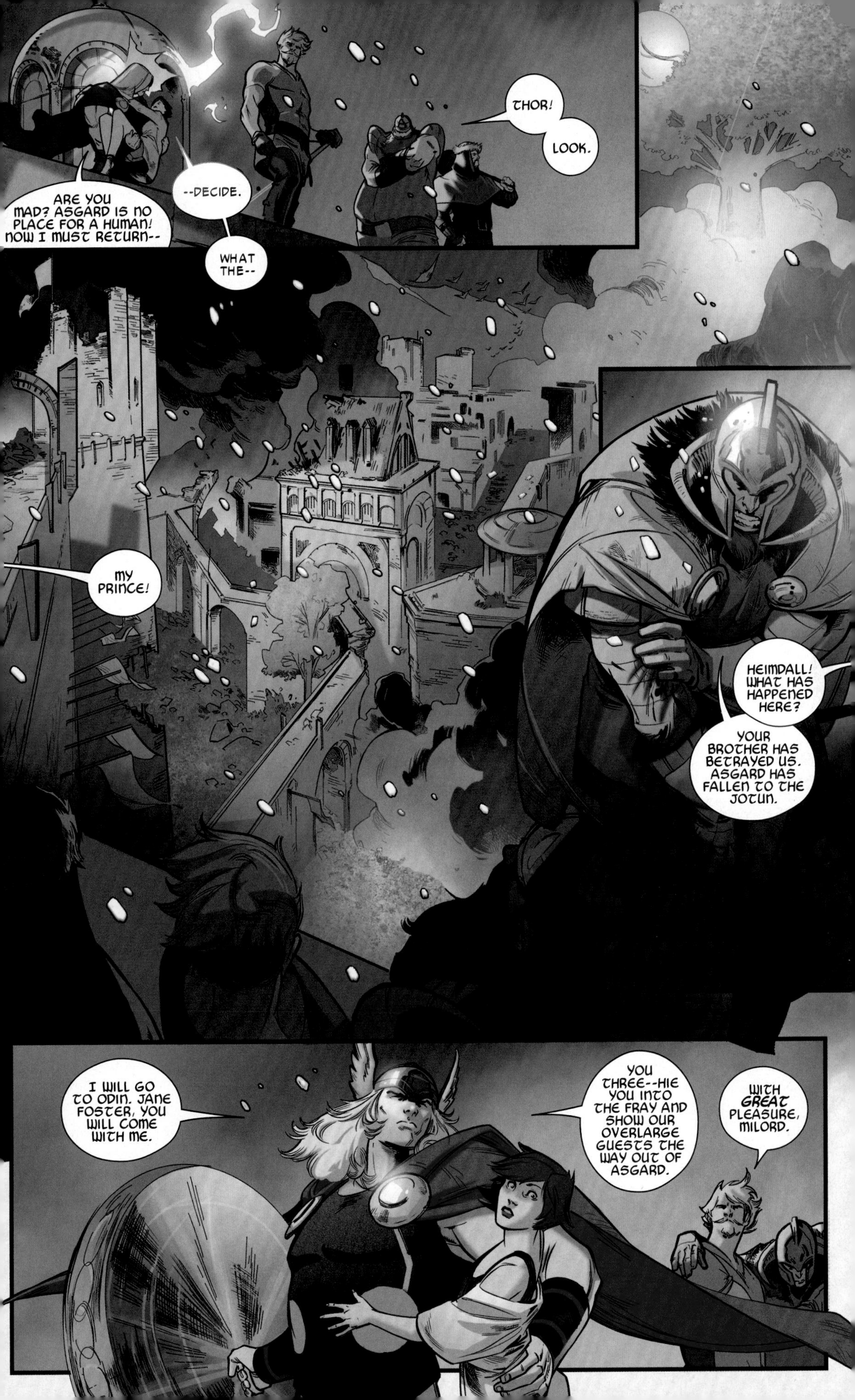
ARE YOU MAD? ASGARD IS NO PLACE FOR A HUMAN! NOW I MUST RETURN--
--DECIDE.
WHAT THE--
THOR!
LOOK.
MY PRINCE!
HEIMDALL! WHAT HAS HAPPENED HERE?
YOUR BROTHER HAS BETRAYED US. ASGARD HAS FALLEN TO THE JOTUN.
I WILL GO TO ODIN. JANE FOSTER, YOU WILL COME WITH ME.
YOU THREE--HIE YOU INTO THE FRAY AND SHOW OUR OVERLARGE GUESTS THE WAY OUT OF ASGARD.
WITH GREAT PLEASURE, MILORD.

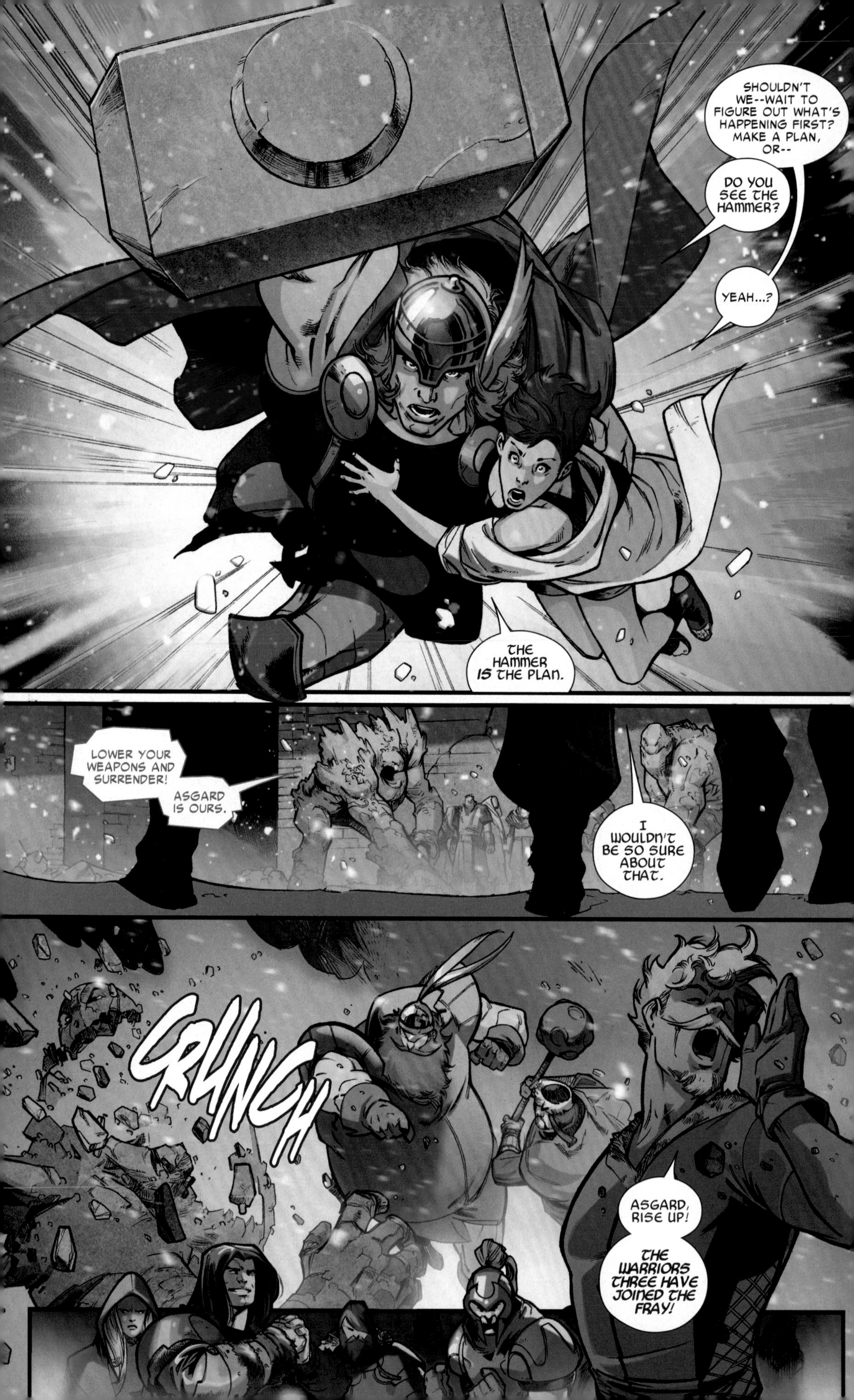
SHOULDN'T WE--WAIT TO FIGURE OUT WHAT'S HAPPENING FIRST? MAKE A PLAN, OR--
DO YOU SEE THE HAMMER?
YEAH...?
THE HAMMER IS THE PLAN.
LOWER YOUR WEAPONS AND SURRENDER!
ASGARD IS OURS.
I WOULDN'T BE SO SURE ABOUT THAT.
CRUNCH
ASGARD, RISE UP!
THE WARRIORS THREE HAVE JOINED THE FRAY!

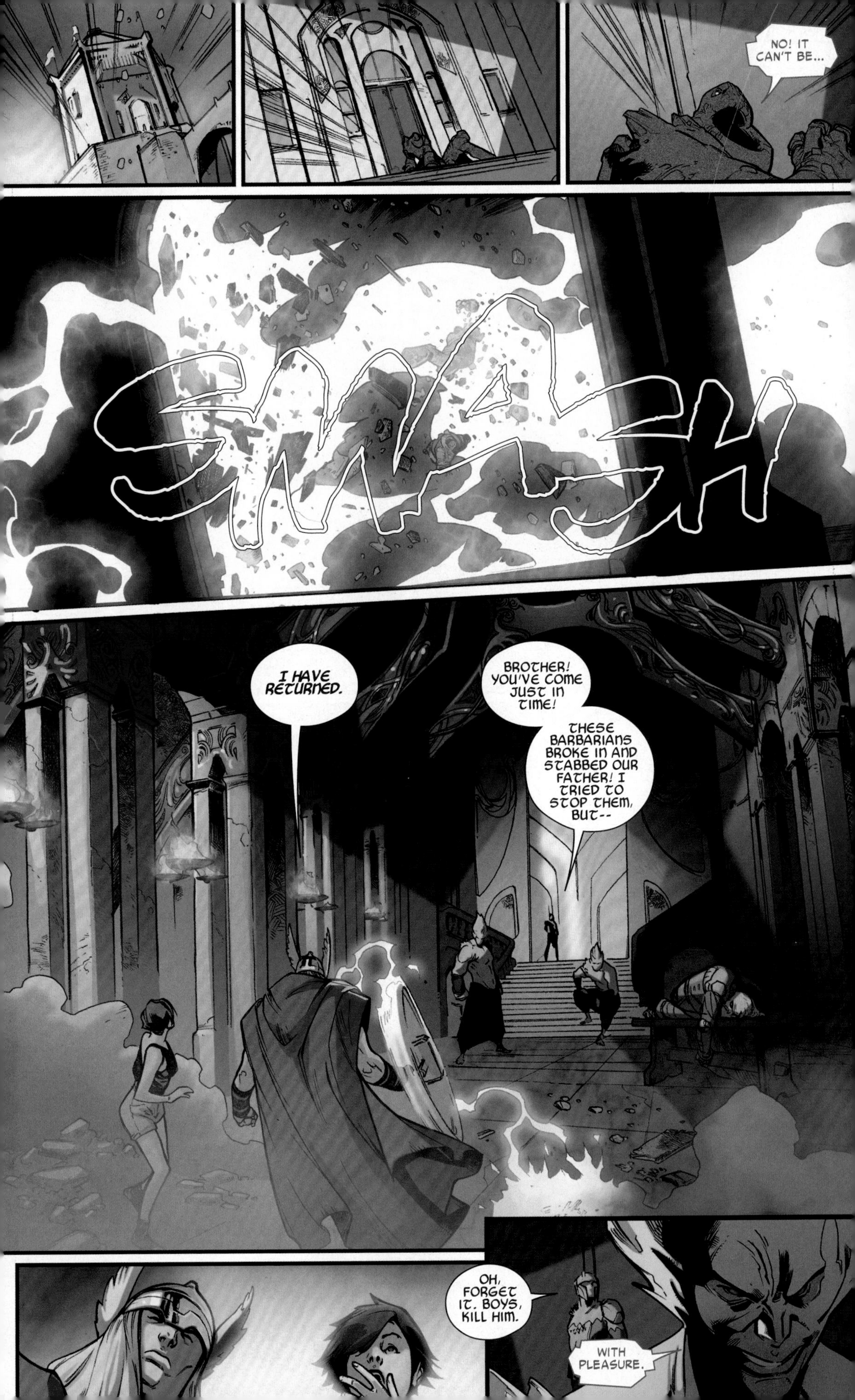
NO! IT CAN'T BE...
SMASH
I HAVE RETURNED.
BROTHER! YOU'VE COME JUST IN TIME!
THESE BARBARIANS BROKE IN AND STABBED OUR FATHER! I TRIED TO STOP THEM, BUT--
OH, FORGET IT. BOYS, KILL HIM.
WITH PLEASURE.

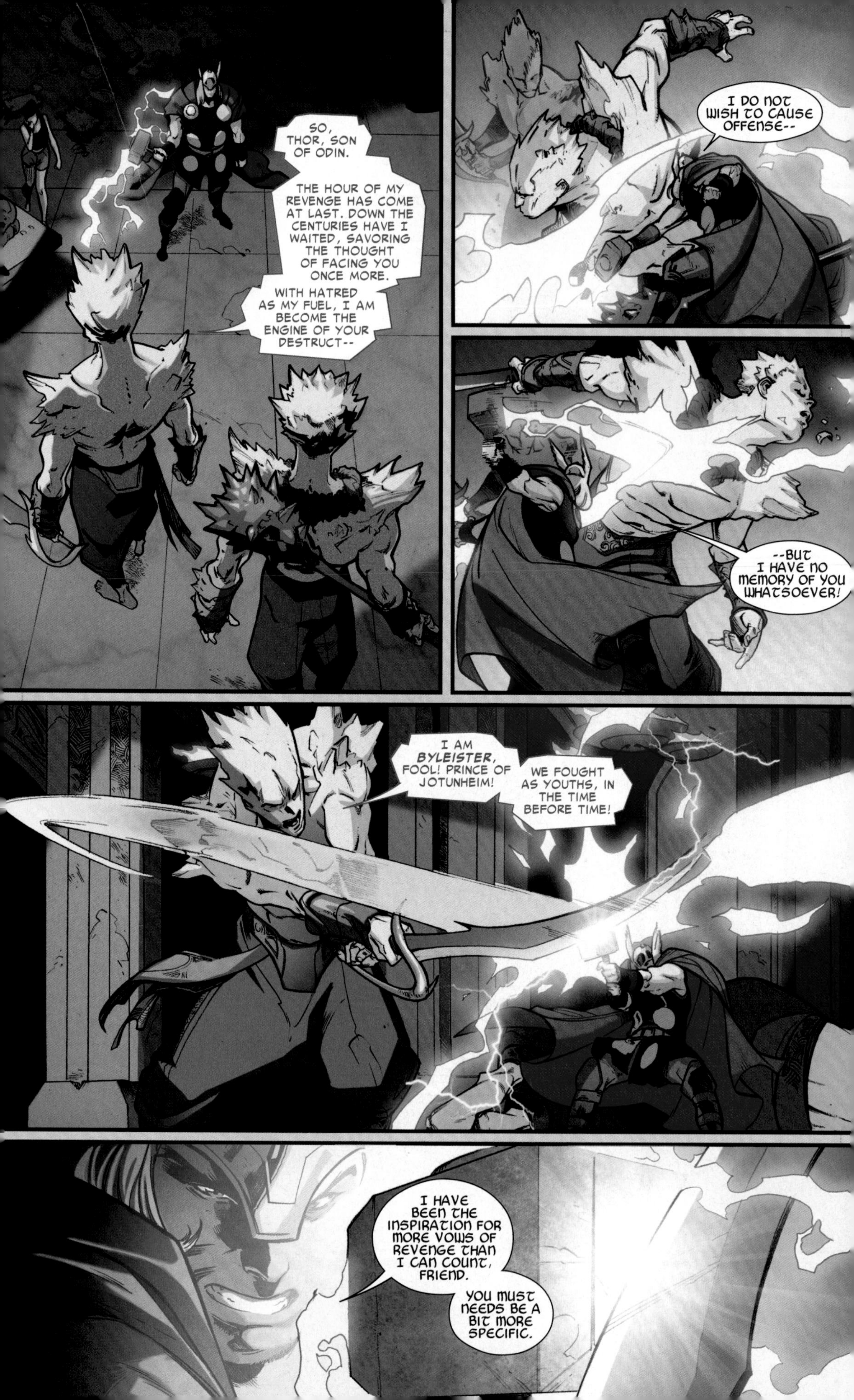
SO, THOR, SON OF ODIN.
THE HOUR OF MY REVENGE HAS COME AT LAST. DOWN THE CENTURIES HAVE I WAITED, SAVORING THE THOUGHT OF FACING YOU ONCE MORE.
WITH HATRED AS MY FUEL, I AM BECOME THE ENGINE OF YOUR DESTRUCT--
I DO NOT WISH TO CAUSE OFFENSE--
--BUT I HAVE NO MEMORY OF YOU WHATSOEVER!
I AM BYLEISTER, FOOL! PRINCE OF JOTUNHEIM!
WE FOUGHT AS YOUTHS, IN THE TIME BEFORE TIME!
I HAVE BEEN THE INSPIRATION FOR MORE VOWS OF REVENGE THAN I CAN COUNT, FRIEND.
YOU MUST NEEDS BE A BIT MORE SPECIFIC.

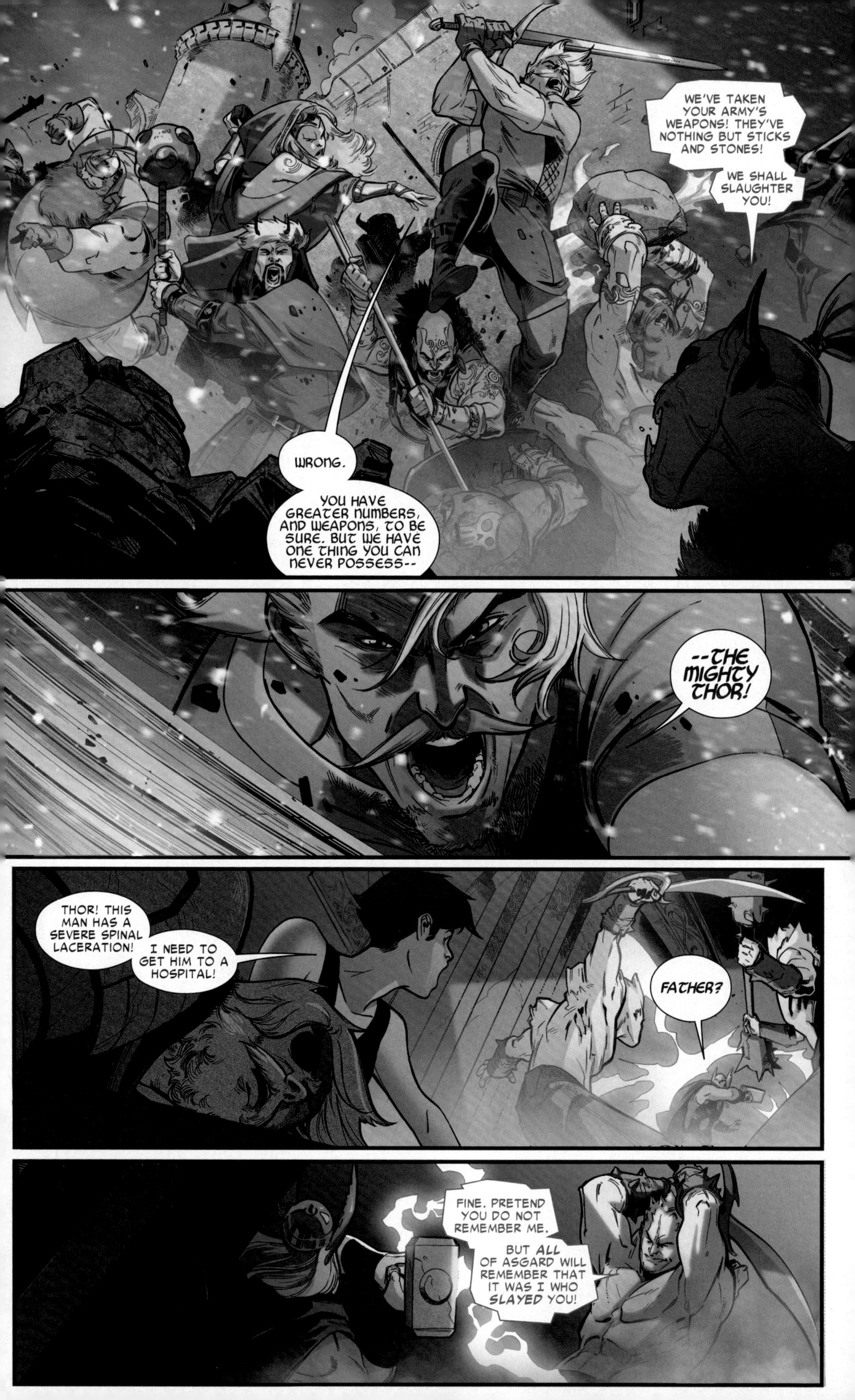
WE'VE TAKEN YOUR ARMY'S WEAPONS! THEY'VE NOTHING BUT STICKS AND STONES!
WE SHALL SLAUGHTER YOU!
WRONG.
YOU HAVE GREATER NUMBERS, AND WEAPONS, TO BE SURE. BUT WE HAVE ONE THING YOU CAN NEVER POSSESS--
--THE MIGHTY THOR!
THOR! THIS MAN HAS A SEVERE SPINAL LACERATION!
I NEED TO GET HIM TO A HOSPITAL!
FATHER?
FINE. PRETEND YOU DO NOT REMEMBER ME.
BUT ALL OF ASGARD WILL REMEMBER THAT IT WAS I WHO SLAYED YOU!

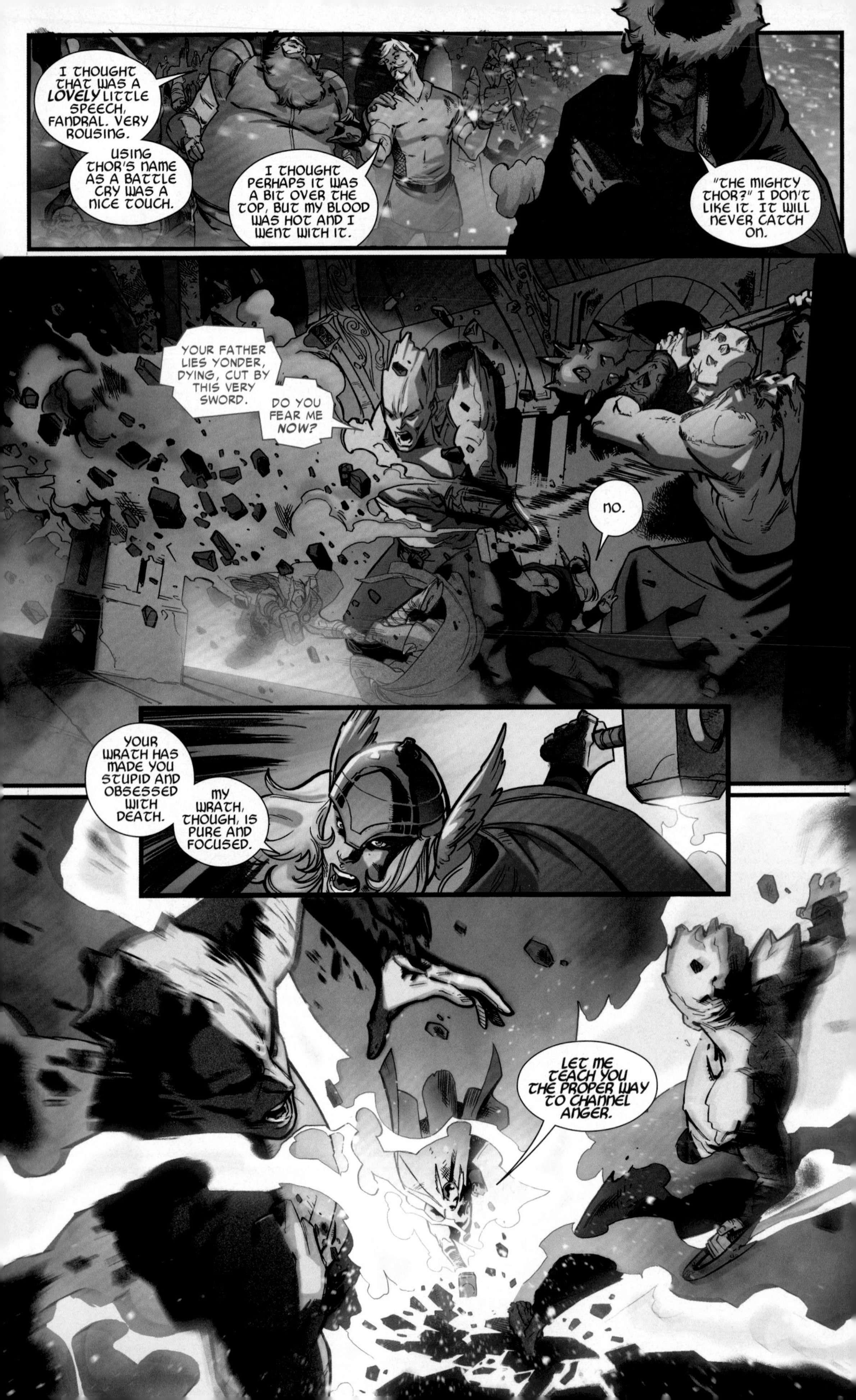
I THOUGHT THAT WAS A LOVELY LITTLE SPEECH, FANDRAL. VERY ROUSING.
USING THOR'S NAME AS A BATTLE CRY WAS A NICE TOUCH.
I THOUGHT PERHAPS IT WAS A BIT OVER THE TOP, BUT MY BLOOD WAS HOT AND I WENT WITH IT.
"THE MIGHTY THOR?" I DON'T LIKE IT. IT WILL NEVER CATCH ON.
YOUR FATHER LIES YONDER, DYING, CUT BY THIS VERY SWORD.
DO YOU FEAR ME NOW?
no.
YOUR WRATH HAS MADE YOU STUPID AND OBSESSED WITH DEATH.
MY WRATH, THOUGH, IS PURE AND FOCUSED.
LET ME TEACH YOU THE PROPER WAY TO CHANNEL ANGER.

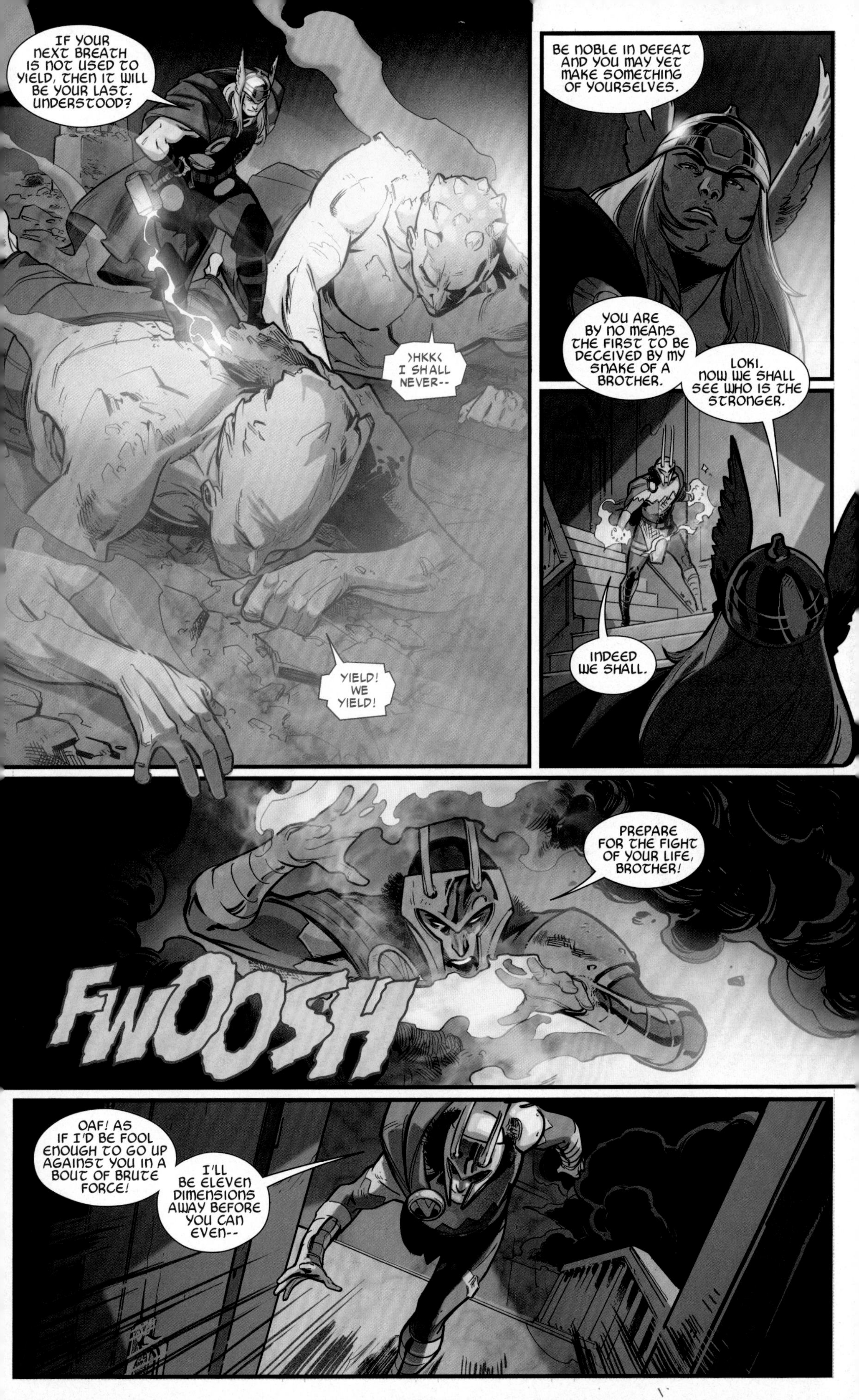
IF YOUR NEXT BREATH IS NOT USED TO YIELD, THEN IT WILL BE YOUR LAST. UNDERSTOOD?
>HKK< I SHALL NEVER--
YIELD! WE YIELD!
BE NOBLE IN DEFEAT AND YOU MAY YET MAKE SOMETHING OF YOURSELVES.
YOU ARE BY NO MEANS THE FIRST TO BE DECEIVED BY MY SNAKE OF A BROTHER.
LOKI. NOW WE SHALL SEE WHO IS THE STRONGER.
INDEED WE SHALL.
PREPARE FOR THE FIGHT OF YOUR LIFE, BROTHER!
FWOOSH
OAF! AS IF I'D BE FOOL ENOUGH TO GO UP AGAINST YOU IN A BOUT OF BRUTE FORCE!
I'LL BE ELEVEN DIMENSIONS AWAY BEFORE YOU CAN EVEN--

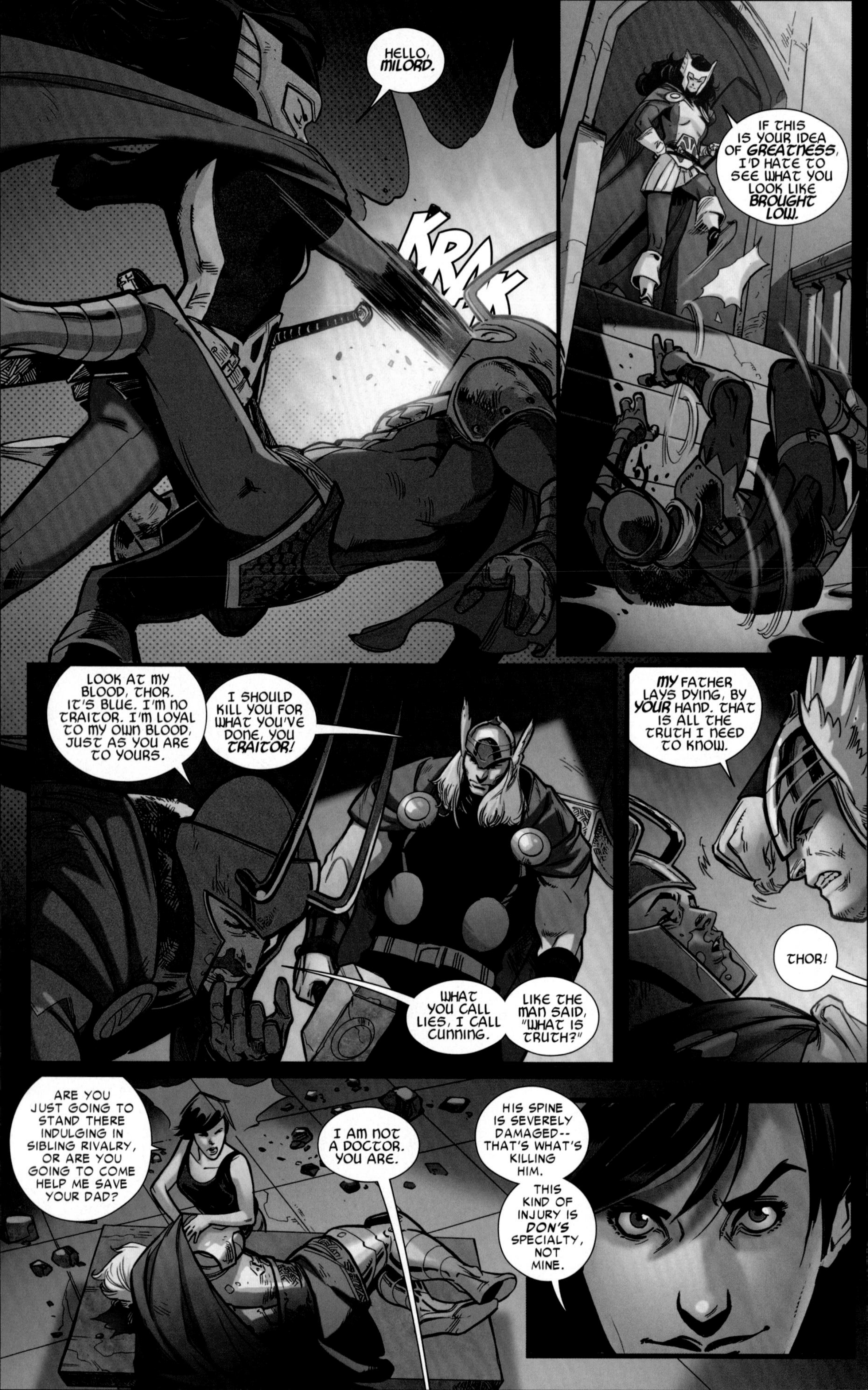
HELLO, MILORD.
KRAK
IF THIS IS YOUR IDEA OF GREATNESS, I'D HATE TO SEE WHAT YOU LOOK LIKE BROUGHT LOW.
I SHOULD KILL YOU FOR WHAT YOU'VE DONE, YOU TRAITOR!
LOOK AT MY BLOOD, THOR. IT'S BLUE. I'M NO TRAITOR. I'M LOYAL TO MY OWN BLOOD, JUST AS YOU ARE TO YOURS.
WHAT YOU CALL LIES, I CALL CUNNING.
LIKE THE MAN SAID, "WHAT IS TRUTH?"
MY FATHER LAYS DYING, BY YOUR HAND. THAT IS ALL THE TRUTH I NEED TO KNOW.
THOR!
ARE YOU JUST GOING TO STAND THERE INDULGING IN SIBLING RIVALRY, OR ARE YOU GOING TO COME HELP ME SAVE YOUR DAD?
I AM NOT A DOCTOR. YOU ARE.
HIS SPINE IS SEVERELY DAMAGED--THAT'S WHAT'S KILLING HIM.
THIS KIND OF INJURY IS DON'S SPECIALTY, NOT MINE.

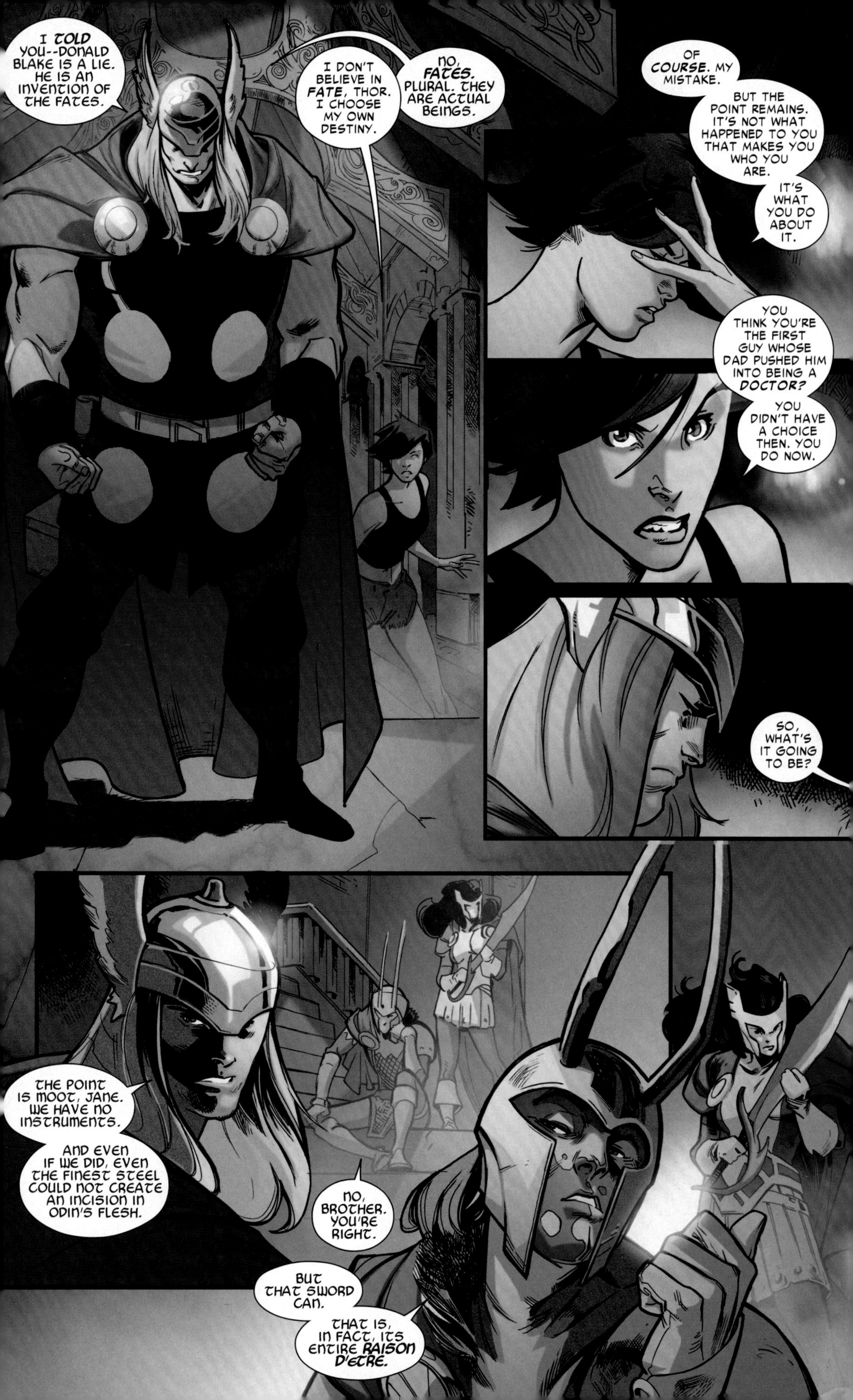
I TOLD YOU--DONALD BLAKE IS A LIE. HE IS AN INVENTION OF THE FATES.
I DON'T BELIEVE IN FATE, THOR. I CHOOSE MY OWN DESTINY.
NO, FATES. PLURAL. THEY ARE ACTUAL BEINGS.
OF COURSE. MY MISTAKE.
BUT THE POINT REMAINS. IT'S NOT WHAT HAPPENED TO YOU THAT MAKES YOU WHO YOU ARE.
IT'S WHAT YOU DO ABOUT IT.
YOU THINK YOU'RE THE FIRST GUY WHOSE DAD PUSHED HIM INTO BEING A DOCTOR?
YOU DIDN'T HAVE A CHOICE THEN. YOU DO NOW.
SO, WHAT'S IT GOING TO BE?
THE POINT IS MOOT, JANE. WE HAVE NO INSTRUMENTS.
AND EVEN IF WE DID, EVEN THE FINEST STEEL COULD NOT CREATE AN INCISION IN ODIN'S FLESH.
NO, BROTHER. YOU'RE RIGHT.
BUT THAT SWORD CAN.
THAT IS, IN FACT, ITS ENTIRE RAISON D'ETRE.

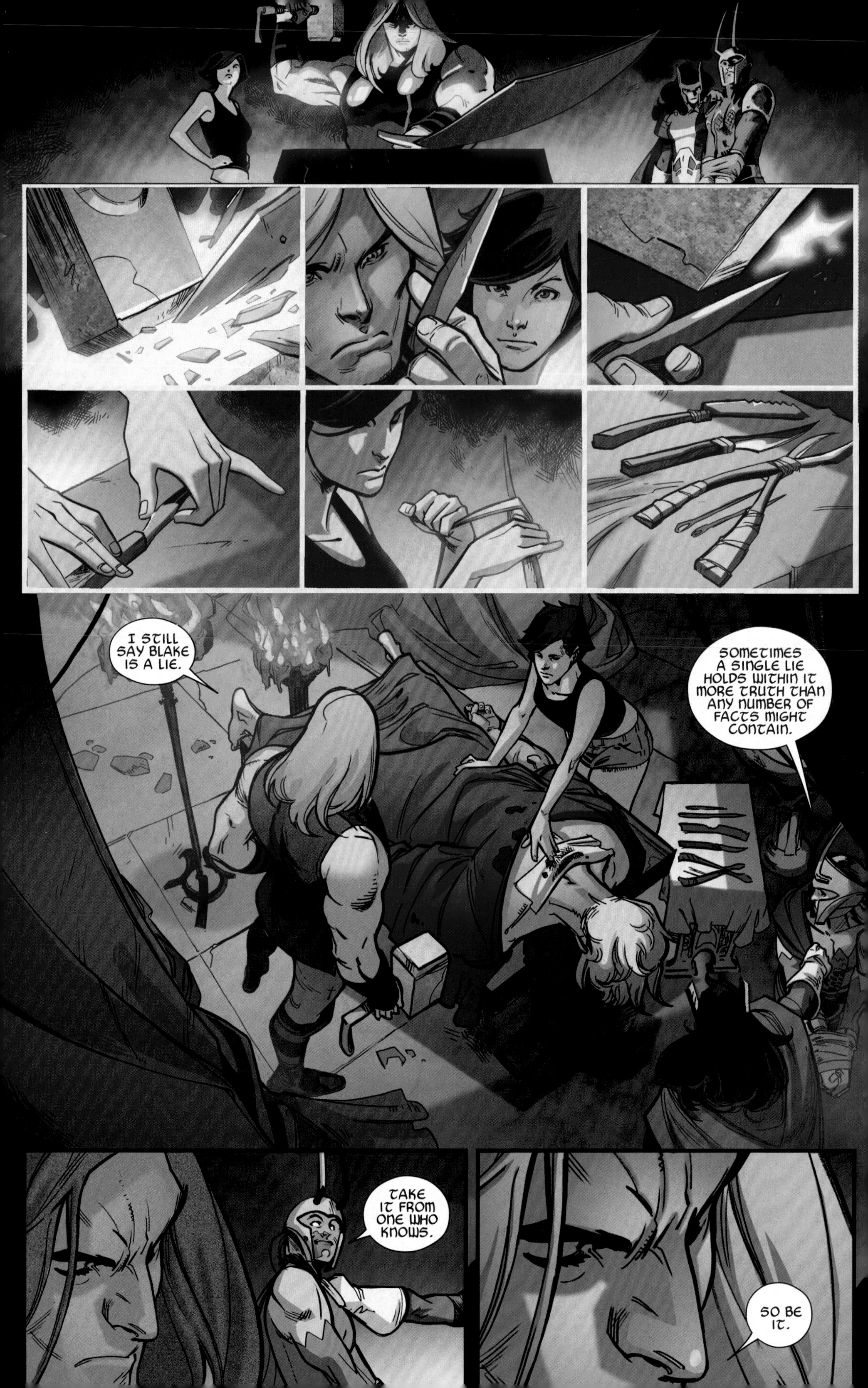
I STILL SAY BLAKE IS A LIE.
SOMETIMES A SINGLE LIE HOLDS WITHIN IT MORE TRUTH THAN ANY NUMBER OF FACTS MIGHT CONTAIN.
TAKE IT FROM ONE WHO KNOWS.
SO BE IT.

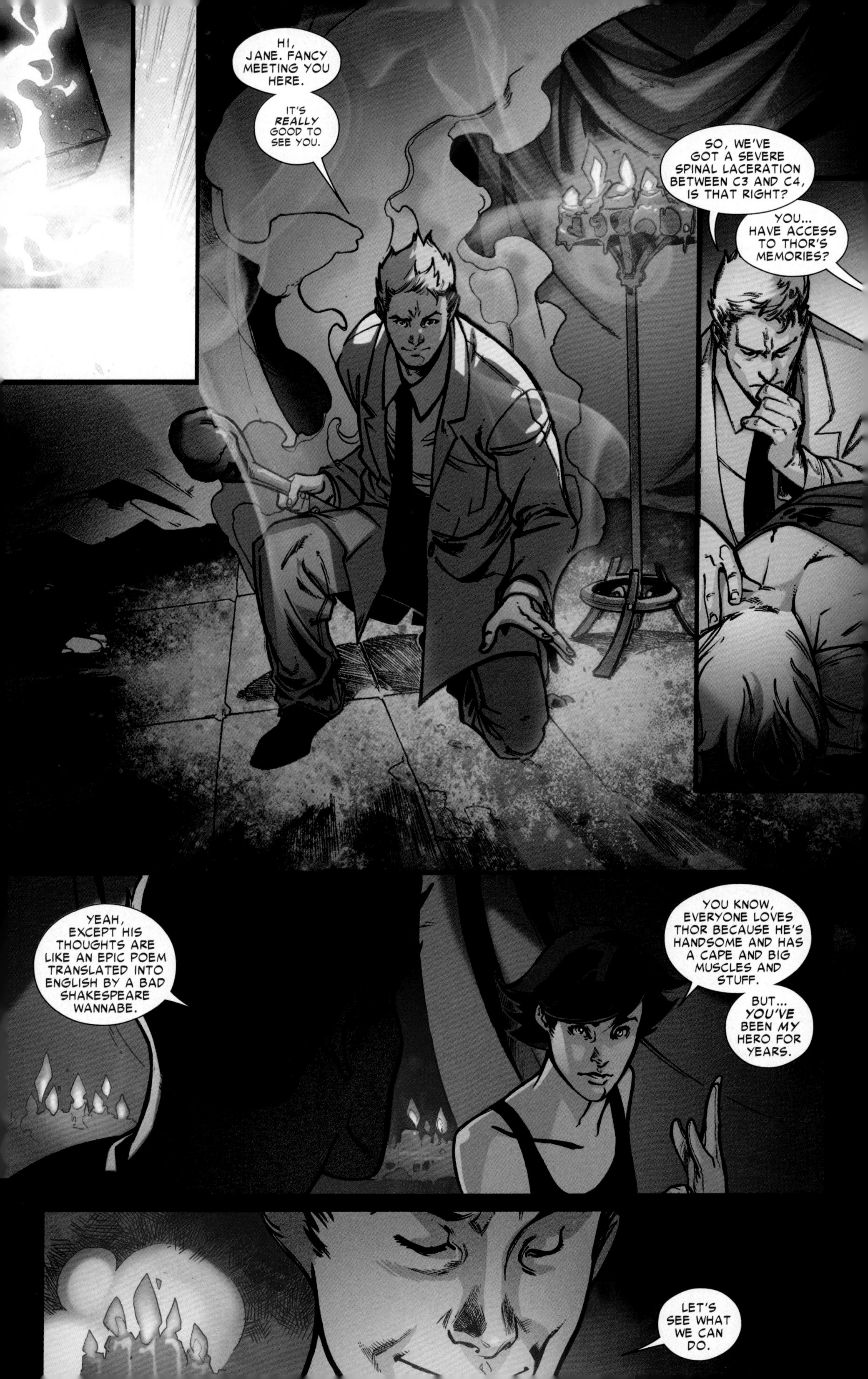
HI, JANE. FANCY MEETING YOU HERE.
IT'S *REALLY* GOOD TO SEE YOU.
SO, WE'VE GOT A SEVERE SPINAL LACERATION BETWEEN C3 AND C4, IS THAT RIGHT?
YOU... HAVE ACCESS TO THOR'S MEMORIES?
YEAH, EXCEPT HIS THOUGHTS ARE LIKE AN EPIC POEM TRANSLATED INTO ENGLISH BY A BAD SHAKESPEARE WANNABE.
YOU KNOW, EVERYONE LOVES THOR BECAUSE HE'S HANDSOME AND HAS A CAPE AND BIG MUSCLES AND STUFF.
BUT... *YOU'VE* BEEN *MY* HERO FOR YEARS.
LET'S SEE WHAT WE CAN DO.

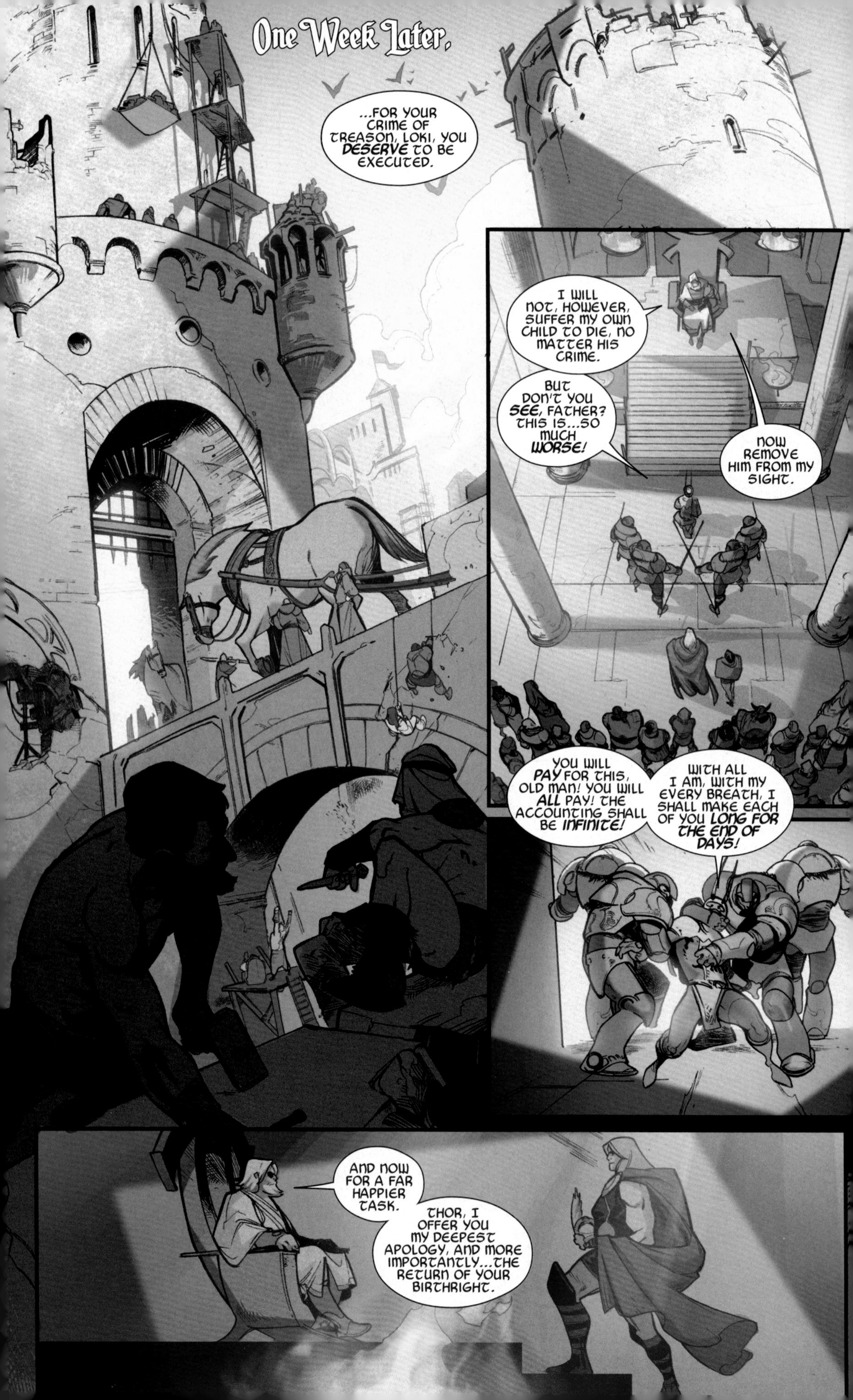

One Week Later,
...FOR YOUR CRIME OF TREASON, LOKI, YOU DESERVE TO BE EXECUTED.
I WILL NOT, HOWEVER, SUFFER MY OWN CHILD TO DIE, NO MATTER HIS CRIME.
BUT DON'T YOU SEE, FATHER? THIS IS...SO MUCH WORSE!
NOW REMOVE HIM FROM MY SIGHT.
YOU WILL PAY FOR THIS, OLD MAN! YOU WILL ALL PAY! THE ACCOUNTING SHALL BE INFINITE!
WITH ALL I AM, WITH MY EVERY BREATH, I SHALL MAKE EACH OF YOU LONG FOR THE END OF DAYS!
AND NOW FOR A FAR HAPPIER TASK.
THOR, I OFFER YOU MY DEEPEST APOLOGY, AND MORE IMPORTANTLY...THE RETURN OF YOUR BIRTHRIGHT.

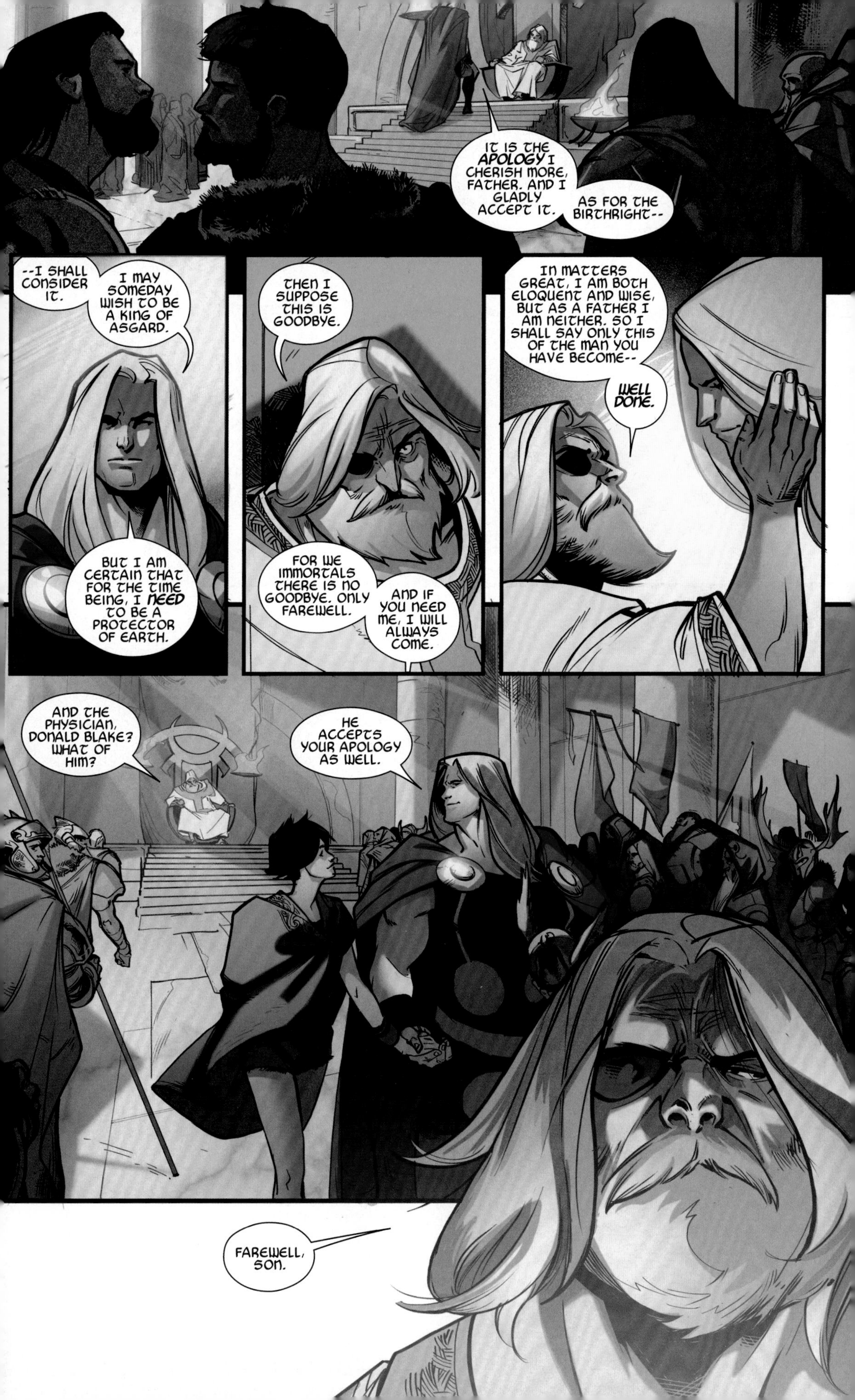
IT IS THE APOLOGY I CHERISH MORE, FATHER. AND I GLADLY ACCEPT IT.
AS FOR THE BIRTHRIGHT--
--I SHALL CONSIDER IT.
I MAY SOMEDAY WISH TO BE A KING OF ASGARD.
BUT I AM CERTAIN THAT FOR THE TIME BEING, I NEED TO BE A PROTECTOR OF EARTH.
THEN I SUPPOSE THIS IS GOODBYE.
FOR WE IMMORTALS THERE IS NO GOODBYE. ONLY FAREWELL.
AND IF YOU NEED ME, I WILL ALWAYS COME.
IN MATTERS GREAT, I AM BOTH ELOQUENT AND WISE, BUT AS A FATHER I AM NEITHER. SO I SHALL SAY ONLY THIS OF THE MAN YOU HAVE BECOME--
WELL DONE.
AND THE PHYSICIAN, DONALD BLAKE? WHAT OF HIM?
HE ACCEPTS YOUR APOLOGY AS WELL.
FAREWELL, SON.

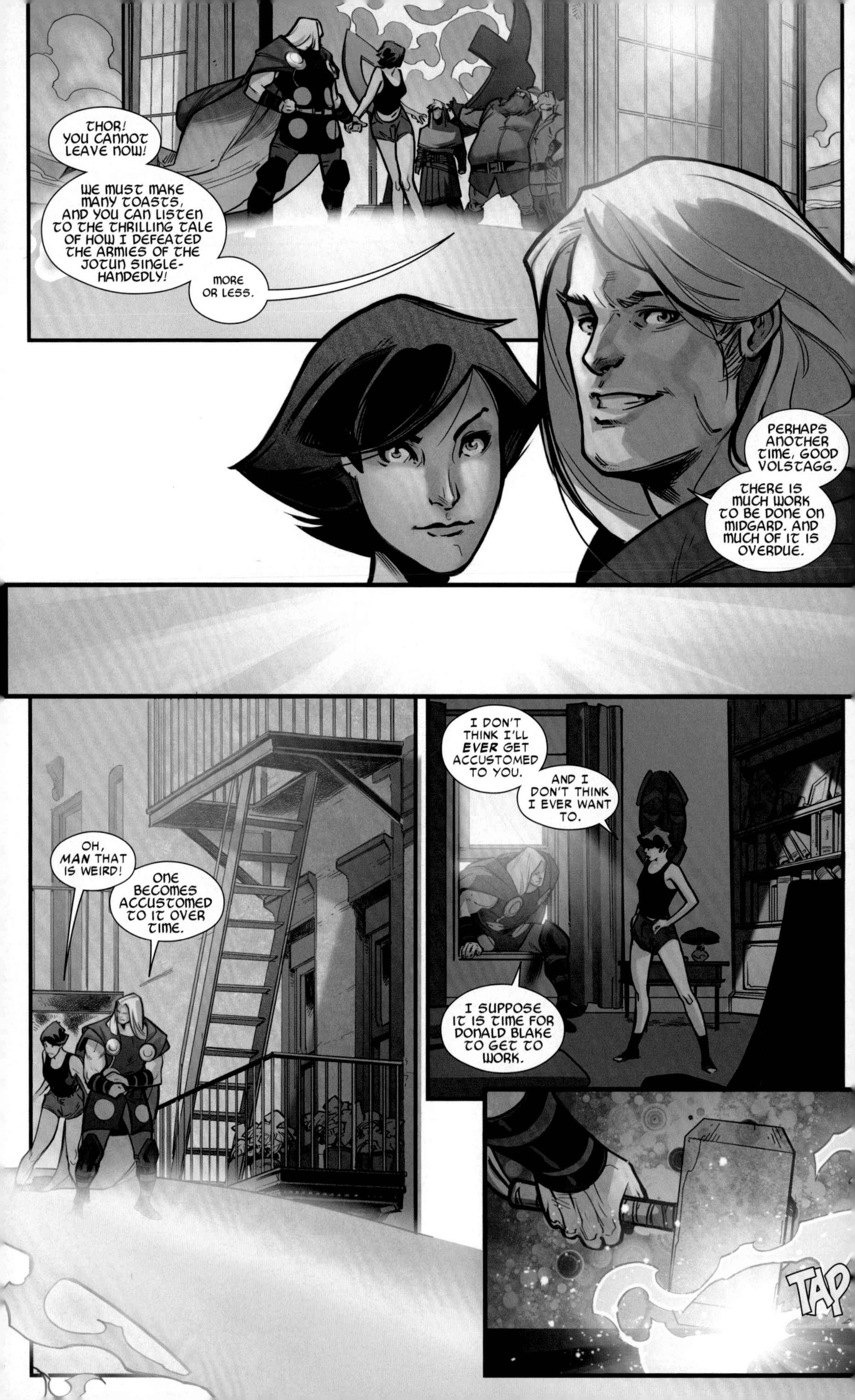
THOR! YOU CANNOT LEAVE NOW!
WE MUST MAKE MANY TOASTS, AND YOU CAN LISTEN TO THE THRILLING TALE OF HOW I DEFEATED THE ARMIES OF THE JOTUN SINGLE-HANDEDLY!
MORE OR LESS.
PERHAPS ANOTHER TIME, GOOD VOLSTAGG.
THERE IS MUCH WORK TO BE DONE ON MIDGARD. AND MUCH OF IT IS OVERDUE.
OH, MAN THAT IS WEIRD!
ONE BECOMES ACCUSTOMED TO IT OVER TIME.
I DON'T THINK I'LL EVER GET ACCUSTOMED TO YOU.
AND I DON'T THINK I EVER WANT TO.
I SUPPOSE IT IS TIME FOR DONALD BLAKE TO GET TO WORK.
TAP

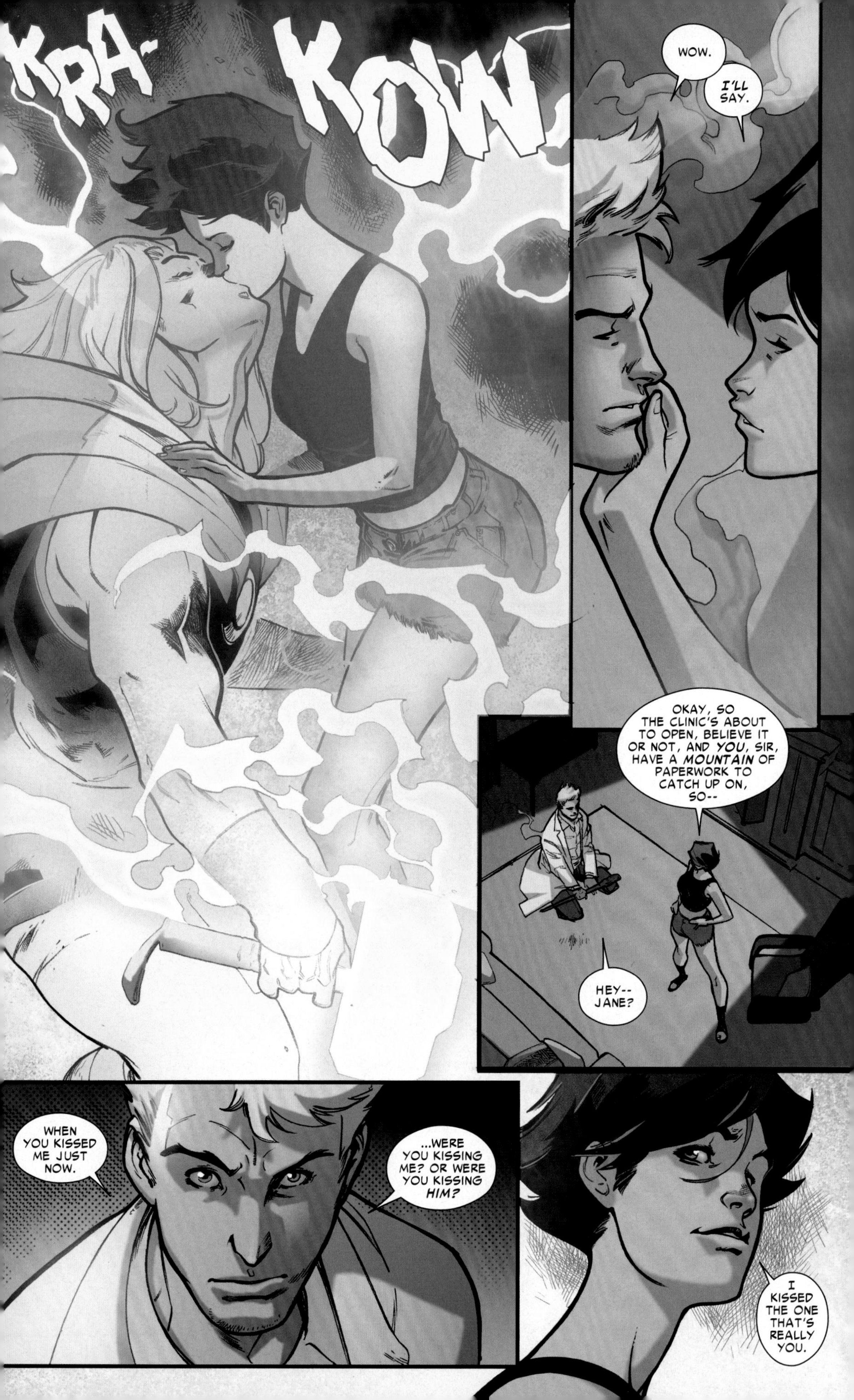
KRA-
KOW
WOW.
I'LL SAY.
OKAY, SO THE CLINIC'S ABOUT TO OPEN, BELIEVE IT OR NOT, AND YOU, SIR, HAVE A MOUNTAIN OF PAPERWORK TO CATCH UP ON, SO--
HEY-- JANE?
WHEN YOU KISSED ME JUST NOW.
...WERE YOU KISSING ME? OR WERE YOU KISSING HIM?
I KISSED THE ONE THAT'S REALLY YOU.

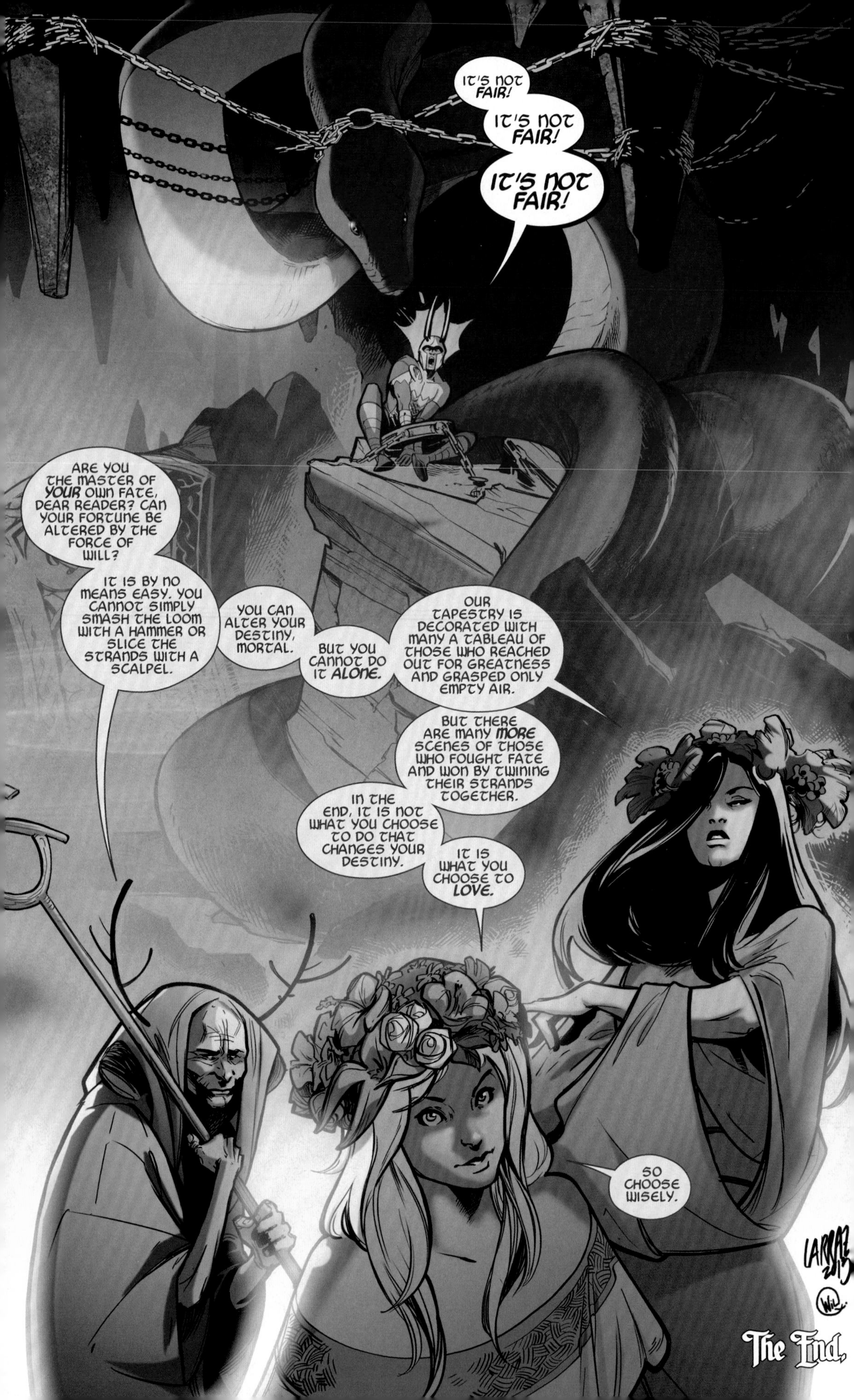
IT'S NOT FAIR!
IT'S NOT FAIR!
IT'S NOT FAIR!
ARE YOU THE MASTER OF YOUR OWN FATE, DEAR READER? CAN YOUR FORTUNE BE ALTERED BY THE FORCE OF WILL?
IT IS BY NO MEANS EASY. YOU CANNOT SIMPLY SMASH THE LOOM WITH A HAMMER OR SLICE THE STRANDS WITH A SCALPEL.
YOU CAN ALTER YOUR DESTINY, MORTAL.
BUT YOU CANNOT DO IT ALONE.
OUR TAPESTRY IS DECORATED WITH MANY A TABLEAU OF THOSE WHO REACHED OUT FOR GREATNESS AND GRASPED ONLY EMPTY AIR.
BUT THERE ARE MANY MORE SCENES OF THOSE WHO FOUGHT FATE AND WON BY TWINING THEIR STRANDS TOGETHER.
IN THE END, IT IS NOT WHAT YOU CHOOSE TO DO THAT CHANGES YOUR DESTINY.
IT IS WHAT YOU CHOOSE TO LOVE.
SO CHOOSE WISELY.
The End.

THOR: GOD OF THUNDER #1 (2013) THE GODS ARE VANISHING, LEADING THOR ON A BLOODY TRAIL THAT THREATENS TO CONSUME HIS PAST, PRESENT AND FUTURE. TO SAVE THESE WORLDS, THOR MUST UNRAVEL THE GRUESOME MYSTERY OF THE GOD BUTCHER!

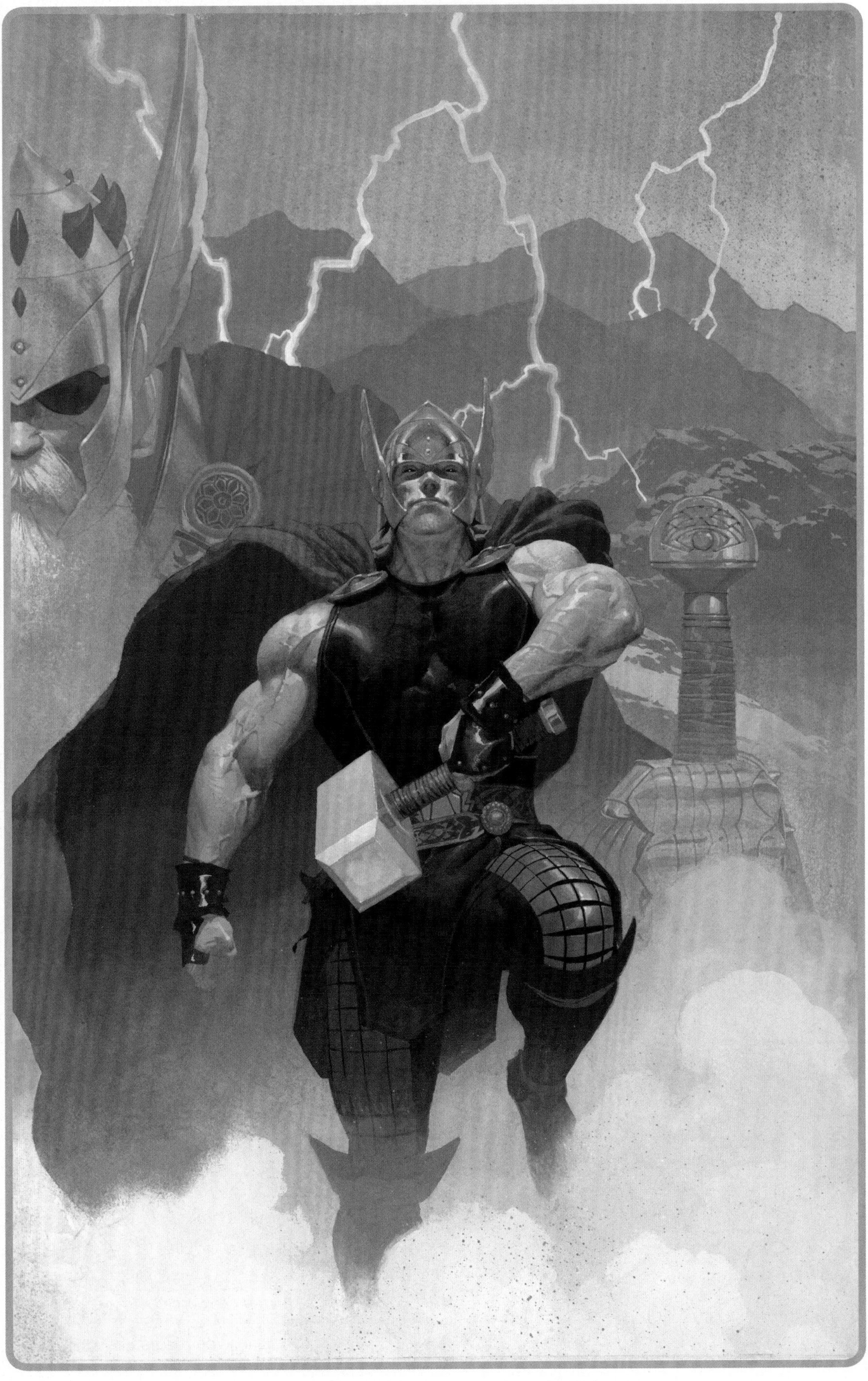

893 A.D.
Earth.
The Western Coast of Iceland.

The **FROST GIANT** had terrorized these people for weeks. It had eaten three goats, four dogs and two children.

The mothers in the village prayed for help from the gods. And help they did receive.

I led a group of twenty men, tracking the giant to its den in the highlands. It battled us for hours, swinging trees and hurling boulders. Many Vikings found their way to Valhalla.

Until my **AXE** hacked its guts to bloody slush and lopped off its head.

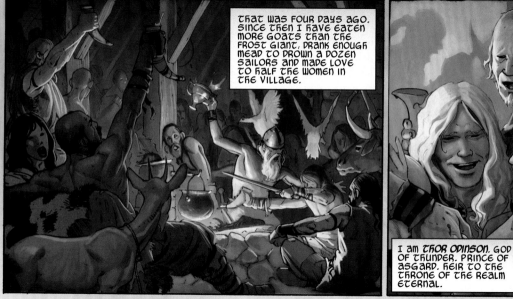

That was four days ago. Since then I have eaten more goats than the frost giant, drank enough mead to drown a dozen sailors and made love to half the women in the village.

I am **THOR ODINSON**. God of thunder. Prince of Asgard. Heir to the throne of the realm eternal.

I **LOVE** my life.

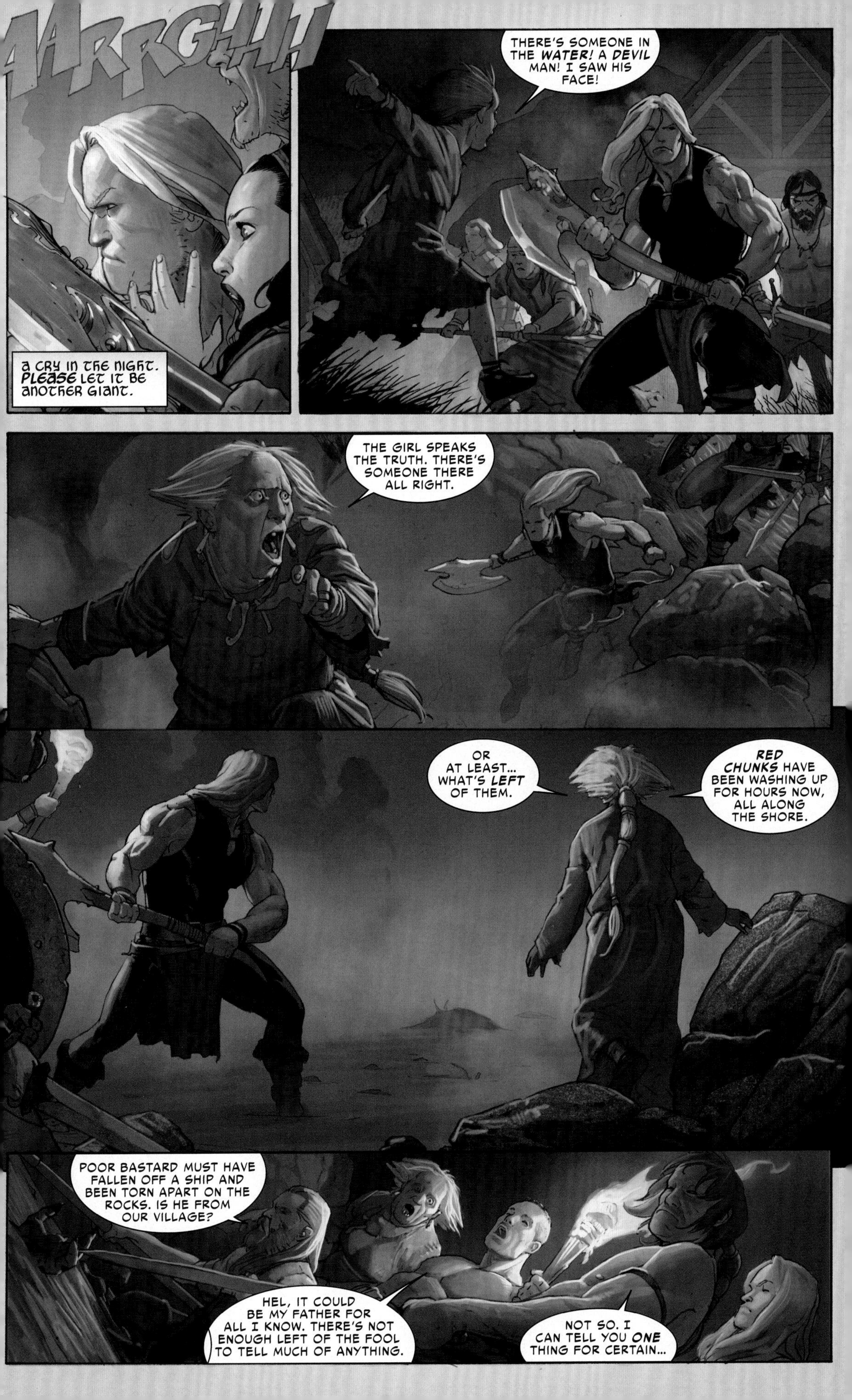
AARRGHH
A CRY IN THE NIGHT. PLEASE LET IT BE ANOTHER GIANT.
THERE'S SOMEONE IN THE WATER! A DEVIL MAN! I SAW HIS FACE!
THE GIRL SPEAKS THE TRUTH. THERE'S SOMEONE THERE ALL RIGHT.
OR AT LEAST... WHAT'S LEFT OF THEM.
RED CHUNKS HAVE BEEN WASHING UP FOR HOURS NOW, ALL ALONG THE SHORE.
POOR BASTARD MUST HAVE FALLEN OFF A SHIP AND BEEN TORN APART ON THE ROCKS. IS HE FROM OUR VILLAGE?
HEL, IT COULD BE MY FATHER FOR ALL I KNOW. THERE'S NOT ENOUGH LEFT OF THE FOOL TO TELL MUCH OF ANYTHING.
NOT SO. I CAN TELL YOU ONE THING FOR CERTAIN...

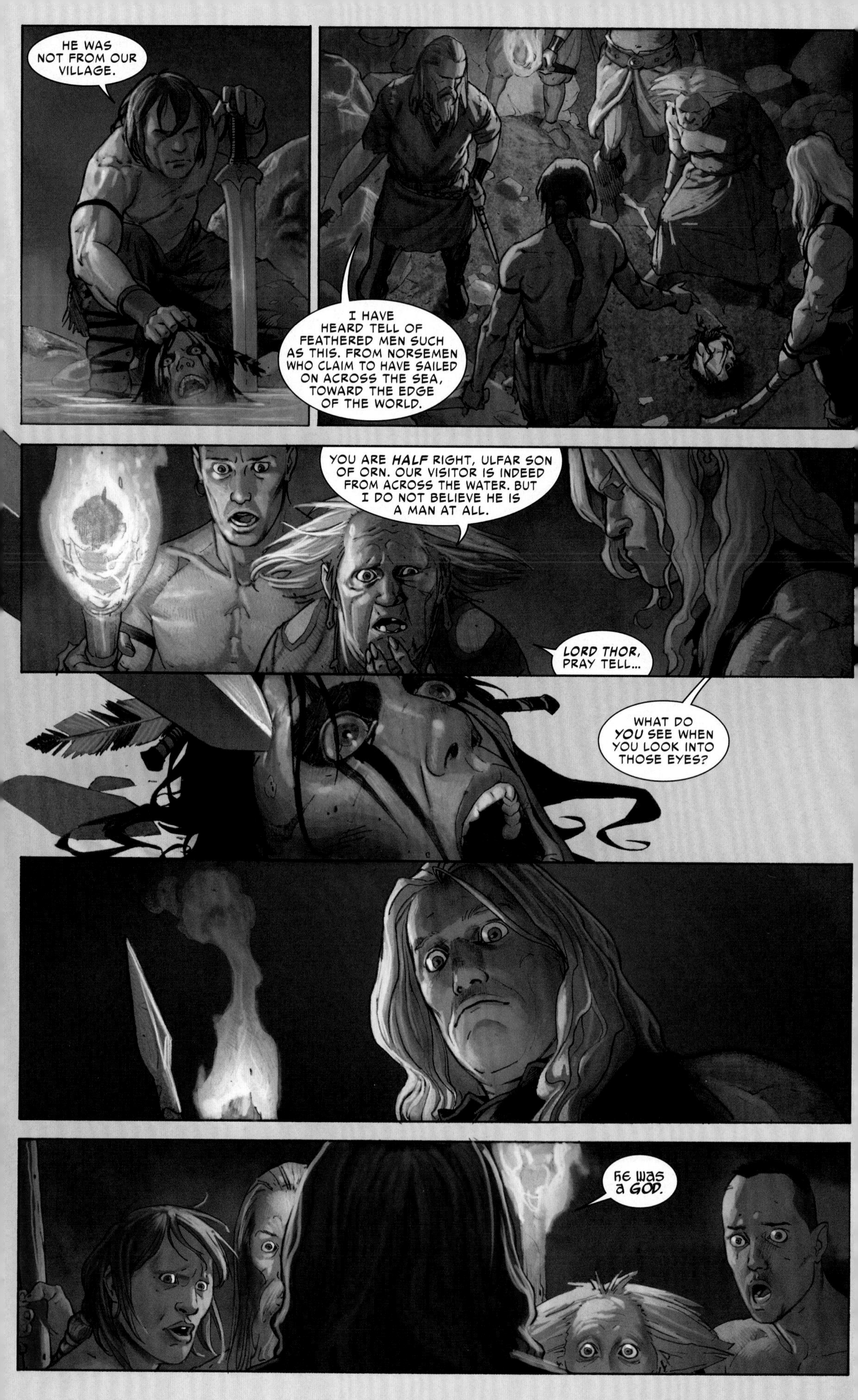
HE WAS NOT FROM OUR VILLAGE.
I HAVE HEARD TELL OF FEATHERED MEN SUCH AS THIS. FROM NORSEMEN WHO CLAIM TO HAVE SAILED ON ACROSS THE SEA, TOWARD THE EDGE OF THE WORLD.
YOU ARE *HALF* RIGHT, ULFAR SON OF ORN. OUR VISITOR IS INDEED FROM ACROSS THE WATER. BUT I DO NOT BELIEVE HE IS A MAN AT ALL.
LORD THOR, PRAY TELL...
WHAT DO *YOU* SEE WHEN YOU LOOK INTO THOSE EYES?
HE WAS A *GOD*.

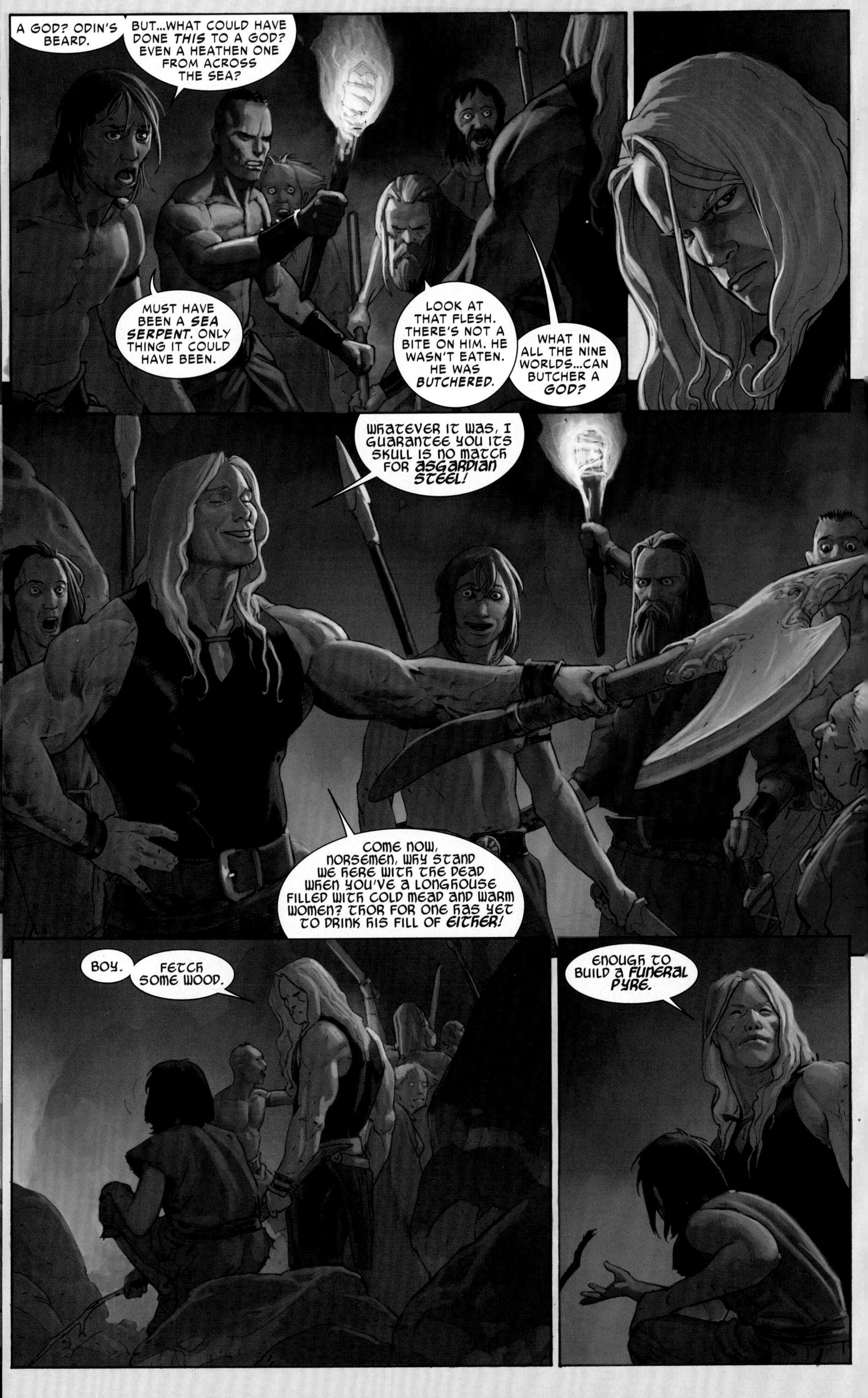
A GOD? ODIN'S BEARD.
BUT...WHAT COULD HAVE DONE THIS TO A GOD? EVEN A HEATHEN ONE FROM ACROSS THE SEA?
MUST HAVE BEEN A SEA SERPENT. ONLY THING IT COULD HAVE BEEN.
LOOK AT THAT FLESH. THERE'S NOT A BITE ON HIM. HE WASN'T EATEN. HE WAS BUTCHERED.
WHAT IN ALL THE NINE WORLDS...CAN BUTCHER A GOD?
WHATEVER IT WAS, I GUARANTEE YOU ITS SKULL IS NO MATCH FOR ASGARDIAN STEEL!
COME NOW, NORSEMEN, WHY STAND WE HERE WITH THE DEAD WHEN YOU'VE A LONGHOUSE FILLED WITH COLD MEAD AND WARM WOMEN? THOR FOR ONE HAS YET TO DRINK HIS FILL OF EITHER!
BOY.
FETCH SOME WOOD.
ENOUGH TO BUILD A FUNERAL PYRE.

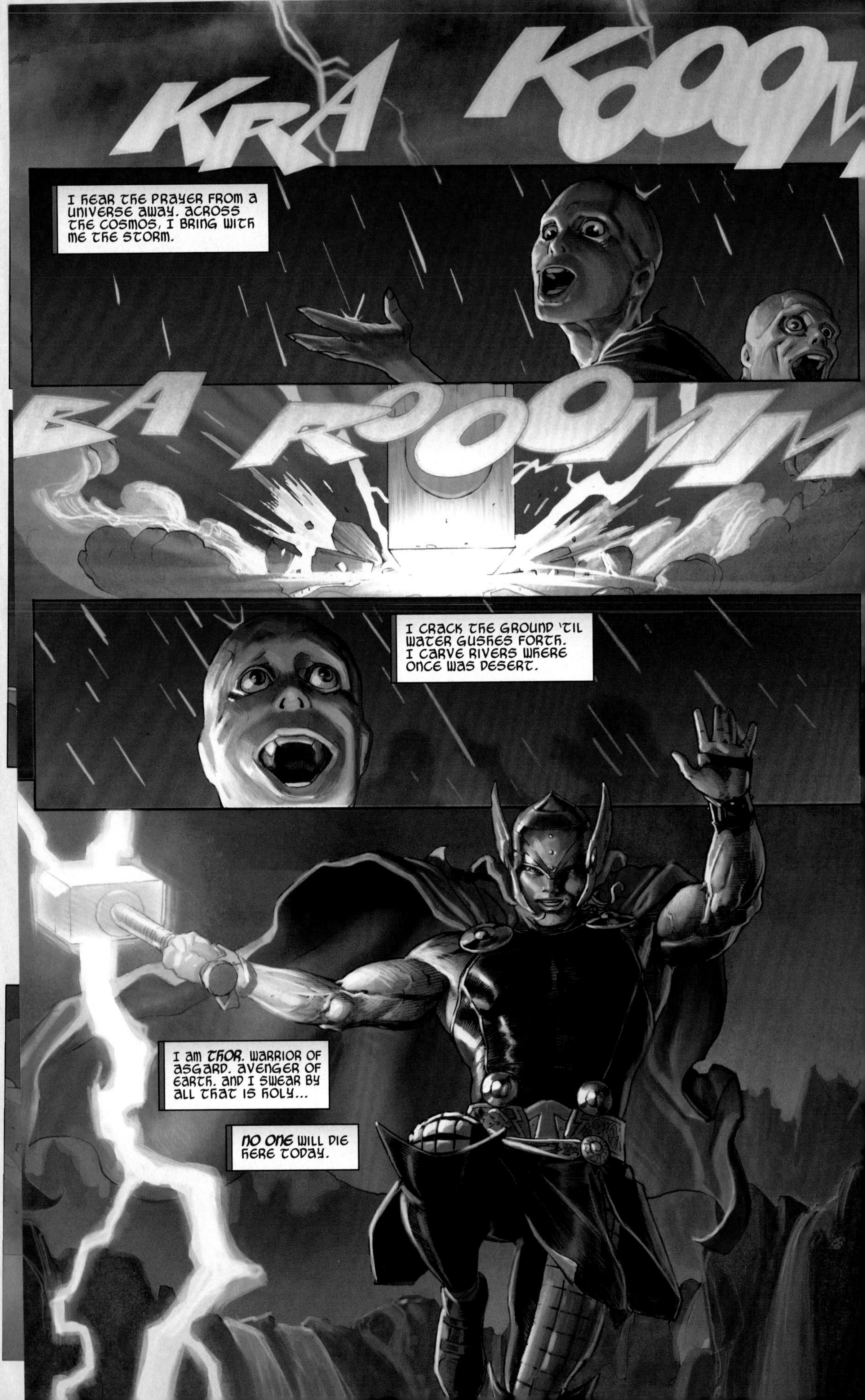
KRA KOOOM
I HEAR THE PRAYER FROM A UNIVERSE AWAY. ACROSS THE COSMOS, I BRING WITH ME THE STORM.
BA ROOOOMM
I CRACK THE GROUND 'TIL WATER GUSHES FORTH. I CARVE RIVERS WHERE ONCE WAS DESERT.
I AM THOR. WARRIOR OF ASGARD. AVENGER OF EARTH. AND I SWEAR BY ALL THAT IS HOLY...
NO ONE WILL DIE HERE TODAY.

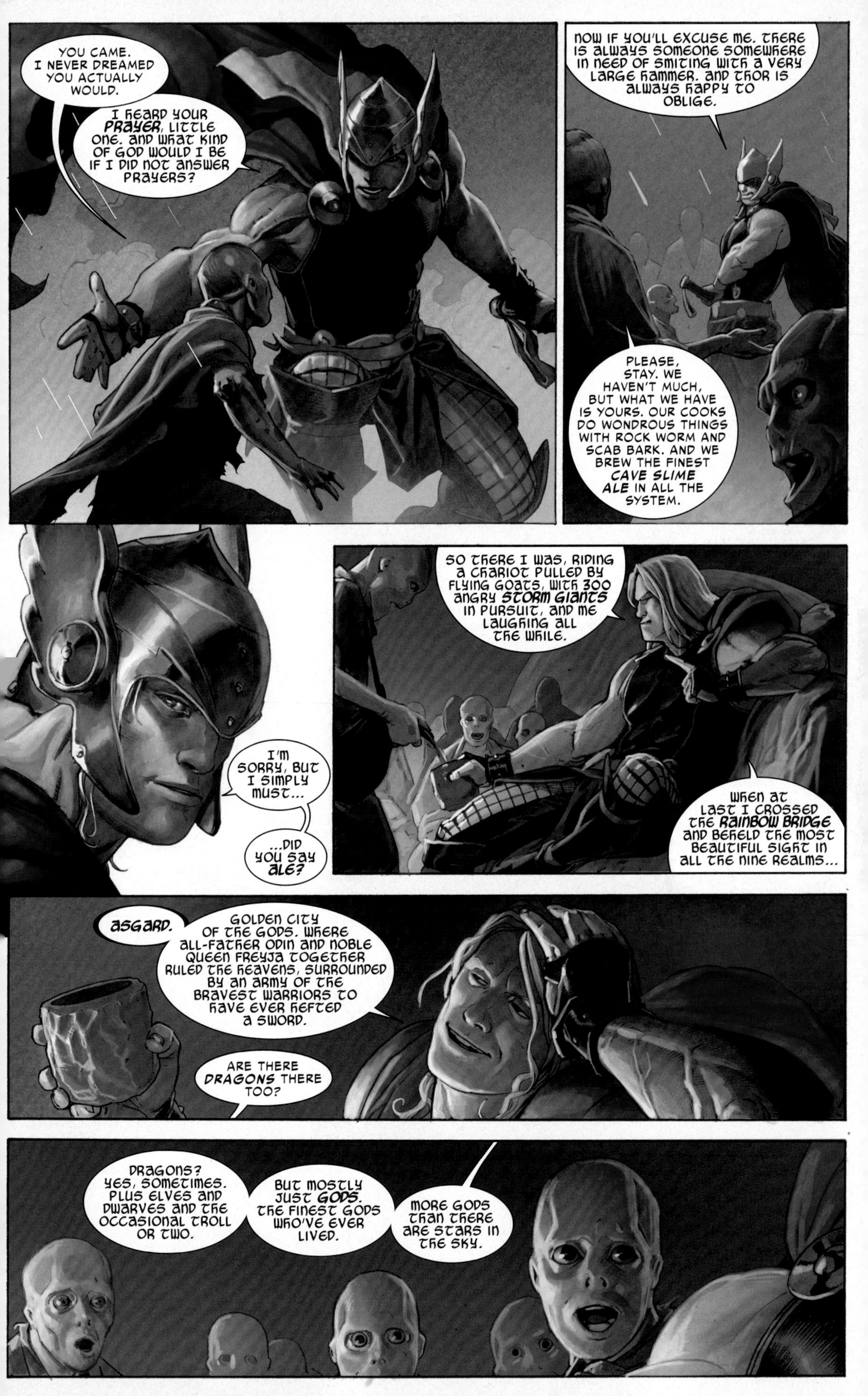
YOU CAME. I NEVER DREAMED YOU ACTUALLY WOULD.
I HEARD YOUR PRAYER, LITTLE ONE. AND WHAT KIND OF GOD WOULD I BE IF I DID NOT ANSWER PRAYERS?
NOW IF YOU'LL EXCUSE ME. THERE IS ALWAYS SOMEONE SOMEWHERE IN NEED OF SMITING WITH A VERY LARGE HAMMER. AND THOR IS ALWAYS HAPPY TO OBLIGE.
PLEASE, STAY. WE HAVEN'T MUCH, BUT WHAT WE HAVE IS YOURS. OUR COOKS DO WONDROUS THINGS WITH ROCK WORM AND SCAB BARK. AND WE BREW THE FINEST CAVE SLIME ALE IN ALL THE SYSTEM.
I'M SORRY, BUT I SIMPLY MUST...
...DID YOU SAY ALE?
SO THERE I WAS, RIDING A CHARIOT PULLED BY FLYING GOATS, WITH 300 ANGRY STORM GIANTS IN PURSUIT, AND ME LAUGHING ALL THE WHILE.
WHEN AT LAST I CROSSED THE RAINBOW BRIDGE AND BEHELD THE MOST BEAUTIFUL SIGHT IN ALL THE NINE REALMS...
ASGARD.
GOLDEN CITY OF THE GODS. WHERE ALL-FATHER ODIN AND NOBLE QUEEN FREYJA TOGETHER RULED THE HEAVENS, SURROUNDED BY AN ARMY OF THE BRAVEST WARRIORS TO HAVE EVER HEFTED A SWORD.
ARE THERE DRAGONS THERE TOO?
DRAGONS? YES, SOMETIMES. PLUS ELVES AND DWARVES AND THE OCCASIONAL TROLL OR TWO.
BUT MOSTLY JUST GODS. THE FINEST GODS WHO'VE EVER LIVED.
MORE GODS THAN THERE ARE STARS IN THE SKY.

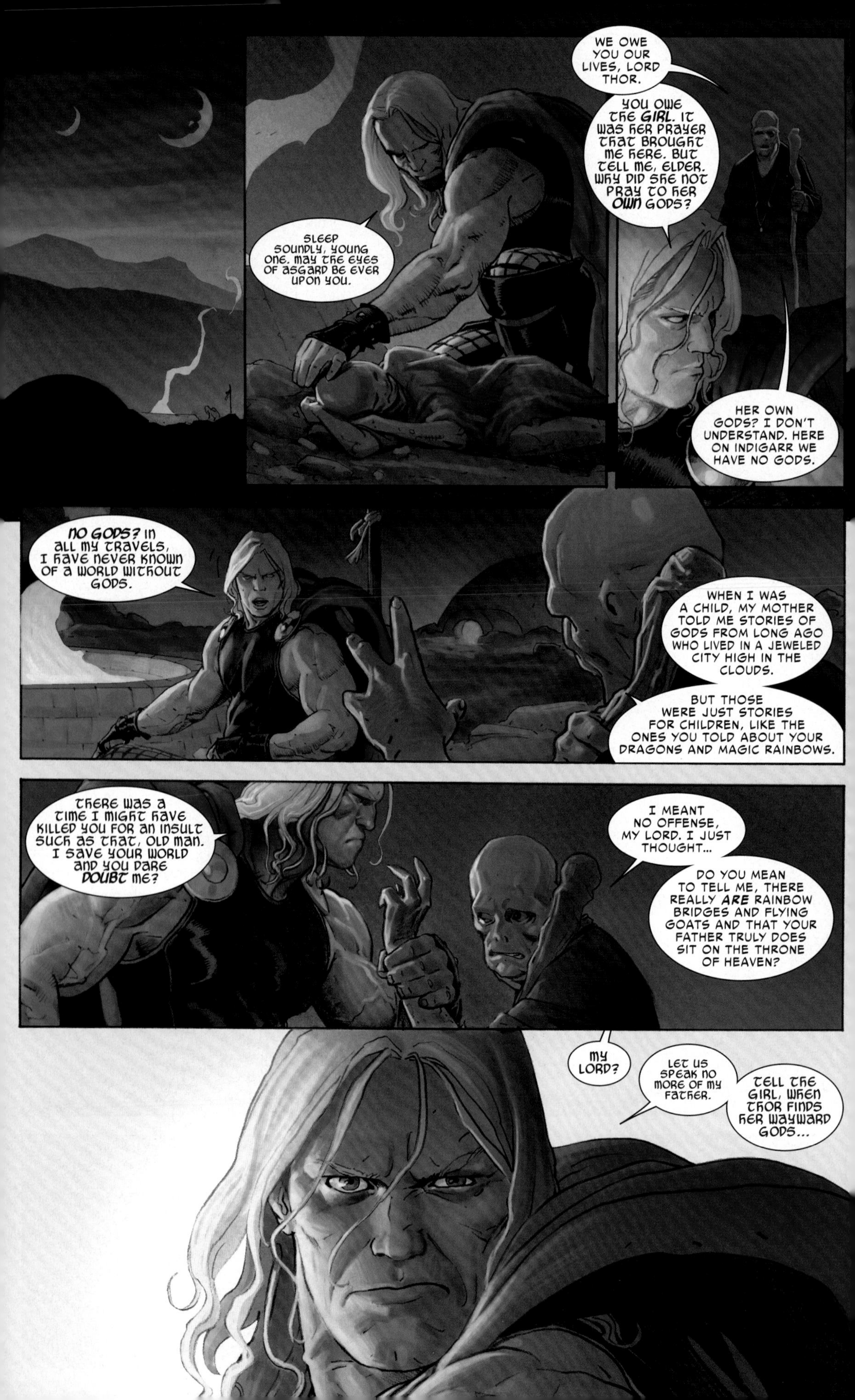
SLEEP SOUNDLY, YOUNG ONE. MAY THE EYES OF ASGARD BE EVER UPON YOU.
WE OWE YOU OUR LIVES, LORD THOR.
YOU OWE THE GIRL. IT WAS HER PRAYER THAT BROUGHT ME HERE. BUT TELL ME, ELDER. WHY DID SHE NOT PRAY TO HER OWN GODS?
HER OWN GODS? I DON'T UNDERSTAND. HERE ON INDIGARR WE HAVE NO GODS.
NO GODS? IN ALL MY TRAVELS, I HAVE NEVER KNOWN OF A WORLD WITHOUT GODS.
WHEN I WAS A CHILD, MY MOTHER TOLD ME STORIES OF GODS FROM LONG AGO WHO LIVED IN A JEWELED CITY HIGH IN THE CLOUDS.
BUT THOSE WERE JUST STORIES FOR CHILDREN, LIKE THE ONES YOU TOLD ABOUT YOUR DRAGONS AND MAGIC RAINBOWS.
THERE WAS A TIME I MIGHT HAVE KILLED YOU FOR AN INSULT SUCH AS THAT, OLD MAN. I SAVE YOUR WORLD AND YOU DARE DOUBT ME?
I MEANT NO OFFENSE, MY LORD. I JUST THOUGHT...
DO YOU MEAN TO TELL ME, THERE REALLY ARE RAINBOW BRIDGES AND FLYING GOATS AND THAT YOUR FATHER TRULY DOES SIT ON THE THRONE OF HEAVEN?
MY LORD?
LET US SPEAK NO MORE OF MY FATHER.
TELL THE GIRL, WHEN THOR FINDS HER WAYWARD GODS...

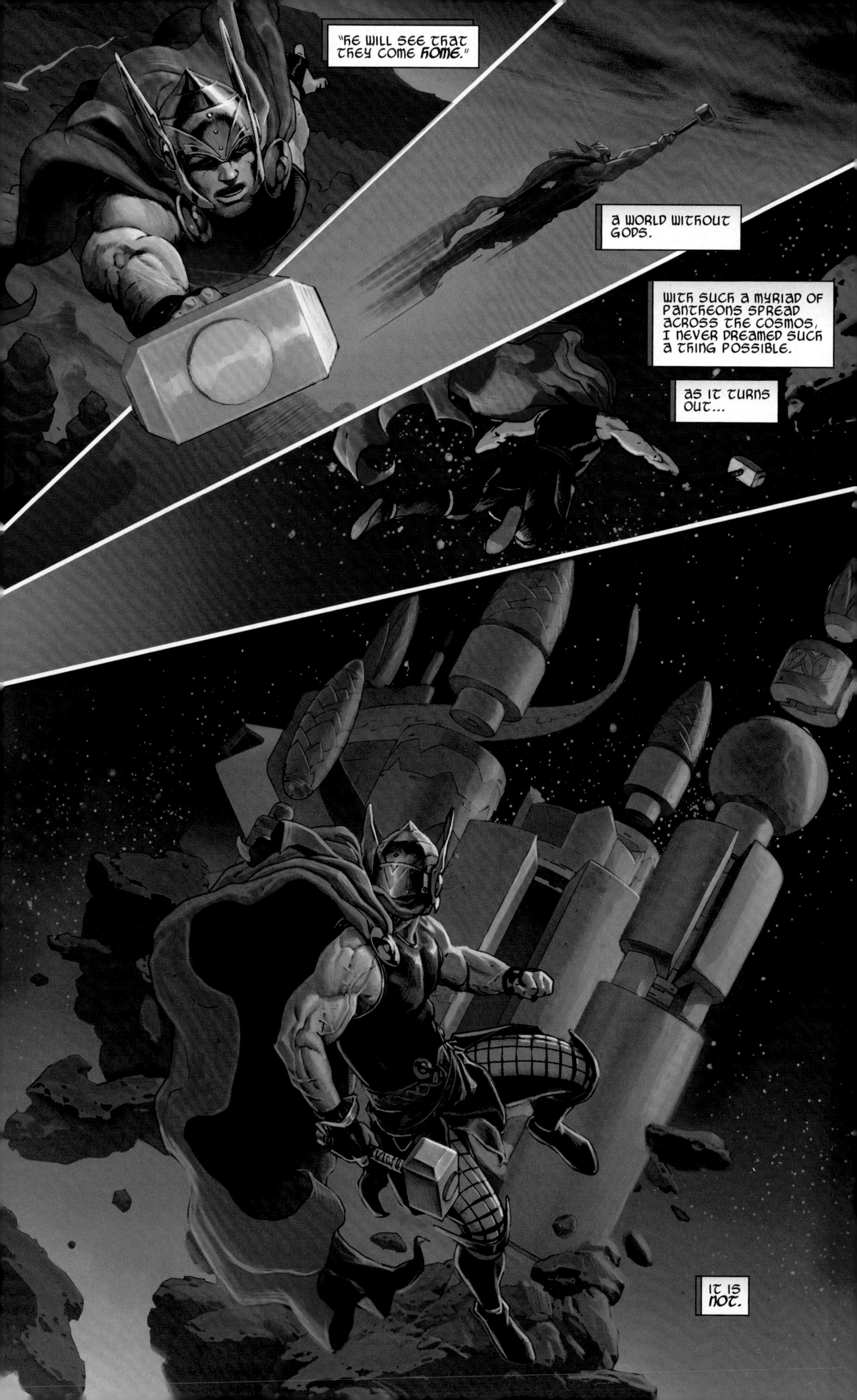
"HE WILL SEE THAT THEY COME HOME."
A WORLD WITHOUT GODS.
WITH SUCH A MYRIAD OF PANTHEONS SPREAD ACROSS THE COSMOS, I NEVER DREAMED SUCH A THING POSSIBLE.
AS IT TURNS OUT...
IT IS NOT.

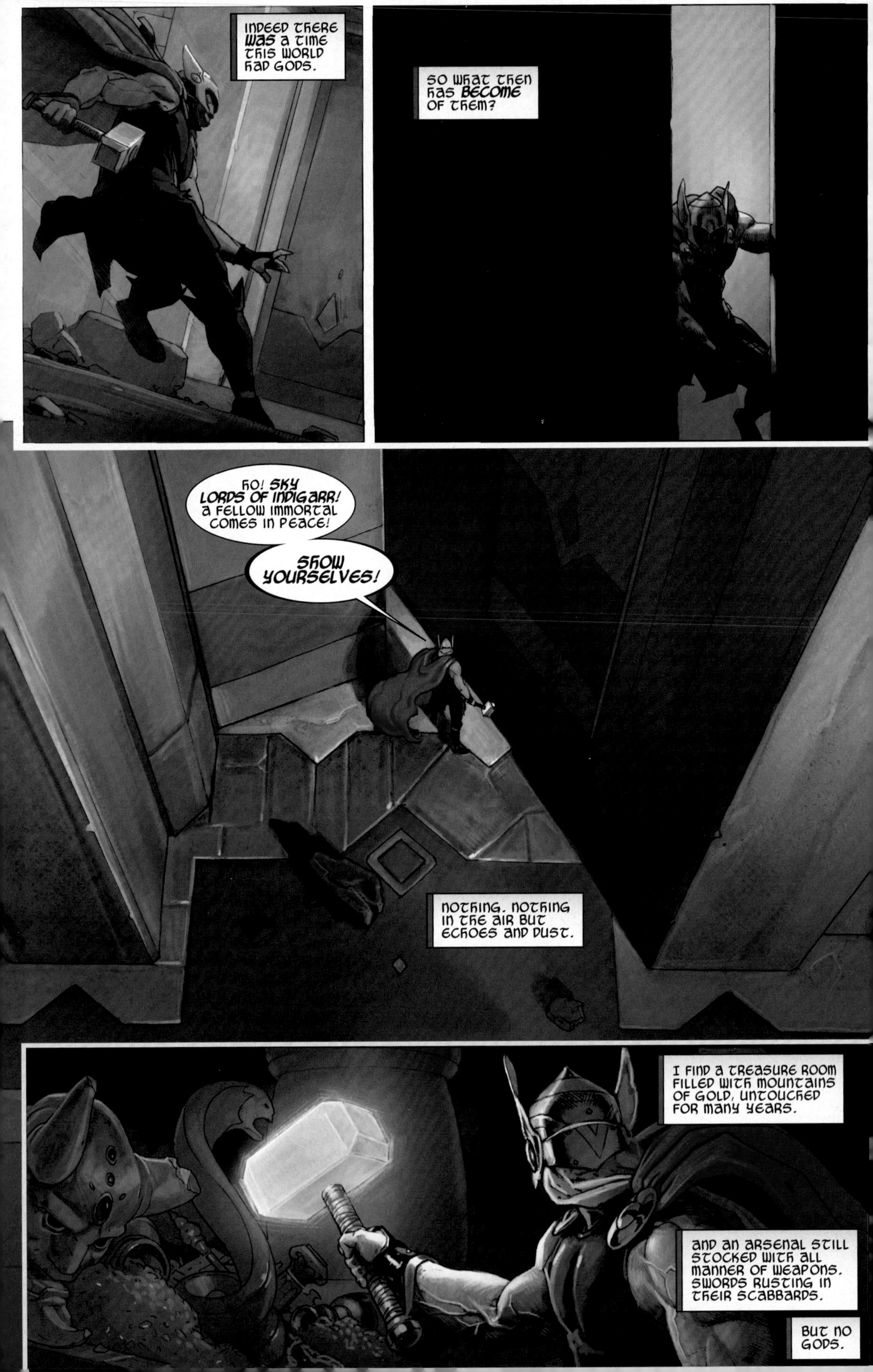
INDEED THERE WAS A TIME THIS WORLD HAD GODS.
SO WHAT THEN HAS BECOME OF THEM?
HO! SKY LORDS OF INDIGARR! A FELLOW IMMORTAL COMES IN PEACE!
SHOW YOURSELVES!
NOTHING. NOTHING IN THE AIR BUT ECHOES AND DUST.
I FIND A TREASURE ROOM FILLED WITH MOUNTAINS OF GOLD, UNTOUCHED FOR MANY YEARS.
AND AN ARSENAL STILL STOCKED WITH ALL MANNER OF WEAPONS. SWORDS RUSTING IN THEIR SCABBARDS.
BUT NO GODS.

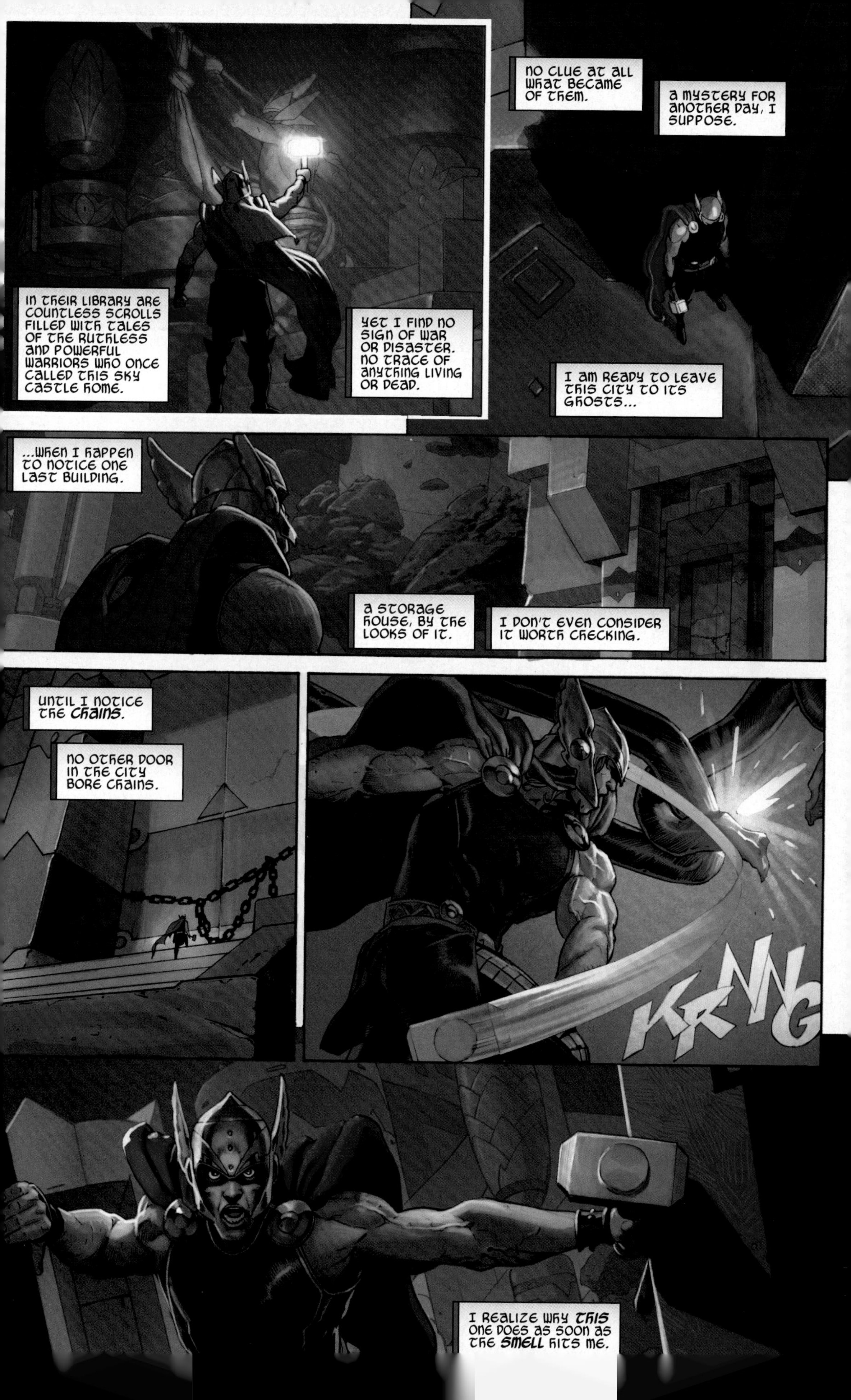
IN THEIR LIBRARY ARE COUNTLESS SCROLLS FILLED WITH TALES OF THE RUTHLESS AND POWERFUL WARRIORS WHO ONCE CALLED THIS SKY CASTLE HOME.
YET I FIND NO SIGN OF WAR OR DISASTER. NO TRACE OF ANYTHING LIVING OR DEAD.
NO CLUE AT ALL WHAT BECAME OF THEM.
A MYSTERY FOR ANOTHER DAY, I SUPPOSE.
I AM READY TO LEAVE THIS CITY TO ITS GHOSTS...
...WHEN I HAPPEN TO NOTICE ONE LAST BUILDING.
A STORAGE HOUSE, BY THE LOOKS OF IT.
I DON'T EVEN CONSIDER IT WORTH CHECKING.
UNTIL I NOTICE THE CHAINS.
NO OTHER DOOR IN THE CITY BORE CHAINS.
KRNNG
I REALIZE WHY THIS ONE DOES AS SOON AS THE SMELL HITS ME.

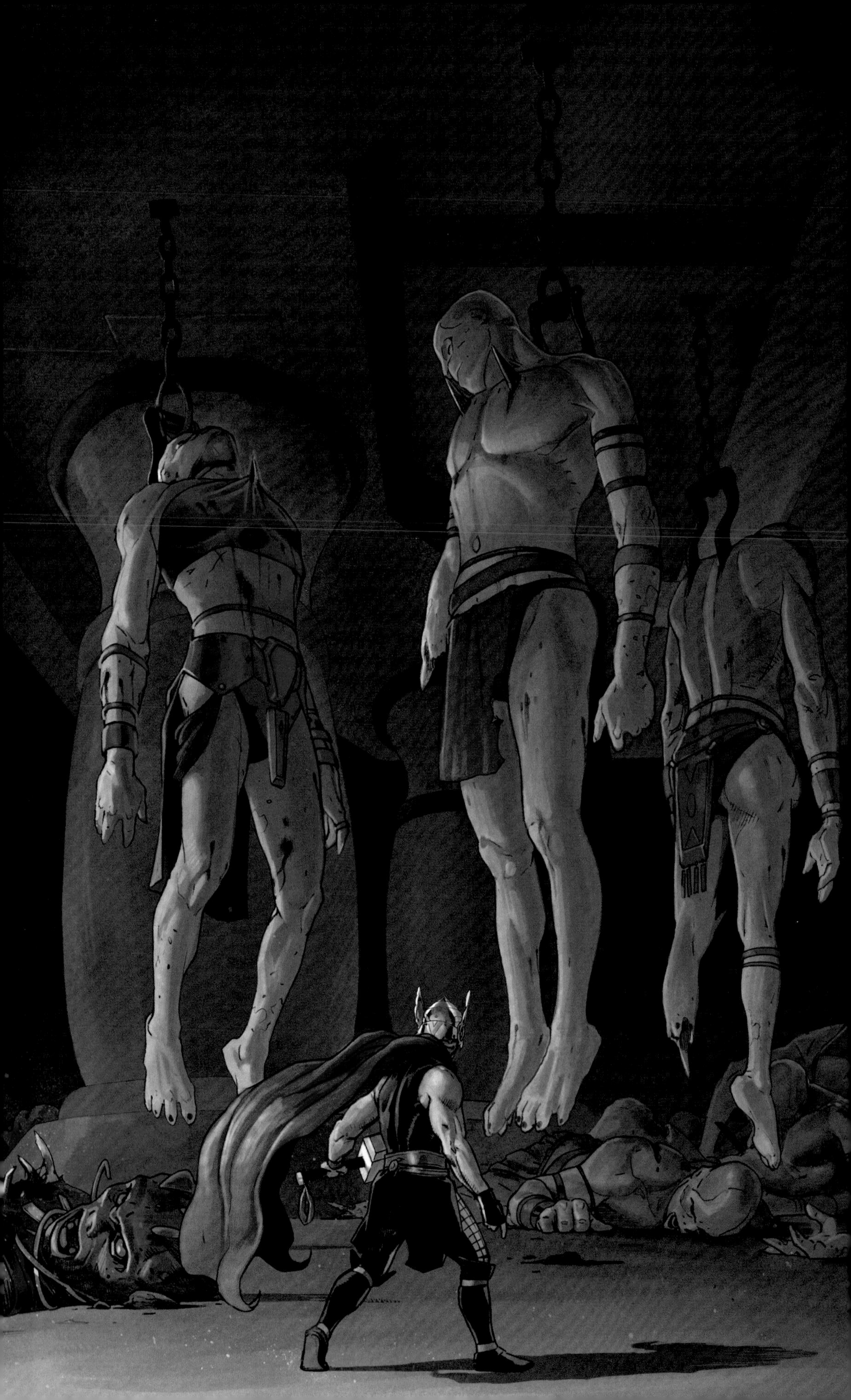

HOGGSCARR THE HARSH. KRAWSKIN THE CRUEL. LADY VYLE THE GODDESS OF ATROCITIES. LORD ALL-BLUD THE INEXORABLE AND HIS THIRTEEN SONS BY THIRTEEN BRIDES. I RECOGNIZE THEM ALL FROM THE STORIES IN THE SCROLLS.

THESE ARE THE MISSING GODS OF INDIGARR.

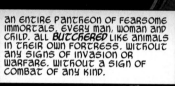

THUS IS ONE MYSTERY SOLVED. AS ANOTHER IS BORN.

AN ENTIRE PANTHEON OF FEARSOME IMMORTALS. EVERY MAN, WOMAN AND CHILD. ALL BUTCHERED LIKE ANIMALS IN THEIR OWN FORTRESS. WITHOUT ANY SIGNS OF INVASION OR WARFARE. WITHOUT A SIGN OF COMBAT OF ANY KIND.

NO, TO EVEN CALL THIS BUTCHERY IS AN INSULT TO HONEST BUTCHERS.

THIS...

THIS WAS SOMETHING ELSE ENTIRELY.

GODFLESH ROTS SLOWLY. BY MY GUESS THEY'VE BEEN HERE A FEW HUNDRED YEARS. UNDISTURBED UNTIL NOW.

NO ARMY DID THIS. NO GIANTS EITHER. NO STENCH OF SORCERY IN THE AIR. THIS WAS NO RITUAL. NO ONE-TIME EXPLOSION OF MADNESS. FLESH WASN'T EATEN, SO NEITHER WAS IT A MINDLESS BEAST.

THERE WAS NOTHING MINDLESS ABOUT THIS.

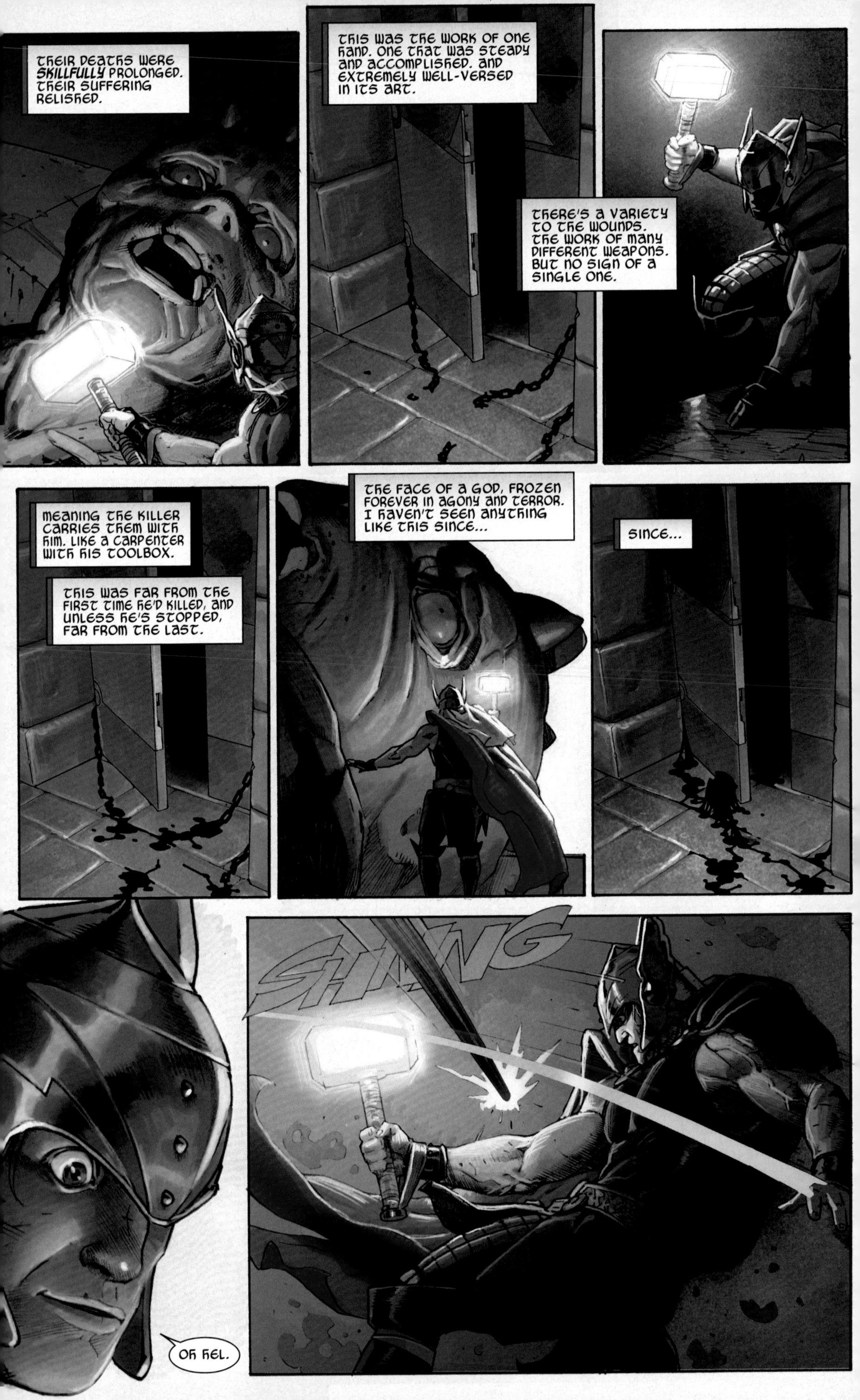
THEIR DEATHS WERE SKILLFULLY PROLONGED. THEIR SUFFERING RELISHED.
THIS WAS THE WORK OF ONE HAND. ONE THAT WAS STEADY AND ACCOMPLISHED. AND EXTREMELY WELL-VERSED IN ITS ART.
THERE'S A VARIETY TO THE WOUNDS. THE WORK OF MANY DIFFERENT WEAPONS. BUT NO SIGN OF A SINGLE ONE.
MEANING THE KILLER CARRIES THEM WITH HIM. LIKE A CARPENTER WITH HIS TOOLBOX.
THIS WAS FAR FROM THE FIRST TIME HE'D KILLED, AND UNLESS HE'S STOPPED, FAR FROM THE LAST.
THE FACE OF A GOD, FROZEN FOREVER IN AGONY AND TERROR. I HAVEN'T SEEN ANYTHING LIKE THIS SINCE...
SINCE...
OH HEL.

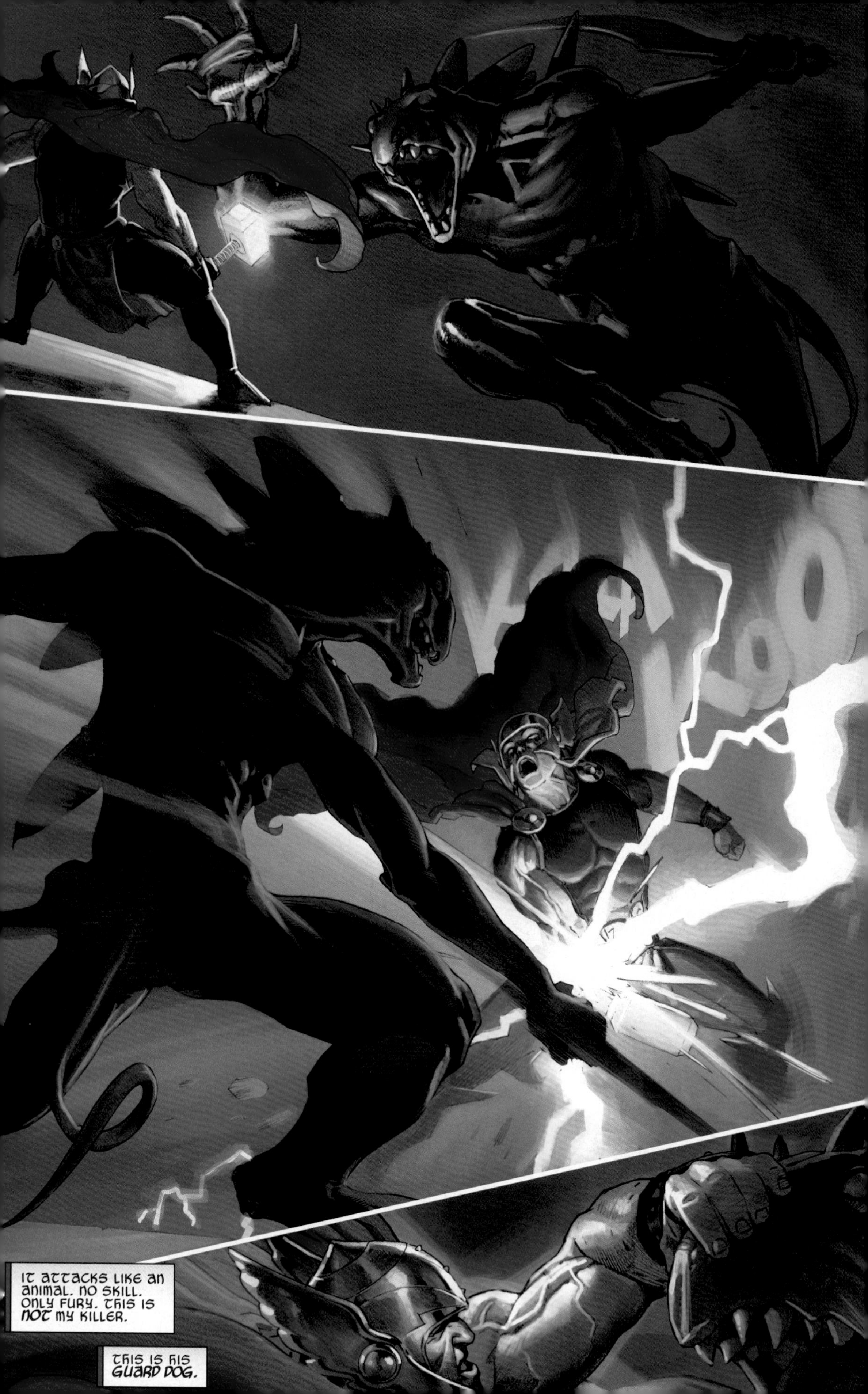
IT ATTACKS LIKE AN ANIMAL. NO SKILL. ONLY FURY. THIS IS **NOT** MY KILLER.
THIS IS HIS ***GUARD DOG.***

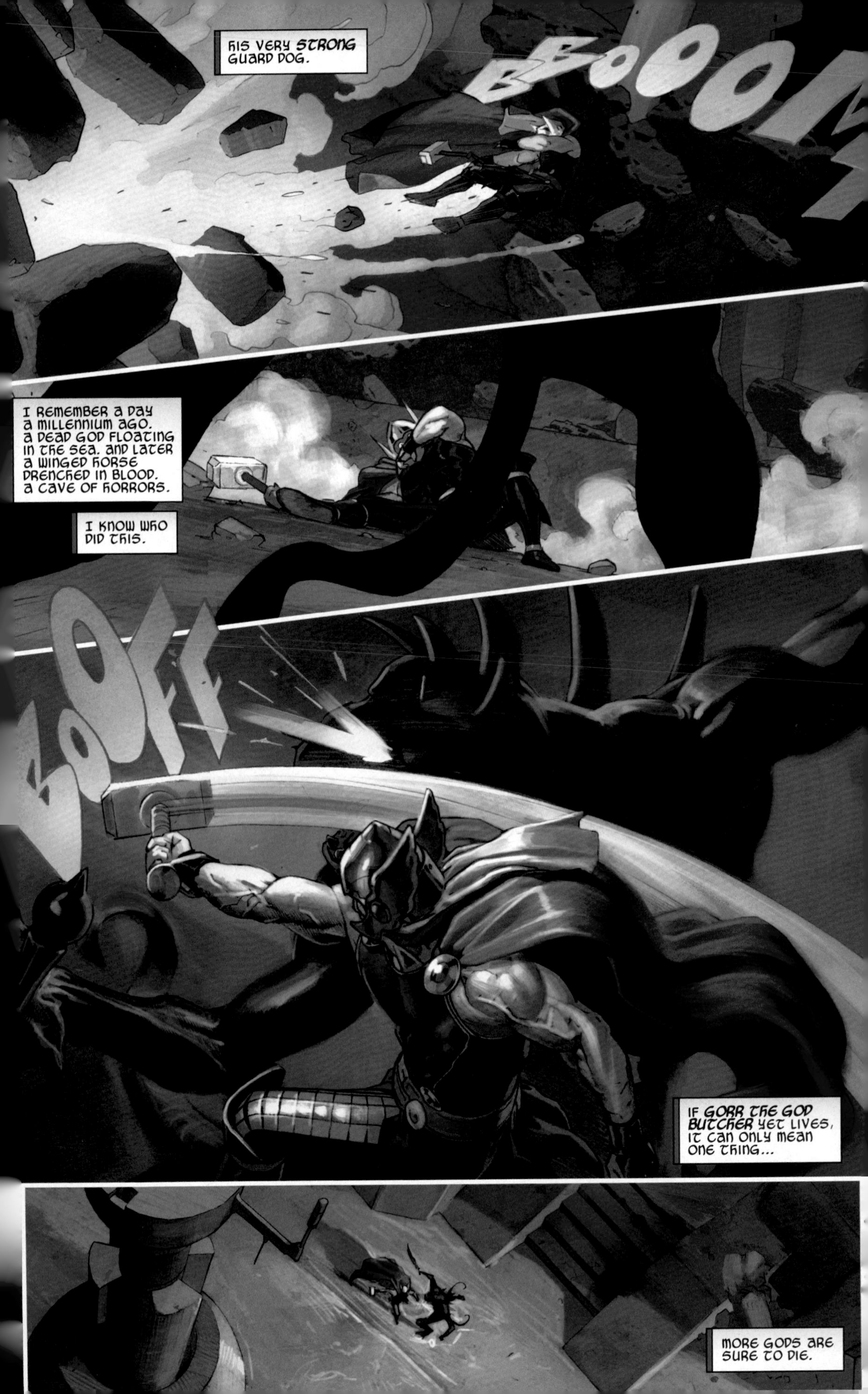
HIS VERY STRONG GUARD DOG.
BBOOOOM
I REMEMBER A DAY A MILLENNIUM AGO. A DEAD GOD FLOATING IN THE SEA. AND LATER A WINGED HORSE DRENCHED IN BLOOD. A CAVE OF HORRORS.
I KNOW WHO DID THIS.
OOFF
IF GORR THE GOD BUTCHER YET LIVES, IT CAN ONLY MEAN ONE THING...
MORE GODS ARE SURE TO DIE.

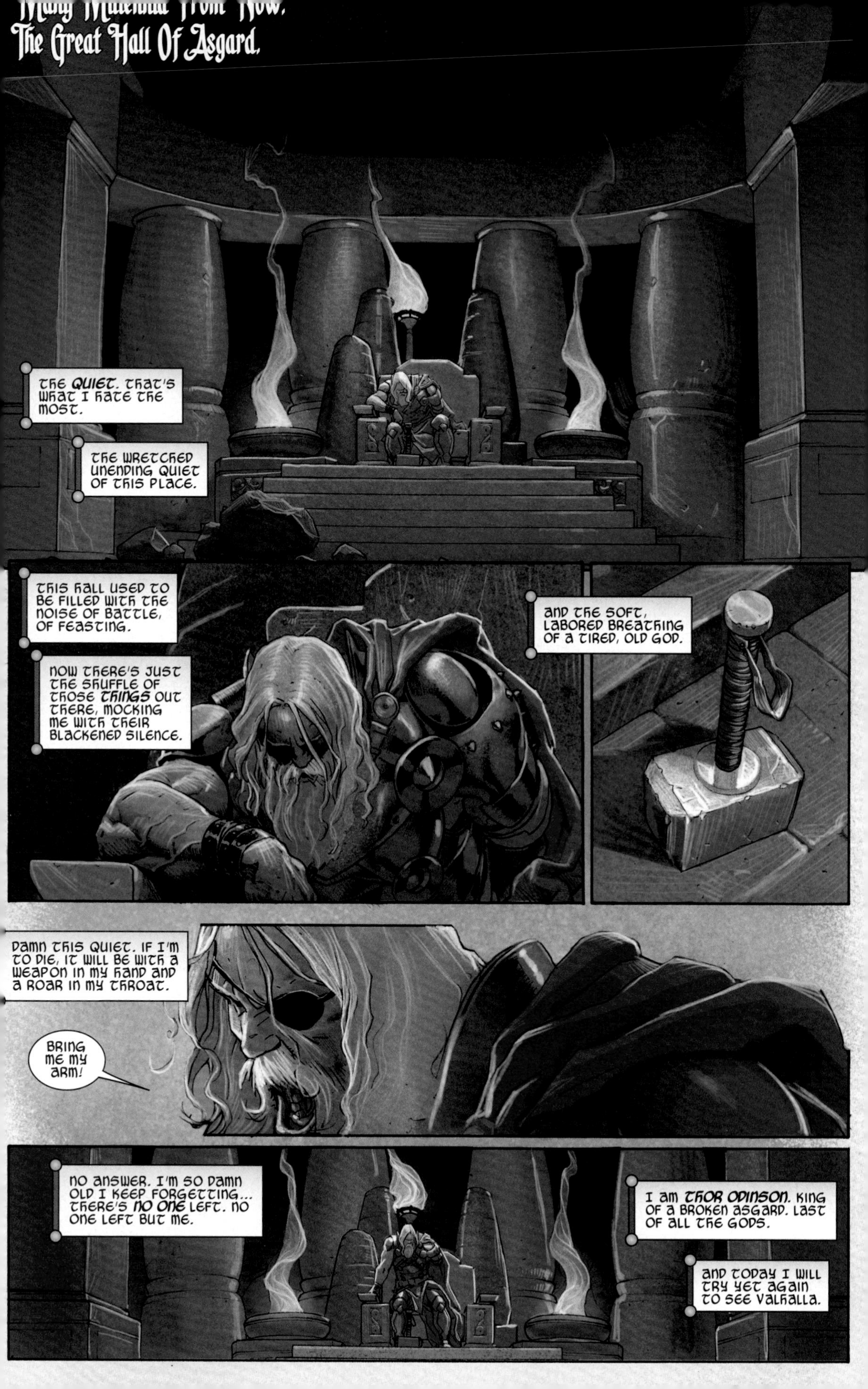

The Great Hall Of Asgard.
THE QUIET. THAT'S WHAT I HATE THE MOST.
THE WRETCHED UNENDING QUIET OF THIS PLACE.
THIS HALL USED TO BE FILLED WITH THE NOISE OF BATTLE, OF FEASTING.
NOW THERE'S JUST THE SHUFFLE OF THOSE THINGS OUT THERE, MOCKING ME WITH THEIR BLACKENED SILENCE.
AND THE SOFT, LABORED BREATHING OF A TIRED, OLD GOD.
DAMN THIS QUIET. IF I'M TO DIE, IT WILL BE WITH A WEAPON IN MY HAND AND A ROAR IN MY THROAT.
BRING ME MY ARM!
NO ANSWER. I'M SO DAMN OLD I KEEP FORGETTING... THERE'S NO ONE LEFT. NO ONE LEFT BUT ME.
I AM THOR ODINSON. KING OF A BROKEN ASGARD. LAST OF ALL THE GODS.
AND TODAY I WILL TRY YET AGAIN TO SEE VALHALLA.

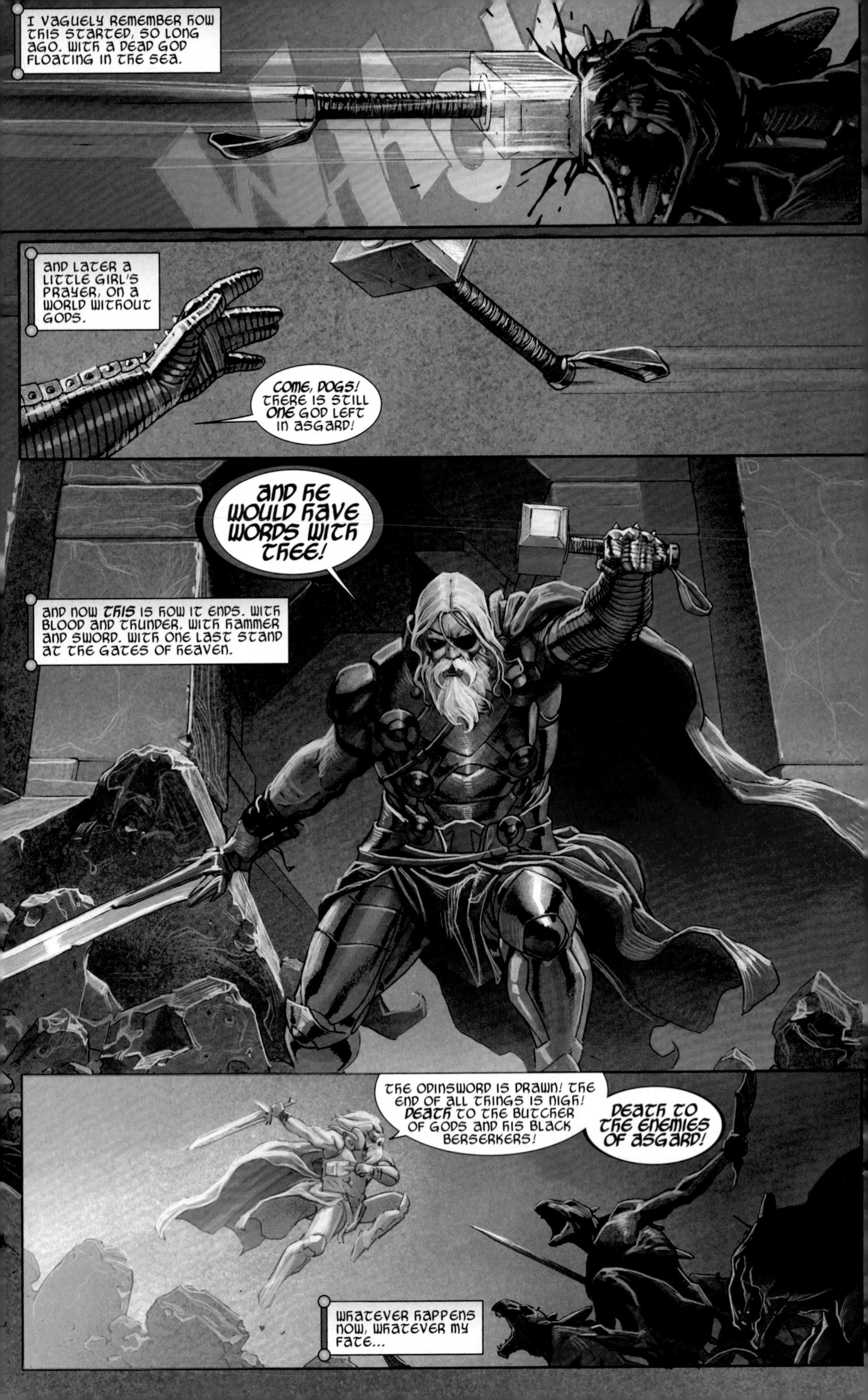
I VAGUELY REMEMBER HOW THIS STARTED, SO LONG AGO. WITH A DEAD GOD FLOATING IN THE SEA.
AND LATER A LITTLE GIRL'S PRAYER, ON A WORLD WITHOUT GODS.
COME, DOGS! THERE IS STILL ONE GOD LEFT IN ASGARD!
AND HE WOULD HAVE WORDS WITH THEE!
AND NOW THIS IS HOW IT ENDS. WITH BLOOD AND THUNDER. WITH HAMMER AND SWORD. WITH ONE LAST STAND AT THE GATES OF HEAVEN.
THE ODINSWORD IS DRAWN! THE END OF ALL THINGS IS NIGH! DEATH TO THE BUTCHER OF GODS AND HIS BLACK BERSERKERS!
DEATH TO THE ENEMIES OF ASGARD!
WHATEVER HAPPENS NOW, WHATEVER MY FATE...

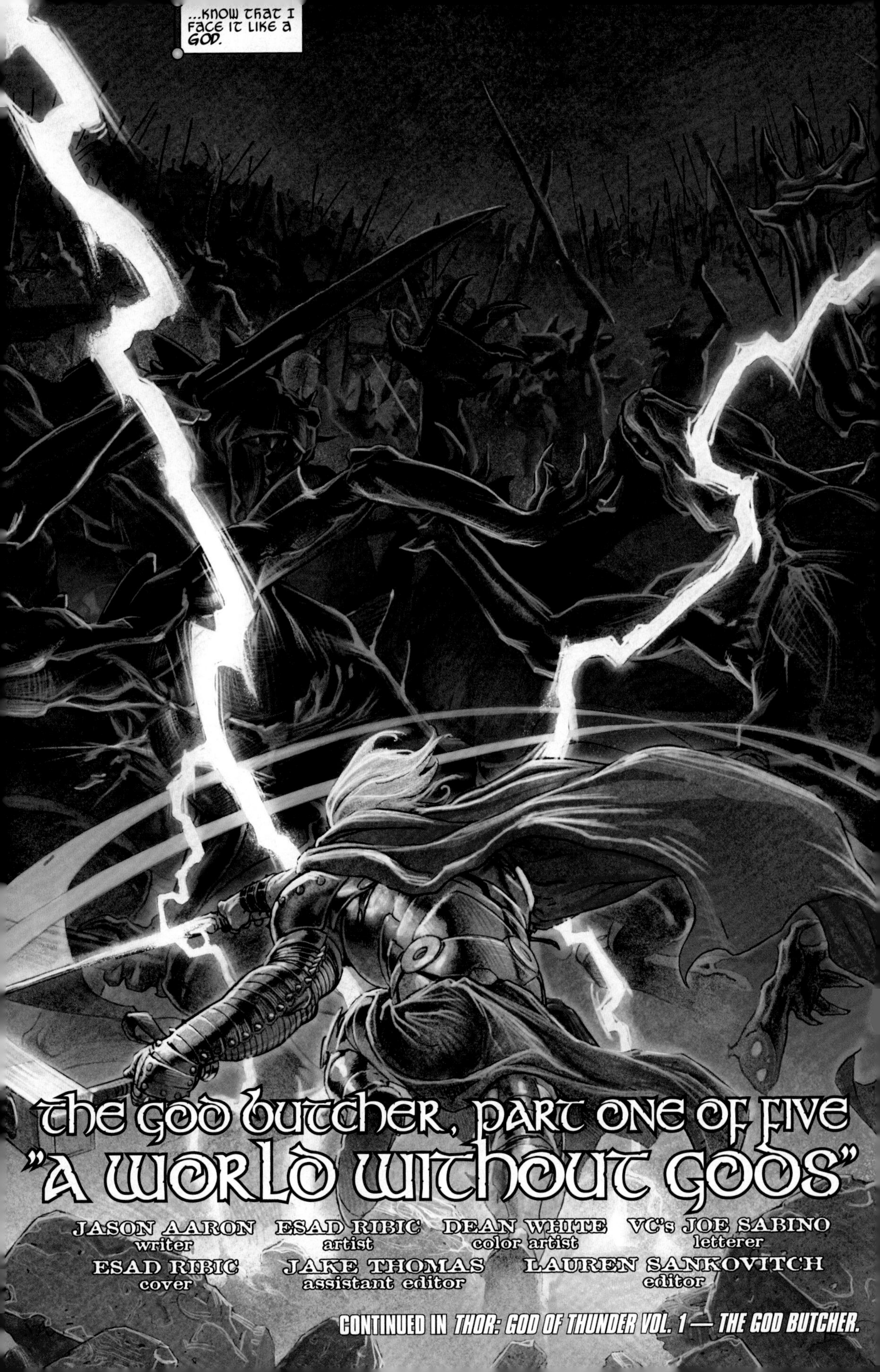
...KNOW THAT I FACE IT LIKE A GOD.
THE GOD BUTCHER, PART ONE OF FIVE
"A WORLD WITHOUT GODS"
JASON AARON writer
ESAD RIBIC artist
DEAN WHITE color artist
VC's JOE SABINO letterer
ESAD RIBIC cover
JAKE THOMAS assistant editor
LAUREN SANKOVITCH editor
CONTINUED IN THOR: GOD OF THUNDER VOL. 1 — THE GOD BUTCHER.

COVER PROCESS

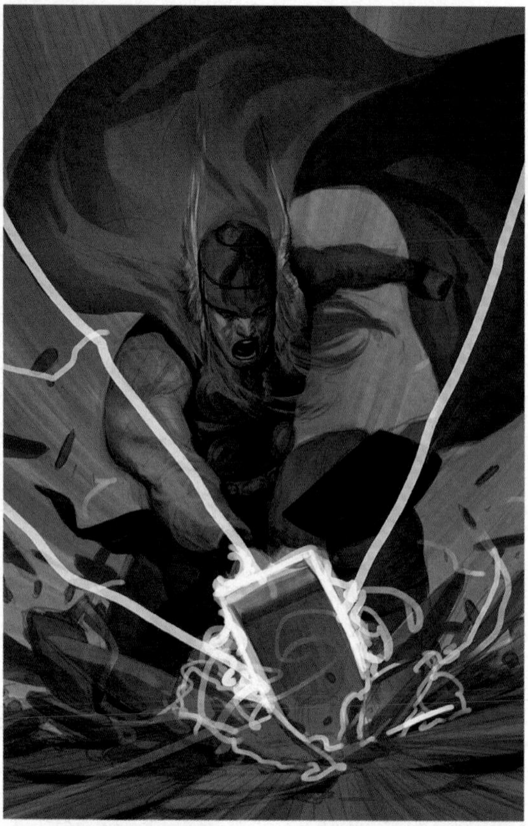

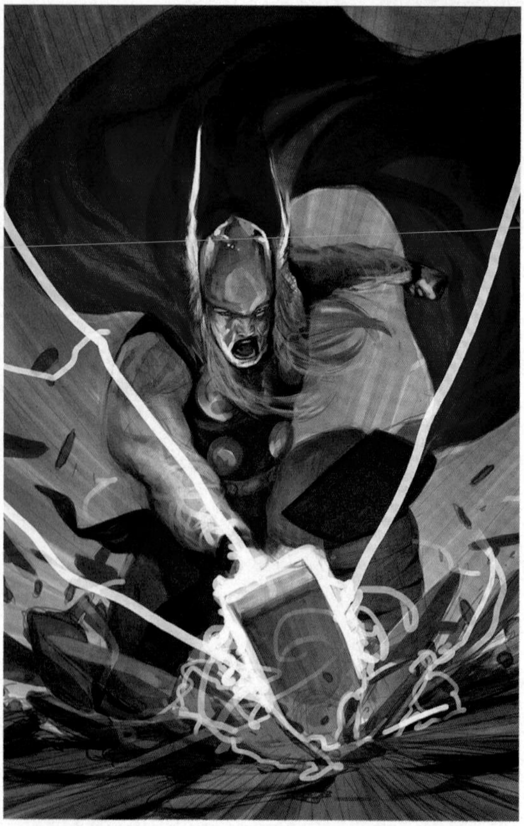

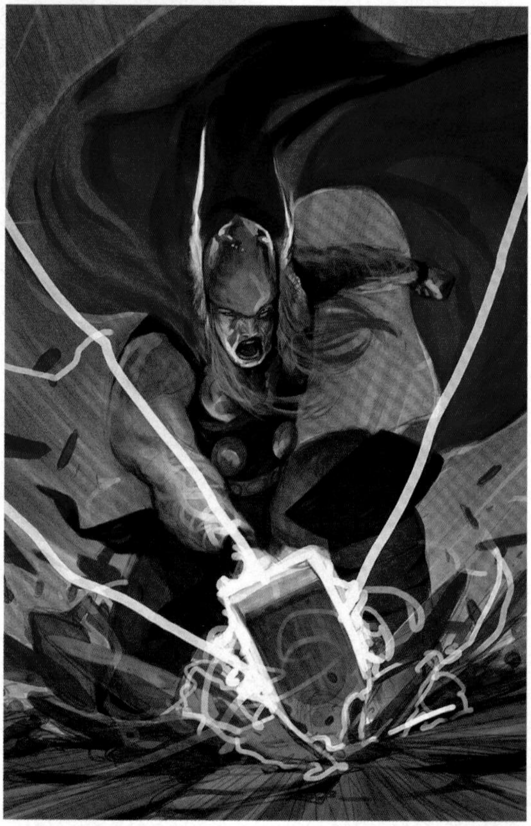

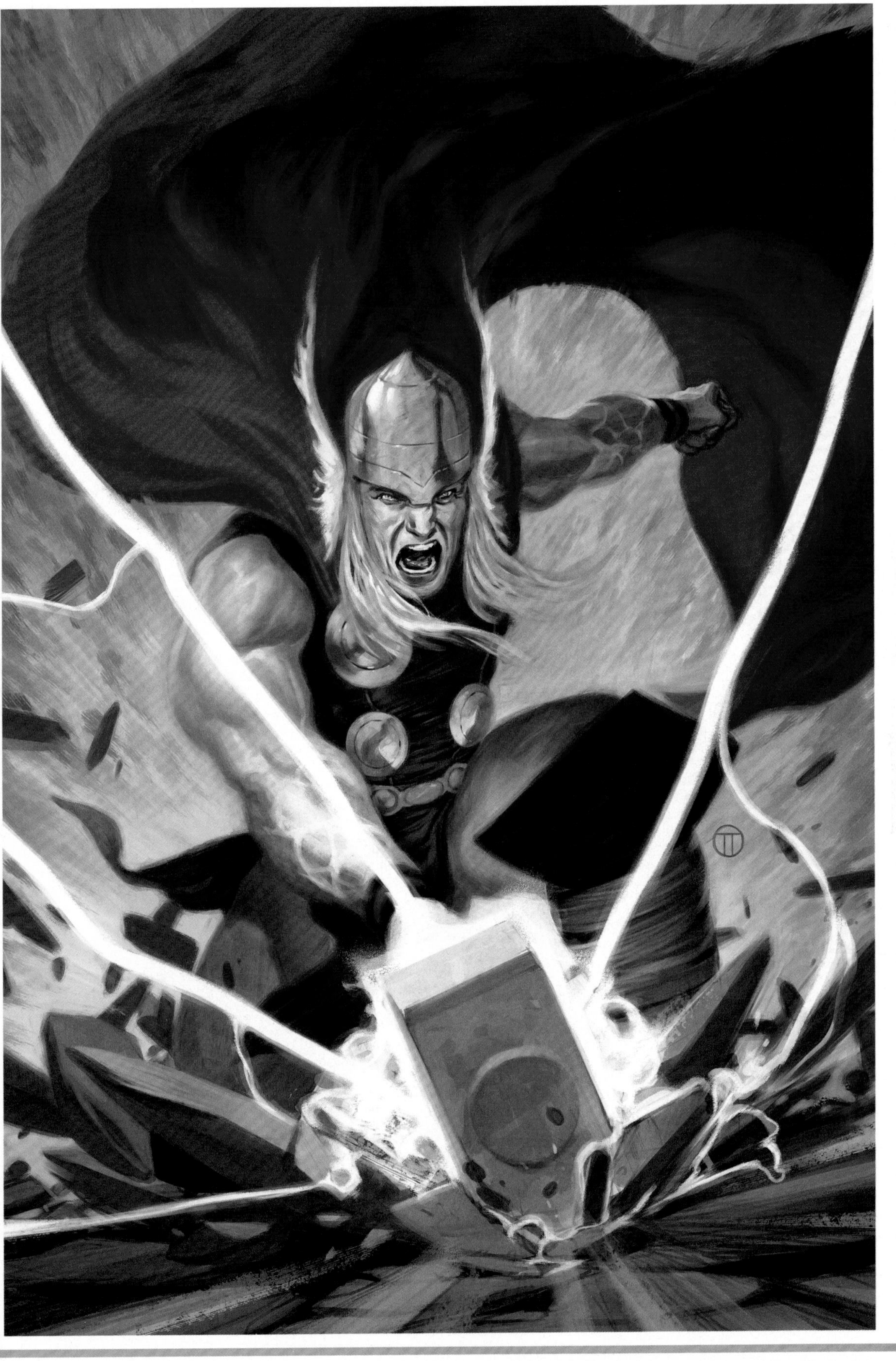

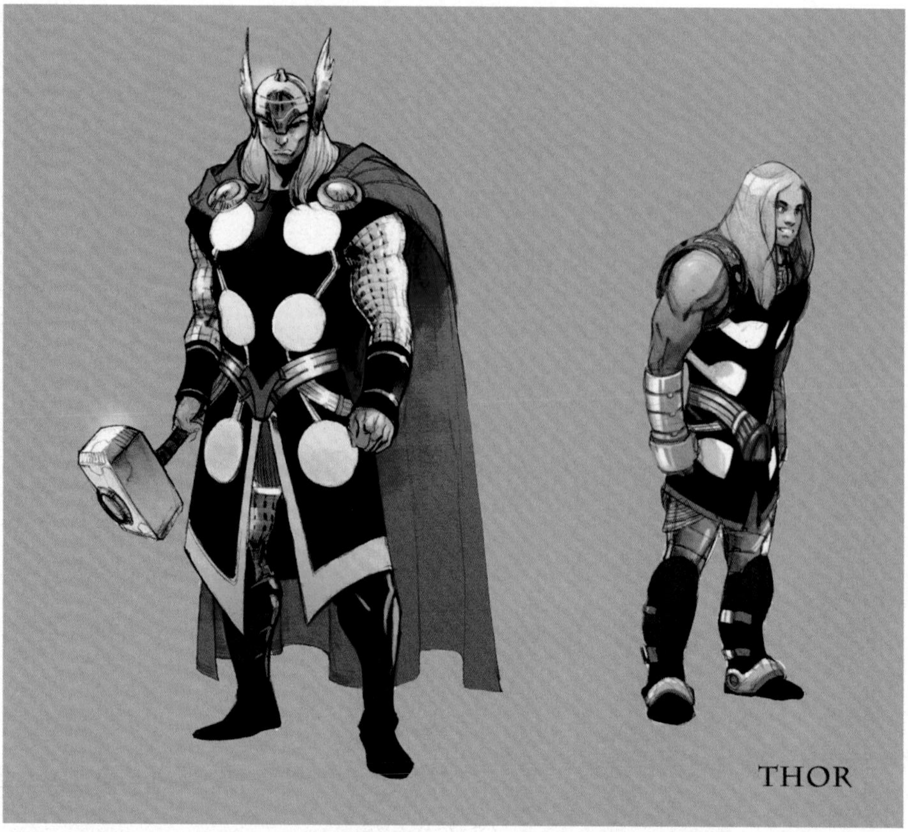

THOR

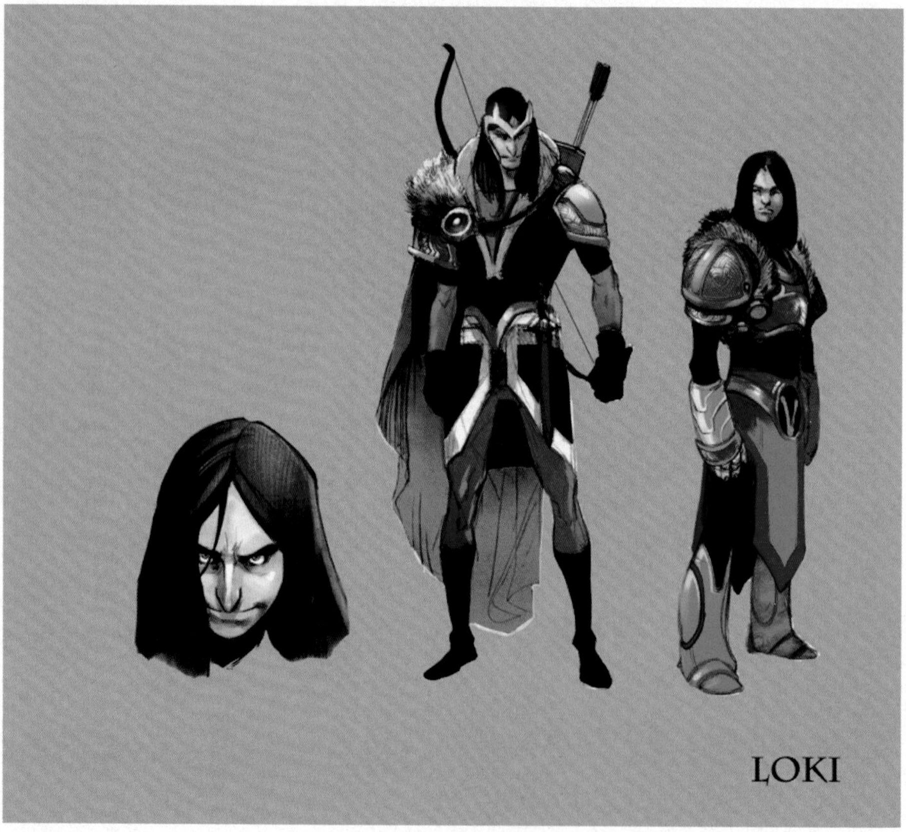

LOKI

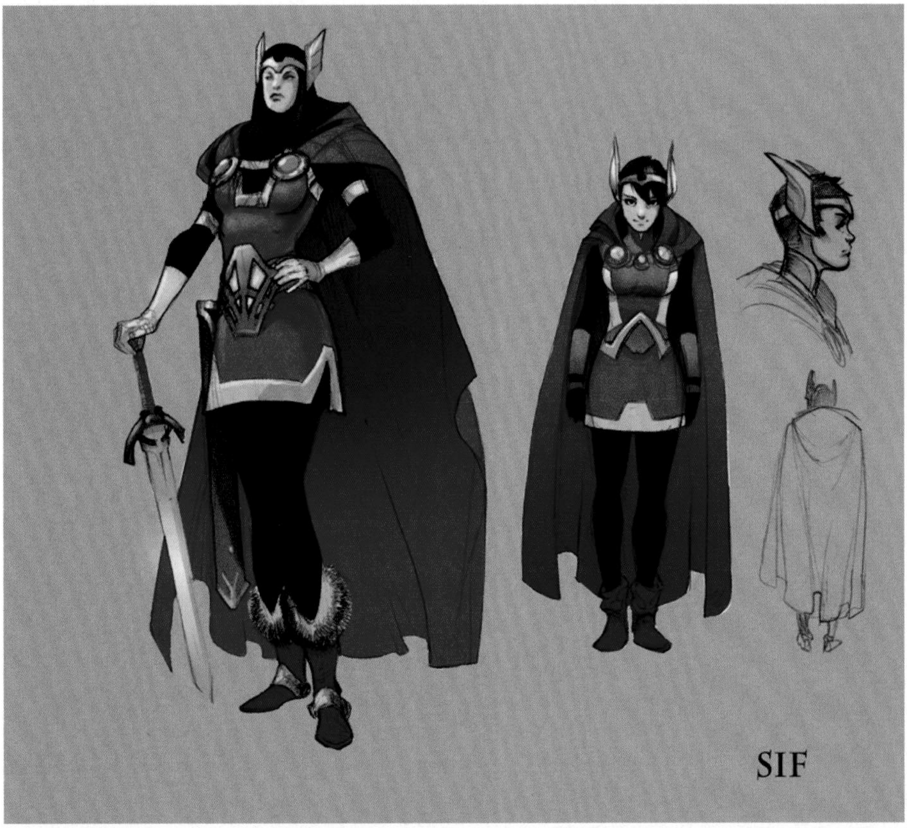
SIF

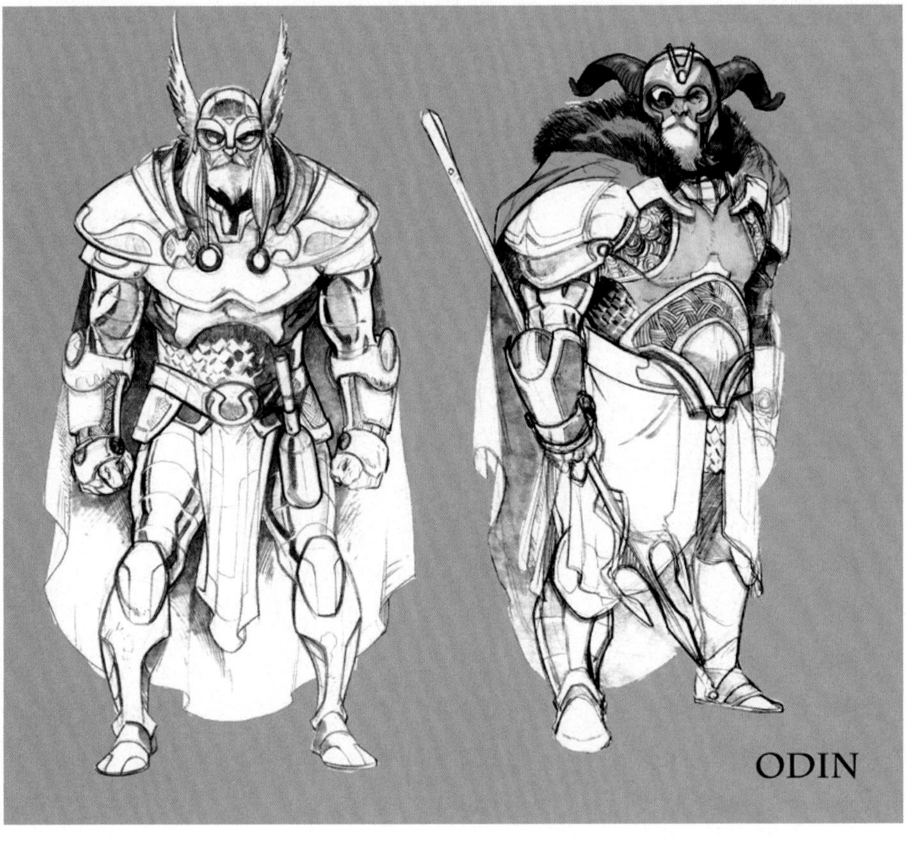
ODIN

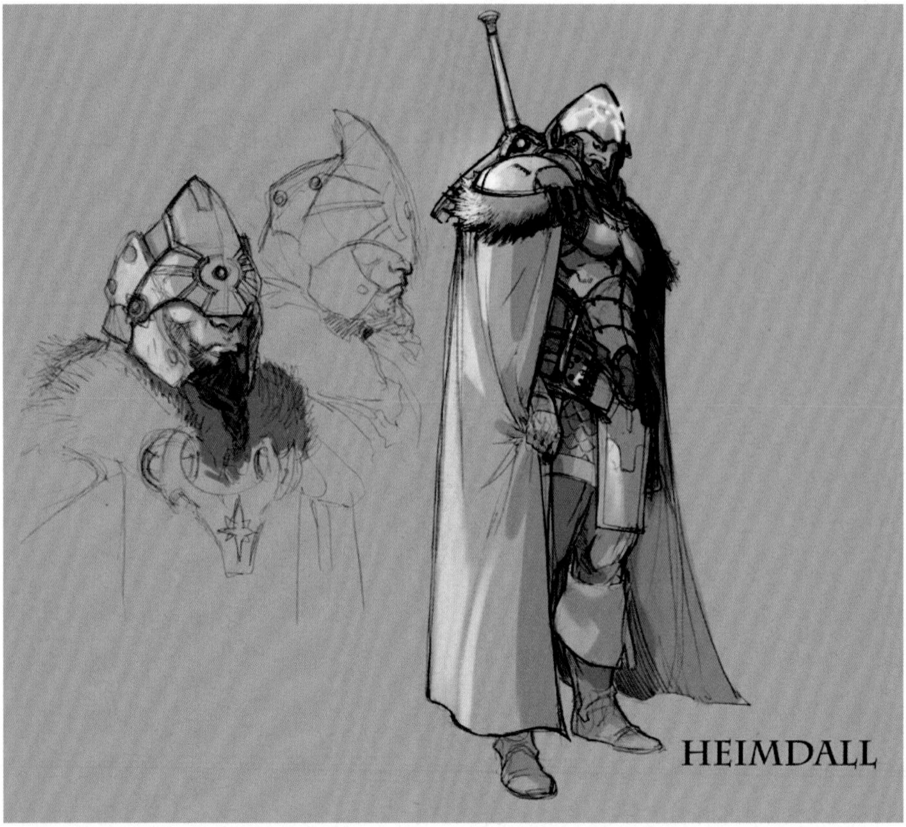
HEIMDALL

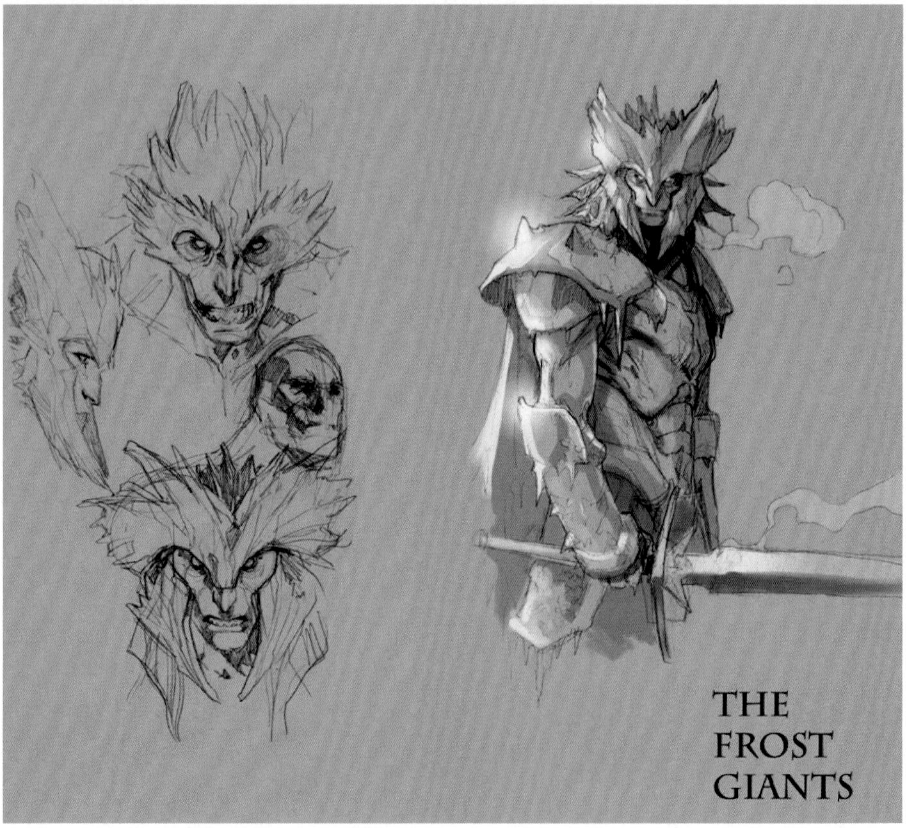
THE FROST GIANTS

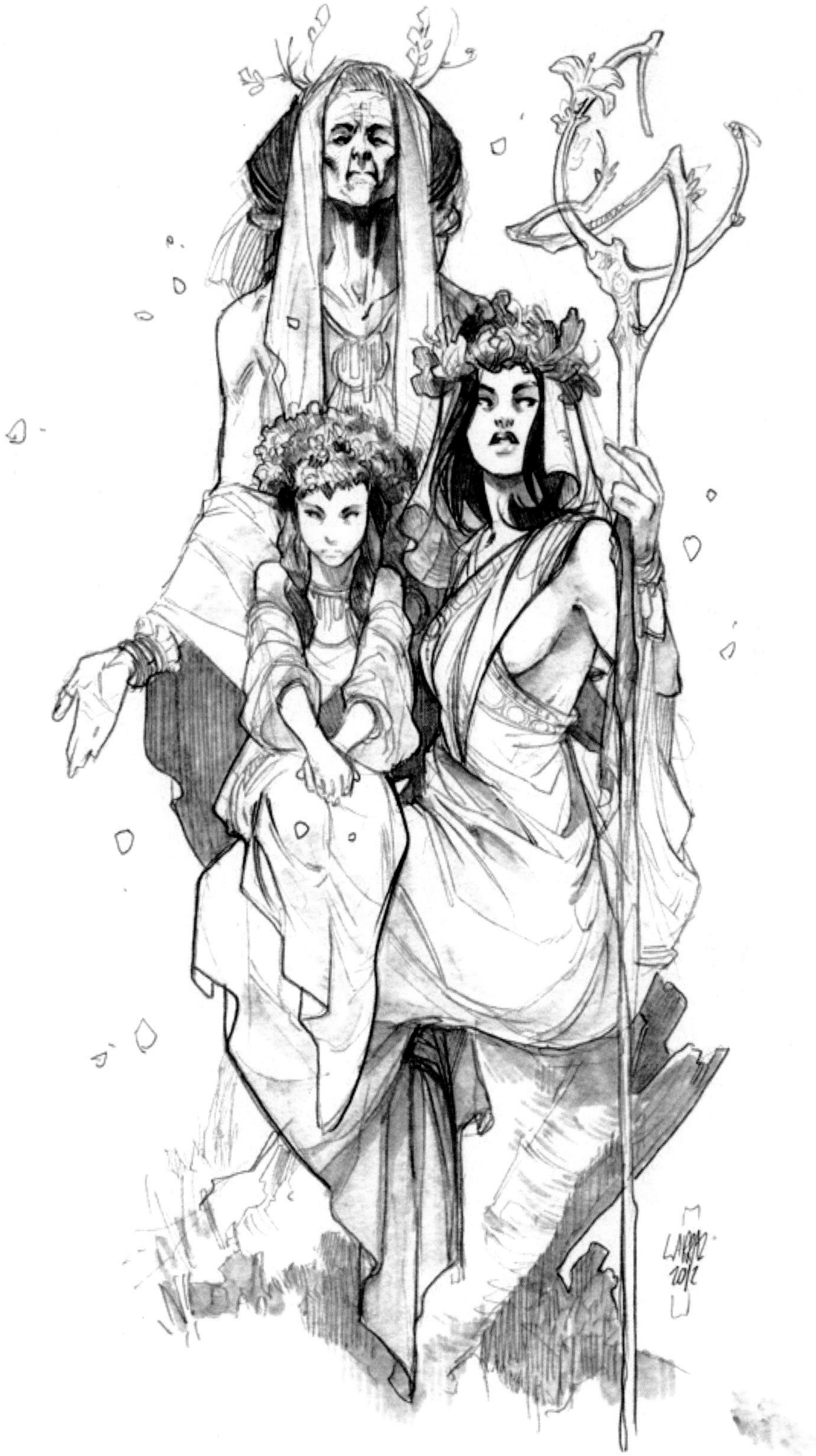

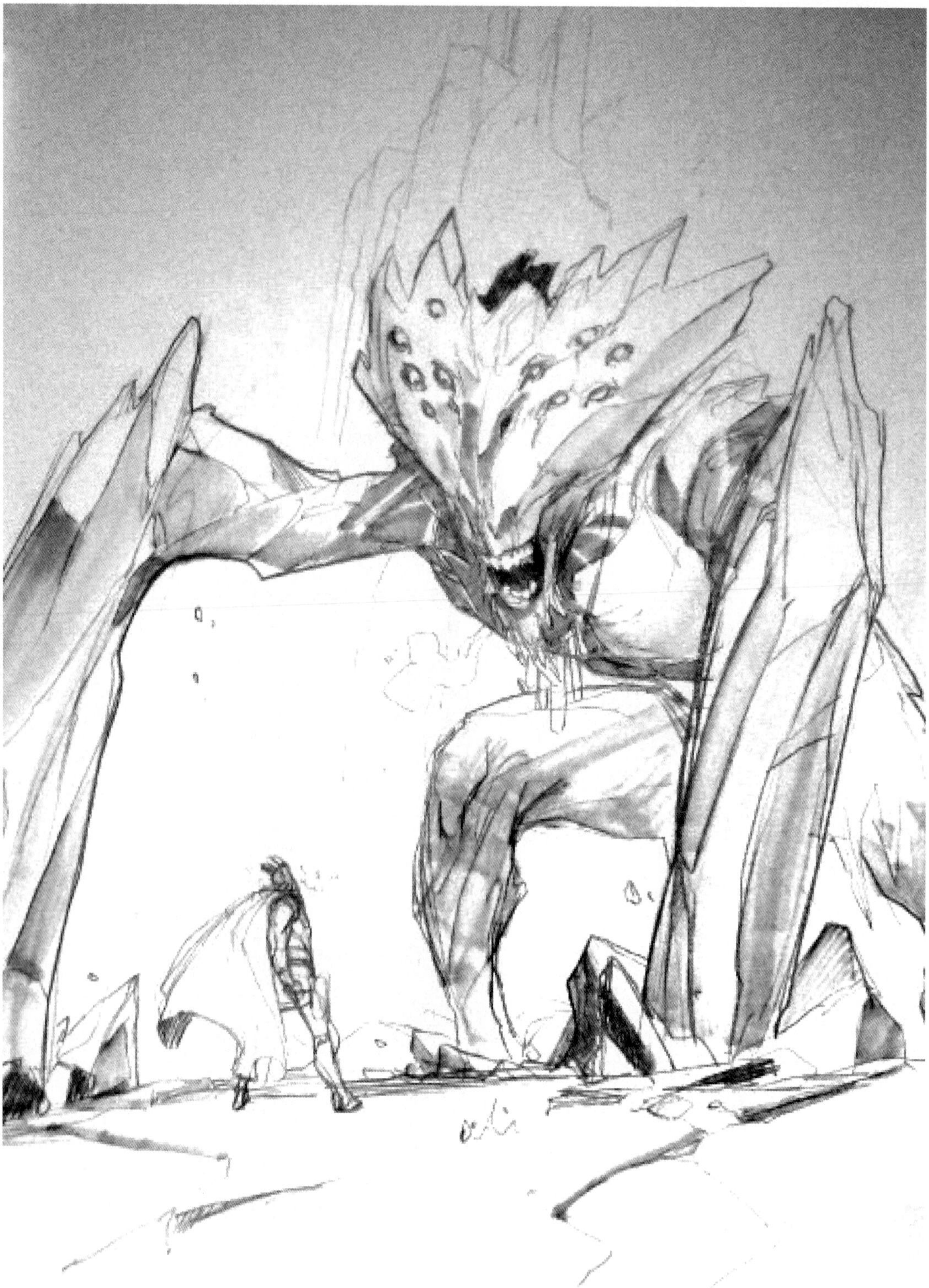

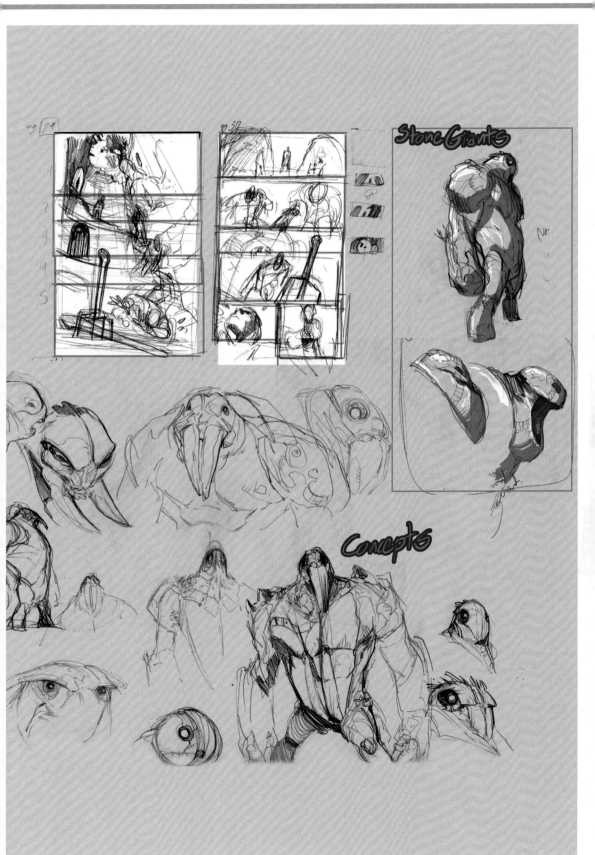

Stone Giants

Concepts

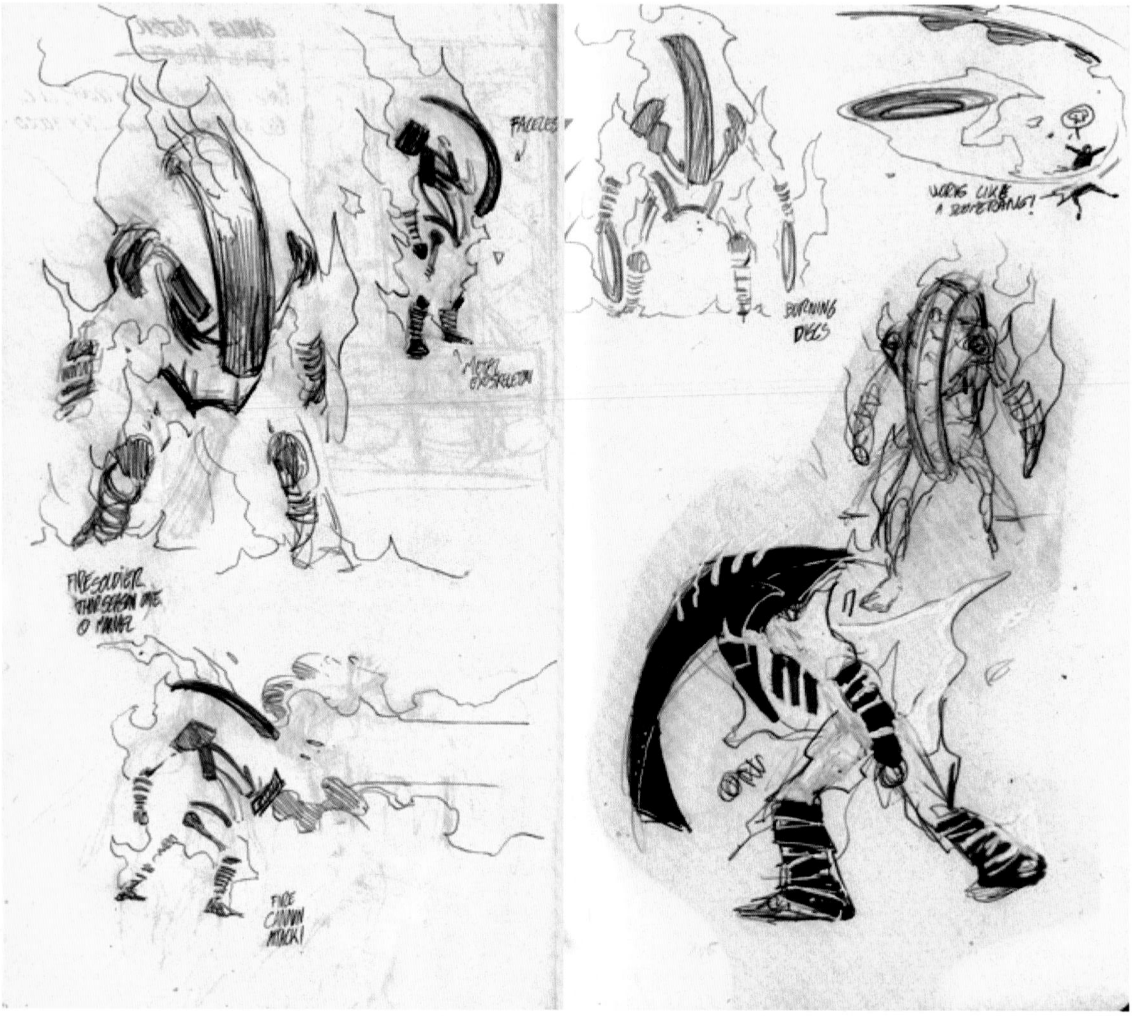
FACELESS
METAL EXOSKELETON
FIRESOLDIER
FIRE CANNON ATTACK!
BURNING DISCS
WORKS LIKE A BOOMERANG?

pg 71

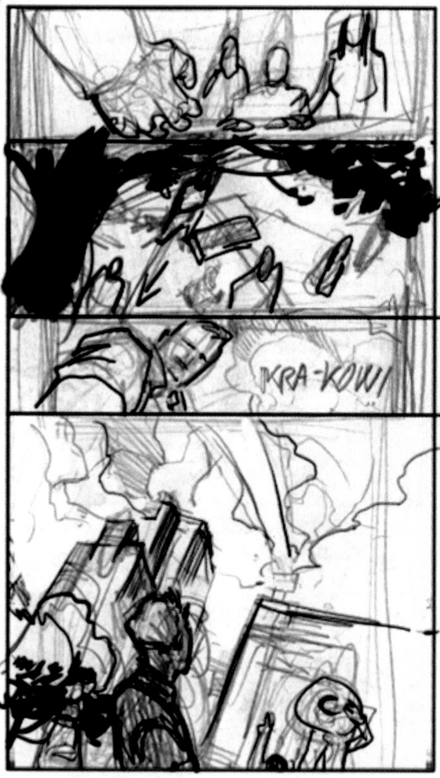
KRA-KOW!

pg 72

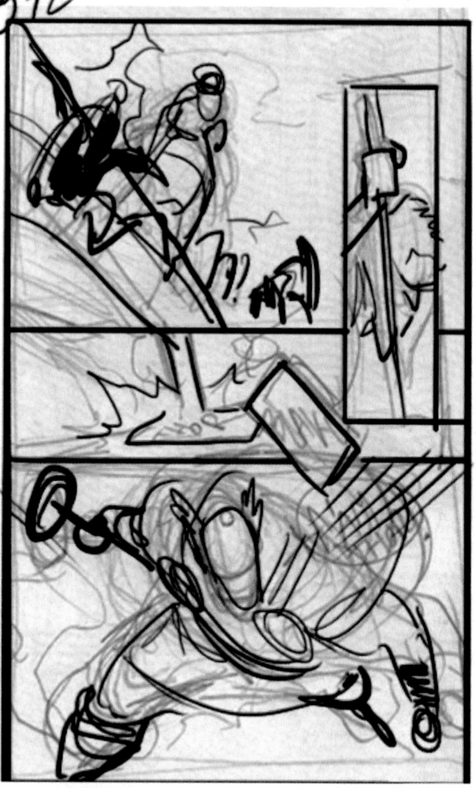

pg 73

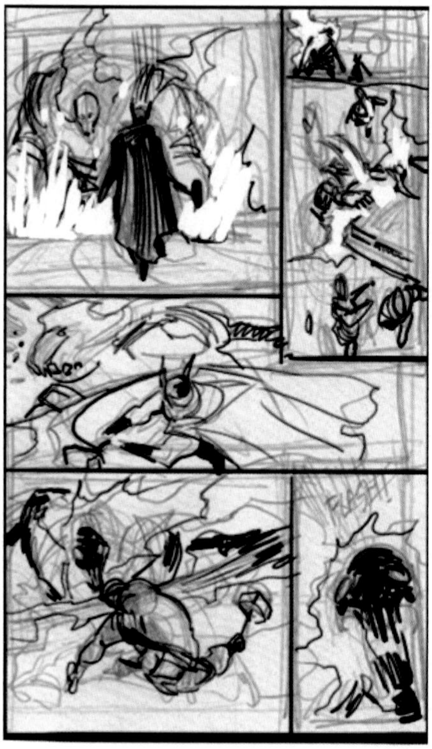

pg 74

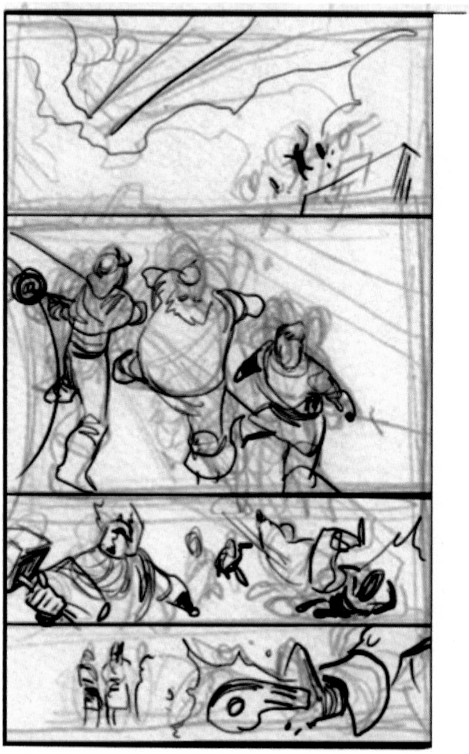

LAYOUTS, PAGES 71-74

pg 75

pg 76

pg 77

LAYOUTS, PAGES 75-77

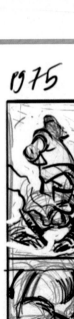

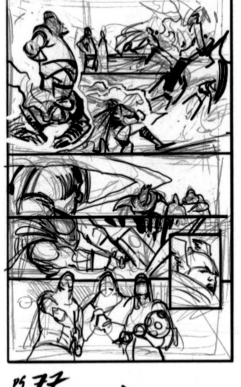

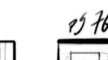

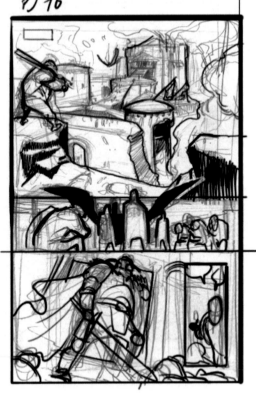

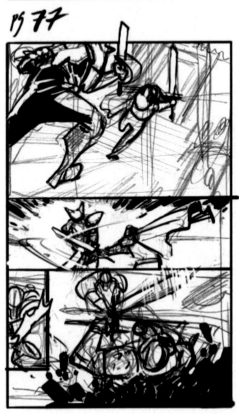